THE WALL STREET JOURNAL.

THE WALL STREET JOURNAL.

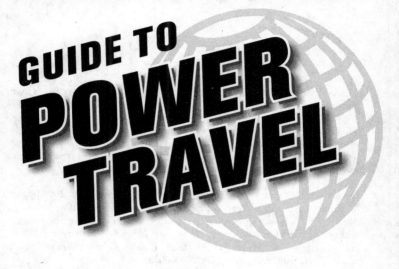

GUIDE TO POWER TRAVEL

HOW TO ARRIVE WITH YOUR DIGNITY, SANITY & WALLET INTACT

Scott McCartney

Middle Seat Columnist
The Wall Street Journal

HARPER

NEW YORK • LONDON • TORONTO • SYDNEY

JUL 07 2009

The Wall Street Journal® is a registered trademark of Dow Jones and is used by permission of Dow Jones.

This book is written as a source of information only. All efforts have been made to ensure its accuracy as of the date published. The author and the publisher expressly disclaim responsibility for any adverse effects arising from the use or application of the information contained herein.

FIRST EDITION

Designed by Renato Stanisic

Library of Congress Cataloging-in-Publication Data
McCartney, Scott.
The Wall Street Journal guide to power travel : how to arrive with your dignity, sanity, & wallet intact / Scott McCartney.
p. cm.
ISBN 978-0-06-168871-3
1. Travel—Guidebooks. I. Wall Street Journal (Firm) II. Title.
G153.4.M275 2009
910.4—dc22

2008049131

09 10 11 12 13   OV/RRD   10 9 8 7 6 5 4 3 2 1

To Karen (again and always),
for making the journey a joy

I travel not to go anywhere, but to go.
I travel for travel's sake. The great affair is to move.
—Robert Louis Stevenson

Contents

Introduction: What This Book Is, and How to Use It xi

CHAPTER 1
The Ten Commandments of Travel *1*

CHAPTER 2
Deciding Where You Want to Go, and How *11*

CHAPTER 3
How Airlines Price Tickets *23*

CHAPTER 4
Hunting That Elusive Low Fare *39*

CHAPTER 5
Up-Sells, First-Class Bargains, and Enhancements *59*

CHAPTER 6
Frequent-Flier Rewards and Rip-offs *71*

CHAPTER 7
Preparing for Takeoff *93*

CHAPTER 8
Baggage Woes *115*

CHAPTER 9
Hassle-Free Security (Hah!) *135*

CHAPTER 10
Bumping, Upgrades, and Boarding *163*

CHAPTER 11
In the Middle Seat *181*

CHAPTER 12
When Bad Things Happen to Good Travelers *205*

CHAPTER 13
Airline/Air-Traffic-Control Operations *215*

CHAPTER 14
The Best Perks *245*

CHAPTER 15
Hotel Secrets and Strategies *263*

CHAPTER 16
Cruise Strategies *277*

Conclusion: Will Travel Ever Get Better? 293
Appendix: Resources 299

Introduction

What This Book Is, and How to Use It

In his 1974 classic, *Zen and the Art of Motorcycle Maintenance*, author Robert M. Pirsig took a journey across America, seeking understanding and knowledge. At the foot of mountains, he remarked on the bittersweet joy of a good trip. "I feel happy to be here, and still a little sad to be here too. Sometimes it's a little better to travel than to arrive."

There is joy in travel. Travel takes us to knowledge. It takes us to happiness, to reunion, to memories, and to new experiences. Travel takes us to work, clients, meetings, sales, and profitable relationships. It takes us to grandchildren and grandparents; to beaches and golf and Disney. And sometimes, best of all, travel takes us home. We soar six miles above the earth and cruise at five hundred miles per hour. The world shrinks—we can be on the other side of the planet in a matter of hours, nonstop. What joy! Travel should be, and indeed can be, one of our greatest pleasures.

But today, travel is not a happy adventure. The days of unfettered, free-spirit, Zen-like travel are long gone. Today, travel is simply the means to an end, a hardship that must be endured to get where we need to be or want to go. It's exhausting, complicated, and frustrating. Sometimes, it's downright mysterious. Often, it just plain stinks. These days, arriving is far better than traveling—but it didn't used to be that way, and there's no reason that should be the case today.

With overcrowded airplanes, airports, and skies, we wait in one line after another to travel. We endure one aggravating rule after another—shoes off, liquids in tiny bottles, bags no heavier than fifty pounds. Or is it forty pounds? Or forty inches? Or is it forty dollars?

Even on board, travelers have different experiences. One person may enjoy ample space, cheerful, attentive service, a pillow and blanket, hot food, decent wine, and perhaps even a delicious hot fudge sundae. A few rows back, another person is wedged in a middle seat between two longshoremen, unable to read with the seat in front reclined into his lap, and hardly able to stomach the experience after finding a dirty diaper left in the seatback pocket.

At least one flight out of every four will be late—your personal odds may be a lot higher if you travel on a delay-prone route. At least one person on a typical airplane will arrive without his or her luggage. In a typical year, U.S. airlines "mishandle" luggage for four to five million passengers. And to add insult to injury, the airline usually can't tell you where your bag is. Despite the bar-coded tags applied to bags (what they are used for remains a mystery to many), the airline doesn't know if the bag is in Manchester or Maui.

The deck is often stacked against travelers. Airlines charge penalties to change plans but delay or reschedule customers without penalty when it's to the airline's advantage. These days, tens of thousands of customers get involuntarily bumped each year from flights they had tickets for—most often a nonrefundable ticket. Imagine the inequity of that—

you have to show up or you lose your money, yet the airline can deny you the seat you bought and change your plans, at little to no penalty at all to the airline.

In 2007, consumer complaints filed about U.S. airlines with the government skyrocketed 65 percent. Flights sit for hours on runways. Passengers must fend for themselves overnight in strange cities, or longer. Woe is the customer who misses a cruise sailing or wedding or graduation or dinner in Paris because an airline flight got canceled and no seats were available for three days. Your compensation? A discount coupon on your next trip, so you can endure it all over again.

It doesn't have to be that way. There are ways to improve travel, whether it's for business or pleasure or both. There are ways to minimize the chances that travel will be disrupted. There are ways to reduce the stress of travel, and find help when things do go bad. There are even ways to *enjoy* travel.

This book will give you the insider's guide needed for smart travel today, showing you how to improve travel, from ways to anticipate trouble and protect your trip to the best strategies for riding in relative luxury at discount prices. Consider it your "easy button" for taking some of the hassle out of airports and airlines.

Power Travel is the culmination of twenty-five years of frequent travel and in-depth reporting on airlines. For more than a decade I was a roving reporter for the Associated Press, racking up many miles and suitcases full of travel tips. After a few years at *The Wall Street Journal*, I got the chance to cover aviation, and in 2002, I began a weekly column called "The Middle Seat," which quickly gained a following of road warriors hungry for any information to improve their difficult travels. In more than fourteen years of reporting on the airline industry, I've tried to explain why things go awry and highlight the delights that can be found on the road. I approach it all as a professional traveler, but it's a private passion, too. I became a pilot myself in 1998.

We'll move through the book just as you would plan a trip, starting with decisions about where to go, when to go, and what to accomplish while you're there. We'll explore the confounding and frustrating world of airline pricing and look at the best ways to buy tickets. No other industry makes it so hard for consumers to buy its products and use its services. As complex as airline pricing is, there are ways to beat the system, get the best deal, and even find affordable first-class seats. We'll detail the best strategies for scoring frequent-flier awards and avoiding frequent-flier rip-offs. You can upgrade your experience at little cost—this book will show you how to do it, plus what's worth a couple of extra dollars and what's not. You can anticipate problems and formulate a backup plan. You can get early warning of snafus and be first on the phone to book a new flight. You can minimize late flights, missed connections, lost baggage, and long lines. You can protect yourself against getting bumped from flights, or being hassled by airport security, or being left stranded overnight at some airport. You can use several key Internet tools to improve the flight experience, on and off the ground, and find great deals on flights, cruises, and hotels.

Before you go, check the tips for preparing for your trips—what to wear, how to avoid getting nickel-and-dimed, whether or not you need travel insurance, and how to get early warning of travel delays and cancellations. We'll study best baggage practices and explain how airline baggage systems work—and break down—so you'll be able to minimize your chances of lost luggage. And then there are some key tips for navigating the maddening world of airport security.

On the plane, boarding and seating become paramount for travelers, and we'll explain how airlines handle over-booking, bumping, and seat upgrades so you'll have a leg up on fellow passengers. If legroom or seat width is impor-tant to you, we'll outline details on which airlines offer the most. We'll catalog the best perks offered to celebrities and CEOs, and show how you can get occasional pampering. From deep vein thrombosis to jet lag, health issues will be explored. And then there are those policy questions that always perplex many, such as why you have to turn off your cell phone (not because of aircraft instrument interfer-ence, as you're always told). We'll look at how air-traffic-control operations work and why some planes get priority over others, and what you can do to try to avoid air-traffic lockdowns. We'll also look at enhancing your experience at hotels and on cruises, too.

In the self-service travel world, you're on your own these days. You need to learn how to travel better. This guide will take you there.

THE WALL STREET JOURNAL.

CHAPTER 1

The Ten Commandments of Travel

A sixteen-year-old girl flying home alone gets stuck in Chicago when typical summer thunderstorms cause her flight to be canceled. The airline claims it can't rebook her for two days. Where should she stay? the girl asks the airline agent. You're on your own, the airline tells her, but the airport is setting up cots and providing blankets. (And unfortunately, the airline can't retrieve her suitcase.)

A family with a reservation for an expensive Caribbean cruise buys travel insurance ten days before departure because they fear a hurricane might disrupt their trip. Smart, right? Sure enough, a storm moves toward the ship's intended path. The cruise line doesn't cancel, but the family is afraid. They decide not to go and seek a refund. Sorry, they are told, their coverage doesn't apply to *that* storm. They're on their own—travel insurance doesn't cover "fear."

A couple takes their golden anniversary trip across Europe—two weeks of fine dining, gorgeous sites, spectacular museums, and romance rekindling. They land in Rome, but their luggage doesn't. What are we to do? they ask their airline. The agent hands them a small amenity kit with a miniature toothbrush and a small tube of tooth-paste. They don't get a "Sorry." Instead, they are told not to expect the bags for four days, maybe. The airline will try to deliver the bags to wherever they may be on their itinerary, but there's a chance that the bags may not catch up to them until they return home. The airline offers a small clothing allowance—forty dollars each should cover them for a few days—call back if you need more. Other than those token gestures, they are left to basically fend for themselves.

An electrician from San Francisco saves up to take his family to Europe for a family reunion. They book one flight—United 991—from San Francisco to Paris, with a stop in Washington, D.C. The flight is late leaving San Francisco because of a mechanical problem, and they arrive in Washington only to be told that their connection to Paris—the same United Flight 991—departed eighteen minutes before they arrived. One flight; two planes. Because they bought a deeply discounted ticket, United won't put them on another airline to Paris. They have to wait two days for seats. Fear not, the airline tells them, because it was the airline's fault they missed the connection (the mechanical problem with the originating leg of Flight 991), the airline will put the family of four in a tiny hotel room with two double beds near Dulles Airport for the next thirty-eight hours. When they reach Paris, they must race to the reunion, losing two days of their eight-day "trip of a lifetime."

In each of these cases, travelers could have prevented their disappointment and disruption. They needed to prepare for potential problems; they needed to know their rights. It's true: When you travel today, you have to fend for yourself. Whether you are traveling on business and booking trips yourself (or with the help of an assistant who may not be any more travel-trained than you are), or planning vacations and hunting for airfares, hotels, and even museum tickets yourself, the travel business has gone the way of the scan-it-yourself grocery store. And even if you do use an expert travel agent, when you get out on the road your-self, you are still far better off being prepared to take your travels into your own hands than in relying on relief from airlines and other travel vendors. Travelers who wait for the airline to rebook them often wait the longest. Customers who stand in line hoping for a hotel room may be the ones to lose out. Fliers who don't know their rights when they get bumped from a flight often end up with less than they are entitled to.

There was a time when travel by air, sea, and rail was elegant and adventurous, and airlines and travel companies took pains to care for their customers. Back then, travel was also far more expensive—and more dangerous—than today. Travelers dressed up for their trips and enjoyed at-tentive service, sometimes even the white-glove treatment. Airlines, cruise lines, and rail lines around the world catered to the elite. It wasn't mass transit; it was an experience.

Over the years, travel has democratized. It has become mass transit, whether in the air, at sea, or on rails. In 1970, 170 million people flew on U.S. airlines. By 2007, airline passengers in the United States zoomed to 769 million, ac-cording to the U.S. Department of Transportation. The U.S. population increased over that time by 50 percent from about 200 million to 300 million. But the number of airline passengers increased by 352 percent. And the count is expected to keep growing—the Federal Aviation Admin-istration estimates airlines will carry one billion passengers in the United States by 2016, only a few years away.

What was once an extravagance is now a necessity. We can live anywhere we want and still see family and friends almost anytime we want because we can move about cheaply. We can work just about anywhere we want because we can be with a client or the boss in a matter of hours. We can load up our grandchildren, cousins, and anyone else and head on a cruise, or to Disney World, or to the Grand Canyon. The ease and relatively small expense of travel has been a boon to economies around the world, and a major sociological factor in spreading out families, companies, cities, and civilizations. The world is simply a smaller place.

But this sweeping change hasn't come without pain. Around the world, the airline industry in particular has been going through upheaval, with many benefits for passengers and also many detriments. In the United States, big airlines are still trying to find their way in the world thirty years after the industry was deregulated. Incumbent airlines have been trying to rework their cost structures to shed the remnants of the days when the government regulated route competition and fares were set not by free-market competition but by the Civil Aeronautics Board, whose purpose was to limit competition and guarantee that fares were high enough to ensure a profit for airlines. At the same time, start-up airlines bring new options and prices for travelers, stiffening the competition even more. Young carriers aren't saddled with expensive labor contracts; long-standing pension obligations to pilots, mechanics, and flight attendants; or employees with enough seniority to reach the top of pay scales. Yet they also don't have many of the advantages of incumbency—prime gates and landing slots at crowded airports, sweeping frequent-flier programs, and vital contracts with major corporations that buy lots of expensive tickets.

The air wars of the past three decades, along with the enormous strains the industry has suffered, from terrorism attacks to severe storms to high oil prices, have made for industry turbulence. Some U.S. airlines have landed in bankruptcy court two or even three times. And many have failed or been subsumed by healthier rivals. The names of Eastern Air Lines, Braniff International, Pan Am World Airways, Western Airlines, Western Pacific, America West Airlines, and many others have been painted over on the sides of jets. And the repainting will continue as more airlines fail and merge. The latest disappearing name: Northwest Airlines.

Declining service has been another constant, especially when oil prices rise. Meals in coach—and even some first-class cabins—have mostly disappeared off airlines, replaced by snacks for sale and passengers carrying on their own food. Carriers have squeezed seats closer and closer together, and now charge passengers for seats with extra legroom. Airlines took away many previously free services and functions and began charging fees—$25 to buy a ticket over the telephone; $30 round-trip to check one piece of luggage; $50 for a second suitcase. Some charge for blankets, pillows, and bottled water. Most charge large penalties for changing nonrefundable fares. If you buy a $300 ticket six months in advance and then need to make a change, you'll pay a $150 penalty at some airlines, plus the difference if seats are more expensive on the new flight. (But if the airline wants to change its schedule, it can do so without any penalty.)

Is there any other industry that makes it so difficult to use its product? (Funeral homes, perhaps.)

Over the past few years, airlines have also found more ways to pack planes fuller—flying empty seats may make a flight more comfortable for a passenger enjoying the extra room, but what carrier can afford that when billions of dollars in losses pile up? The crowds have made air travel far more difficult. And airlines have, for several years, been moving to leaner and leaner operations. Some airlines used technology to eliminate some jobs—kiosks to check in customers, for example, or online booking to replace reservationists. And many jobs were scaled back simply because airlines were trying to stay afloat. Unable to afford extra airport staff during disruptions, airlines put their employees, and customers, often in terrible situations. Many customers found themselves stranded in long lines at airports, for example, while two agents tried to rebook ten planeloads of angry, tired, and hungry passengers. Likewise, fewer baggage handlers mean more lost luggage—and no one to answer the phone in the baggage office when things go missing. Planes sometimes sit after arrival and wait for a ground crew to marshal the aircraft into the gate. Passengers fume while waiting to race off a plane because the airline doesn't have anyone available to open the aircraft door after it pulls up to a jet-bridge.

In a sense, today's traveler has to open that aircraft door herself. That's the mind-set required today—you can't expect an airline or even a hotel or tour company or car rental firm to take care of you, as odds are they won't. If you want things to go well and want to get where you need to be on time and intact, then you have to open that aircraft door yourself—at least metaphorically.

Good travel starts with good preparation. Simple steps can save you time and money. The right research at home can lead to exciting, enjoyable experiences on the road. Preparing for potential trouble can save you from getting waylaid or stranded. Working the upgrade game can be the difference between happiness and misery.

Here are some Power Travel basics—ten commandments to guide your life away from home. Each will be explored in detail, but here are the essential rules to travel by.

THE POWER TRAVEL COMMANDMENTS

1. **Travel's difficult. And it costs too much.** An editor of mine provided this edict. No matter the season or the continent, travel can be hard, and it will almost always cost more than you might like. This commandment comes before all others—know it and you will understand why the others are necessary.

2. **Book smartly.** There's a wealth of information out there at your fingertips—use it to improve your travels. Pick the right time to fly; choose the right flights; avoid loser flights; know when you're getting a good price and when you aren't; vaccinate yourself against getting bumped or arriving without your luggage. Get warnings of delays or cancellations even before the gate agent does.

3. **Plan for trouble.** Build itineraries with delays in mind, because if you don't, you're sure to get stuck. Always have a backup plan—where will you stay if you miss a connection or get stranded by a storm? How do you know when it's time to quit hoping and take action? How will you get there if you can't go as planned?

4. **Learn something.** Have fun when you travel, even when it's a tedious business trip. Explore a new city, try a new regional cuisine, go see a movie—even if you don't speak the local language. Too often we jet from hotel room to hotel room, even on vacation, without giving ourselves the freedom for adventures.

5. **Enjoy perks that pay.** To get more, you often have to spend more. You can get a lot more in your travels

without spending a lot more. Learn how to find value in paying for access to airport clubs, more legroom, quicker security screening, frequent-flier awards, and upgrades at airlines, hotels, and even rental car companies. Consider popping for the kind of perks that VIPs enjoy—valet parking, perhaps, or a car service to or from the airport. Even a private jet can be more "affordable" than you think.

6.   **Stay loyal.** You have to pick the right airline program for you, the right hotel loyalty program, the right car rental elite program, and even the right credit card. Better yet, find one program that pays you for all your purchases. Concentrating your spending can generate quicker connections to free perks.

7.   **Never check what you can't do without.** There are times when you have to check luggage with airlines; there are times when you may even want to check luggage. But if you're traveling with something you can't do without, don't give it to the airline or the TSA for safekeeping.

8.   **Play the upgrade game.** Even if you don't travel one million miles a year and have Super Precious Elite Status, you can still upgrade. With airlines, hotels, and car rental companies, each has a different game to play, but there are opportunities for everyone to score.

9.   **Ask nicely.** Sure, the gate agent was curt, the flight attendant surly, and the baggage clerk unsympathetic, but don't stoop to their level. Take the high road—it's hard enough, why be angry? It turns out that in the

travel business, whether it's landing a hotel suite for the night or sleeping in a bigger airline seat, you get more with sugar than with salt.

10. **Be kind to your fellow travelers.** The window-seat occupant asked me to move so he could get out and fetch a blanket. "Would you like a blanket?" he asked me. How considerate. Flight attendants weren't about to offer blankets, but passengers can help one another. We can all improve our travel by recognizing that we're all in it together.

CHAPTER 2

Deciding Where You Want to Go, and How

The most important travel preparations begin with the decision we most often give short shrift: deciding where you want to go, and how. Too often we go straight to a computer and start punching up prices and schedules. But that's not the most important consideration. Wait . . . Is that really where I want to go? Is that the best place to go? Is that the best order for visiting those cities? Is there a better way? There's an art to business trips—making them more enjoyable and less stressful while still efficient, productive, and effective. And there's a science to leisure travel—we often pick the wrong vacation, something that we think sounds like fun, but in reality isn't a good fit. The first point to consider is how you can enhance your trip before you even decide where and when you're going.

POWER TRIPS

There are two kinds of successful road warriors. Some skilled travelers navigate the perils of frequent flying by sticking to exact routines and by relying on acquired habits to help them steer through the quirks and complexities of life on the road. They book the same airline every time, even if it involves a connection, because they know what kind of service they'll get most of the time, and because they want the perks that come with elite status, such as early boarding, first-class upgrades, and priority on standby lists. They go through airport security the same way every time. They have a routine once on board airplanes—aisle seat, noise canceling headphones, club soda with a lime. I know frequent travelers who have a specific routine for overnight international flights—wear your suit on board and carry a jogging suit in your bag. Once in the air, change clothes in the bathroom, hanging the suit and sleeping in the jogging suit. About forty-five minutes before landing, change back into the suit and you're good to go, with nary a wrinkle. These kinds of travelers use the same car service or rental car company every trip. They stay in the same chain of hotels because they like the familiarity—and the points. Some even stay in the same room at the same hotel over and over and over and over and over again.

Then there are the free spirits, who see business travel not as one giant headache or sales call, but as an adventure—a chance to explore the world on an expense account. They relish exotic airlines—Oh, the stories they'll be able to tell! They never eat at the hotel restaurant but hunt for the best local cuisine. Exercise means finding the local park. Entertainment may be a trip to the local cinema or a night out at a trendy club. If there is any downtime, they seek out museums or the theater, or simply do some sightseeing. They go with the flow—no worries if security takes a little longer, or they don't get an upgrade. They learn to shrug off delays—just an opportunity to explore more, even if it's some strange airport with little to offer other than a newsstand and hot dogs left too long on a rotisserie.

Both kinds of travelers are successful because they learn to navigate the system in a way suited to their needs and personality. That's the key to the art of business travel: Whether you are ying or yang, particular or free-spirited, you can learn not only how to beat the system, but also how to do it without raising your blood pressure.

Most business travelers know that traveling on the day of a meeting or event can be dicey. If you are making a sales call to your biggest client, you better get to the city a day early. If you are connecting to an overseas trip, don't book a flight that arrives just an hour or two before your international flight departure. You can't depend on a flight being on time. In summer, about one-third of all flights are "late," which the industry defines as arriving at the gate fifteen minutes or more beyond the scheduled arrival time. The frequency of "excessive" delays of forty-five minutes or more is growing. As are cancellations. Cancellations are still rare—generally 3 percent to 4 percent of all flights. But they come in bunches at airlines hit by problems and at cities overwhelmed by storms. These days, never assume the flight will take off or arrive as scheduled.

Getting to town a day ahead of time gives you the luxury of checking into your hotel at a reasonable hour, assuming your air travel worked out and you didn't spend the day waiting and wondering. It gives you time for a workout in the hotel gym; it gives you a chance to explore the city you are visiting. There are lots of resources to use to find fun things to do. You can check local newspapers online for listings of events, concerts, museum exhibitions, and restaurant reviews. Restaurant suggestions also can be found online at Zagat.com, Fodors.com, MobilTravelGuide.com, and other travel guide companies. TripAdvisor.com has restaurant reports and suggestions from travelers about "Things to Do" along with its hotel reviews from customers. And OpenTable.com not only ranks restaurants but also allows you to book reservations online. You can see what's available at popular restaurants with just a couple of clicks, and narrow your choices based on preferences, whether you want a place for foodies, a romantic setting, a neighborhood gem, a vibrant bar scene, or places great for groups. And if you haven't planned ahead or prefer personal recommendations, use hotel concierges. Just remember that their recommendations may be based on establishments that pay them fees for sending travelers their way.

Beyond a good time or a good meal and avoiding travel hassles, time spent getting to know cultures and cities can pay off in any business. Clients and contacts may be impressed and even flattered that you took the time to learn about their home. Knowledge of other countries and histories and customs can pay off in sales or analysis.

Giving yourself a "travel day" does not have to make you any less productive, either. Life on the road these days means being every bit as connected and online as you are when you are in the office. Cellular phones, BlackBerrys, and laptops with wireless Internet service keep many of us plugged in. Airports have gotten better about providing power plugs and work spaces, and lots of business travelers find membership in an airport club program helpful. For an annual fee of around $400 (it varies by airline), you get quiet places to work around the world—not just with that particular airline, but often reciprocal membership at partner airlines as well. Clubs have shower facilities, bars, and meeting rooms. More important, some of the best airline agents are assigned to the clubs, so if you need rebooking or are anxious about an upgrade, those employees know best how to work the system in your favor.

POWER VACATIONS

If the key to successful business travel is finding a strategy you are comfortable with and executing it smartly, do the same rules apply to leisure travel? Yes, and a bit more. Successful vacations depend on proper preparation and careful itinerary selection that suit your personality. The difference, of course, is that we often don't pick our destination when we travel for business—we go where the job takes us. With vacations, we pick the destination as well as how to get there. Too often, vacationers make the wrong choice when picking a place to vacation, opting for bike-riding adventures when they would be happier lying on a beach, or driving to Disney World when they would be more suited to hiking in Alaska.

Cruise lines, airlines, resort operators, and tourism bureaus have long helped fund research in academic and corporate circles to predict traveler preferences and figure out how best to sell trips. These researchers have identified ways to match people with appropriate trips, and the dean of this somewhat obscure cadre of travel experts is a man named Stanley Plog.

Dr. Plog, founder of Plog Research Inc., has spent forty years researching travel preferences and decisions, from which coach seats are most comfortable on airplanes to how resorts and European capitals might best sell themselves to tourists abroad. He has found that we all have a "travel personality"—and most of us fit into one of six different profiles. Figuring out which type of traveler you are can help you pick appropriate vacations. If you pick a destination not well suited for you, you're likely to have a lousy vacation. But if you choose the perfect place for your personality, you'll have an agreeable journey, maybe even the trip of a lifetime.

We all have different desires and needs when we vacation. Some people like to relax on the beach; others prefer to climb mountains. Some people love crowds. Many are most comfortable driving to someplace close to home, and often the same place as last year and the year before. Others jump on airplanes to see new, unfamiliar places, far, far away.

It's not always obvious. Sometimes we feel that we need to seek out rough-edge adventures when really we'd be happier lying by a pool with a cocktail. What's more, some couples have different travel personalities, so one type of trip may not be compatible for both.

"People choose the wrong vacation all the time, and they come back really disappointed," Dr. Plog says. To solve this problem, he developed a questionnaire, available at his Web site www.BestTripChoices.com, that pegs personalities and then recommends appropriate travel choices. The quiz presents fifteen statements and asks people to agree or disagree with each on a seven-point scale. Some seem obviously related to travel, such as "I prefer to go to undiscovered places before big hotels and restaurants are built." Others are more obscure, such as "Chance has little to do with success in my life."

The trick is that only seven or eight of the questions drive the results—the rest are thrown in for cover, Dr. Plog says. He doesn't disclose which questions are the true revealers of personality, except to say they are not the obvious travel questions. How much you read, for example, and how much TV you watch are indicators of the trips you'll prefer, Dr. Plog says.

If you don't want to bother with the questionnaire—I

recommend it, because several friends, family members, and I found it enlightening and at least amusing—then have a look at the six different categories here and see where you think you most likely fit.

1. **Venturers.** At one end of the vacation personality scale are "venturers"—people who like to find undiscovered destinations and explore unique cultures. Venturers, who amount to only 3 percent to 4 percent of the U.S. population, hate to drive to a vacation because it takes too long. They are explorers who would rarely enjoy the services of a tour guide or the comforts of a group. They want freedom in their travels, according to Dr. Plog, and seek uncommon destinations long before travel writers—or worse, resort developers—discover them. "Venturers," likely the first among their friends to have a hybrid car or high-definition television, are a confident bunch who enjoy adventure travel, whether trekking in Nepal or canoeing in the Amazon.

2. **Mid-Venturers.** These people are jet-setters. They want to visit the newest spa or resort. They love to tell friends about the great trips they have taken. They may venture out for a bike trip across New England or New Zealand, but they want to bed down at a quaint inn rather than sleep under the stars, in Dr. Plog's definitions. History holds great fascination for "mid-venturers," and they are way beyond watching the changing of the guard at Buckingham Palace or climbing the Eiffel Tower. They seek the discovery of an ancient monastery. They are disciplined in their personal habits—consumers of vitamins, regulars at the gym, devotees of a good night's sleep.

3. **Centric-Venturers.** Centric-venturers like exotic places, but they want good hotels and restaurants, too. According to Dr. Plog's definition, "centric-venturers" read newspapers a lot and are selective about television. They'd be happy on a Greek cruise or a tour of California ghost towns or even a New York shopping trip. They are the people whom airlines, resorts, cruise lines, and other travel vendors most want to reach, as they are flexible, adaptable, and swayed by advertising. They comprise about 30 percent of the U.S. population and don't stick to regular travel patterns. For one trip they may drive if it's convenient; for the next they will fly. They are turned off by souvenir shops and tourist buses. When they travel, they shop for native products—wool sweaters in Scotland or silver in Mexico. They've been to the big capitals of Europe and now seek out smaller European towns.

4. **Authentics.** At the other end of the spectrum are what Dr. Plog calls "authentics"—travelers who prefer everything familiar and predictable and like going where there are lots of people. After all, it must be a good place if there are crowds. In the bell curve of travel personality, "authentics" comprise only 3 percent to 4 percent of travelers. These folks are quiet, easygoing, and dependable—the ones who get asked to do something often because people know they will do it right. Authentics would "rather go to places that have earned a well-deserved reputation as being great, rather than experiment with more recently discovered and potentially less satisfying destinations," Dr. Plog says. They are comfortable in tour groups, often don't venture too far from home, and like to pick up souvenirs that serve

as visual reminders of a trip—a plastic Statute of Liberty or a Hawaiian shirt. They prefer the predictability and control of driving by car to the unpredictability and hassles of air travel.

5. **Mid-Authentics.** These are steady, unwavering people like authentics, but they are also a little more flexible and have broad circles of friends. They are the most easygoing, unruffled sorts, casual and carefree in their travels. They may get labeled as "mellow" by family and friends. Mid-authentics are particularly social people who love golf and vacations in the sun. About one out of every six people fall into this category, Dr. Plog says. They are movie renters and TV watchers and enjoy household chores and spending time in the backyard. For travel, mid-authentics may be mobile-home aficionados. They go back year after year to places they like, perhaps Florida, perhaps Caribbean cruises. They are happy to relax on a beach—with no need for go-go exploration or adventure.

6. **Centric-Authentics.** These are the people who show up for work on time every day and take few sick days. Others turn to centric-authentics to solve problems— they have lots of common sense and good people skills. They stick with what works, or at least wait before buying new technology until prices drop. Centric-authentic women often cook and sew for fun, Dr. Plog says, while centric-authentic men are good at making repairs around the house or on cars. When they shop, centric-authentics stick to popular brands. When they travel, centric-authentics may head out for a relaxing place to fish, or enjoy just being outdoors in a beautiful

setting. If they do decide to go abroad, escorted tour groups are a good choice for them.

Some travel destinations do offer something for everyone, and the key to an enjoyable vacation lies in selecting activities that fit your profile. Hawaii is a good example: There are beaches for the authentics, although some of them may find a long flight to the islands far less appealing than an easier drive to the coast. For those who want predictable souvenirs, crowded tourist areas, and plenty of familiar hotels and restaurants, Hawaii is a good choice. So, too, for golfers and people who enjoy casual sports, hiking, and history. And for the venturers, there are all kinds of exotic places to explore and even extreme sports—such as surfing or canoeing, volcano hiking, or helicopter tours. Likewise, Alaska can be a place for adventure, and yet authentics can still enjoy scenery from a train or relax on a cruise ship. Massachusetts ranked high as a destination for five of the six different personality groups. Venturers can find lots of sports excitement—run the Boston Marathon, sail in Marblehead, cross-country ski in the Berkshires, make a baseball pilgrimage to Fenway Park. Centrics might like relaxing at the Tanglewood Music Festival in the western part of the state or deep-sea fishing off Cape Cod. Authentics can find lots of history to explore—the Freedom Trail, Plimoth Plantation, Old Sturbridge Village, Longfellow's Wayside Inn in Sudbury. Shopping in Boston, from the elegant boutiques of Newbury Street to the ravenous crowds at Filene's Basement, might highlight a vacation as well.

That's the rub in all of this science: The key to a good vacation is not only the destination, but also careful selection of what to do while there. Even if you're on a cruise ship, decide if rugged shore excursions or exploration on your own is what gets you most excited, or whether you'd prefer daily bingo to working up a sweat. Whether traveling for business or pleasure, spend some time thinking about what you want to accomplish and how you can get the most out of a trip before you ever start shopping for tickets.

CHAPTER 3

How Airlines Price Tickets

There's a Laurel and Hardy–type routine that can be found on the Internet where airline pricing is applied in a paint store. It goes something like this: A man walks in and says he needs a gallon of paint for a home project, and inquires about the price.

"That depends," the store clerk says. "When do you want to paint?"

"I'd like to paint tomorrow—my day off. But why does that matter?" the shopper says. "Just tell me the cost of your paint."

"Our paint ranges in price from twenty-five dollars a gallon to three hundred dollars a gallon," the clerk says.

"Three hundred dollars a gallon! What's the difference between that and the twenty-five-dollar paint?"

"No difference—it's the same paint. It's just a matter of when you want to paint, and how far ahead of time you buy it."

"I'd like the twenty-five-dollar paint," the do-it-yourselfer says.

"That paint can only be used three weeks from now on a

Tuesday, and it can't be applied on a holiday week," the clerk says. "I do have some paint that can be used tomorrow night at two hundred dollars a gallon. Or if you buy for next weekend, the price is only a hundred and twenty-five dollars a gallon."

"That's outrageous," the man says. "But I'll take six gallons of the twenty-five-dollar paint."

"Just remember that the paint must be used under the terms it was sold," the clerk says, "or you'll have to pay us the difference in price, plus a penalty. And if you don't use it all, there will be a penalty."

Buying airline tickets is one of the most confusing and maddening purchases a consumer can make—right up there with shopping for a car. Airlines advertise prices but make it difficult to find that price. What's more, airline prices change several times a day—sometimes as much as seven times a day. And the availability of tickets at a certain price can disappear in a flash. It all makes travelers crazy. Different people on the same plane pay vastly different prices. Ask the other people in your row sometime what they paid. You'll either feel great, or feel like you've been had.

Consider the rules and restrictions that airlines attach to tickets. The fine print on an American Airlines nonrefundable discounted ticket, for example, fills pages and pages in devilishly small type. You can find it under "Terms and Conditions" and "Contract of Carriage." The legalese even spells out what happens to the ticket in case you die before you take your trip. (Fortunately, there's not a penalty for dying—American will refund the ticket to the estate of the dead passenger via the original form of payment if the dead passenger's survivors provide a copy of the death certificate to American. Nothing is easy—even dying.) Here's a sample, just in case you've never read all the terms and conditions you agree to every time you fly. This is just the provisions on a typical nonrefundable American ticket under the "Refunds/Reissues" section. There are several other sections, covering penalties and the like, of equal length and density.

IN THE EVENT OF CHANGES TO TICKETED FLIGHTS BEFORE DEPARTURE OF JOURNEY AND WITHIN TKT VALIDITY CERTAIN DOMESTIC REISSUE PROVISIONS MAY BE OVERRIDDEN BY THOSE OF AA INTERNATIONAL FARES APPLY CARRIER COMPENSATION FEE OF USD 150.00 FOR REISSUE OR HIGHEST FEE OF ANY CHANGED FARE COMPONENT WITHIN JOURNEY—INFANT DISCOUNT APPLIES AND REPRICE USING FARES IN EFFECT TODAY PROVIDED ALL OF THE FOLLOWING CONDITIONS ARE MET- 1. WHEN NO INTL COUPONS REMAIN—ALL NEW TRAVEL MUST BE DOMESTIC 2. AA FARES ARE USED 3. PRIVATE TARIFFS ARE INCLUDED 4. VALIDATE ADVANCE RES REQUIREMENTS WHEN BOOKING DATE KNOWN 5. ADV RES IS MEASURED FROM REISSUE DATE TO DEPARTURE OF PRICING UNIT WHEN CHANGE RESULTS IN LOWER FARE SUBTRACT RESIDUAL FROM THE PENALTY THEN ADD-COLLECT/REFUND—REFUND VIA VOUCHER ENDORSEMENT BOX- HIGHER NON-REF AMT AND NEW ENDORSEMENTS. OR—ANYTIME WITHIN TKT VALIDITY CERTAIN DOMESTIC REISSUE PROVISIONS MAY BE OVERRIDDEN BY THOSE OF AA INTERNATIONAL FARES APPLY CARRIER COMPENSATION FEE OF USD 150.00 FOR REISSUE OR HIGHEST FEE OF ANY CHANGED FARE COMPONENT WITHIN JOURNEY—INFANT DISCOUNT APPLIES AND REPRICE A. CHANGED FARE COMPONENTS USE FARES IN EFFECT TODAY B. ALL OTHERS USE CURRENTLY TKTD FARE PROVIDED ALL OF THE FOLLOWING CONDITIONS ARE MET- 1. NO CHANGE TO STOPOVERS/1ST FARE COMPONENT/ FARE BREAKS 2. SAME FARE ON 1ST FARE COMPONENT IS USED 3. WHEN NO INTL COUPONS REMAIN— ALL NEW TRAVEL MUST BE DOMESTIC 4. FULLY FLOWN FARE NOT REPRICED TO FURTHER POINT 5. AA FARES ARE USED 6. PRIVATE TARIFFS ARE INCLUDED 7. NEW FARE IS EQUAL OR HIGHER THAN PREVIOUS FARE 8. WHEN SAME FARE USED—ALL RULE AND BOOKING CODE PROVISIONS ARE MET EXCEPT DAYTIME—OTHERWISE ALL PROVISIONS MUST BE MET 9. VALIDATE ADVANCE RES REQUIREMENTS WHEN BOOKING DATE KNOWN 10. ADV RES IS MEASURED FROM ORIGINAL TKT DATE TO DEPARTURE OF PRICING UNIT WHEN CHANGE RESULTS IN LOWER FARE SUBTRACT RESIDUAL FROM THE PENALTY THEN ADD-COLLECT/REFUND—REFUND VIA VOUCHER ENDORSEMENT BOX- HIGHER NON-REF AMT AND NEW ENDORSEMENTS. OR—AFTER DEPARTURE OF JOURNEY AND WITHIN TKT VALIDITY CERTAIN DOMESTIC REISSUE PROVISIONS MAY BE OVERRIDDEN BY THOSE OF AA INTERNATIONAL FARES APPLY CARRIER COMPENSATION FEE OF USD 150.00 FOR REISSUE OR HIGHEST FEE OF ANY CHANGED FARE COMPONENT WITHIN JOURNEY—INFANT DISCOUNT APPLIES AND REPRICE A. FULLY FLOWN FARE COMPONENTS USE FARES IN EFFECT WHEN TKT WAS ISSUED B. ALL OTHERS USE FARES IN EFFECT TODAY PROVIDED ALL OF THE FOLLOWING CONDITIONS ARE MET- 1. NO CHANGE TO FARE BREAKS OF FULLY FLOWN FARE COMPONENTS 2. WHEN NO INTL COUPONS REMAIN—ALL NEW TRAVEL MUST BE DOMESTIC 3. AA ONE-WAY FARES ARE USED 4. PRIVATE TARIFFS ARE INCLUDED 5. ALL RULE AND BOOKING CODE PROVISIONS ARE MET 6. VALIDATE ADVANCE RES REQUIREMENTS WHEN BOOKING DATE KNOWN 7. ADV RES IS MEASURED FROM REISSUE DATE TO DEPARTURE OF PRICING UNIT WHEN CHANGE RESULTS IN LOWER FARE SUBTRACT RESIDUAL FROM THE PENALTY THEN ADD-COLLECT/REFUND—REFUND VIA VOUCHER ENDORSEMENT BOX- HIGHER NON-REF AMT AND NEW ENDORSEMENTS. OR—BEFORE DEPARTURE OF JOURNEY AND WITHIN TKT VALIDITY CERTAIN DOMESTIC REISSUE PROVISIONS MAY BE OVERRIDDEN BY THOSE OF AA INTERNATIONAL FARES CHARGE USD 150.00 FOR REISSUE OR HIGHEST FEE OF ANY CHANGED FARE COMPONENT WITHIN JOURNEY AND REPRICE USING CURRENT FARES—ONLY BOOKING CODE CHANGES PERMITTED PROVIDED ALL OF THE FOLLOWING CONDITIONS ARE MET- 1. NO CHANGE TO STOPOVERS 2. WHEN NO INTL COUPONS REMAIN—ALL NEW TRAVEL MUST BE DOMESTIC 3. AA FARES ARE USED 4. PRIVATE TARIFFS ARE INCLUDED 5. VALIDATE ADVANCE RES REQUIREMENTS WHEN BOOKING DATE KNOWN 6. ADV RES IS MEASURED FROM ORIGINAL TKT DATE TO DEPARTURE OF PRICING UNIT WHEN CHANGE RESULTS IN LOWER FARE SUBTRACT RESIDUAL FROM THE PENALTY THEN ADD-COLLECT/REFUND—REFUND VIA VOUCHER ENDORSEMENT BOX- HIGHER NON-REF AMT AND NEW ENDORSEMENTS. OR—ANYTIME WITHIN TKT VALIDITY CERTAIN DOMESTIC REISSUE PROVISIONS MAY BE OVERRIDDEN BY THOSE OF AA INTERNATIONAL FARES APPLY CARRIER COMPENSATION FEE OF USD 150.00 FOR REISSUE OR HIGHEST FEE OF ANY CHANGED FARE COMPONENT WITHIN JOURNEY—INFANT DISCOUNT APPLIES AND REPRICE USING CURRENTLY TKTD FARE PROVIDED ALL OF THE FOLLOWING CONDITIONS ARE MET- 1. NO CHANGE TO STOPOVERS/1ST FARE COMPONENT/FARE BREAKS 2. WHEN NO INTL COUPONS REMAIN—ALL NEW TRAVEL MUST BE DOMESTIC 3. FULLY FLOWN FARE NOT REPRICED TO FURTHER POINT 4. AA SAME FARE CLASS GOVERNED BY SAME RULE IS USED 5. PRIVATE TARIFFS ARE INCLUDED 6. NEW FARE IS EQUAL OR HIGHER THAN PREVIOUS FARE 7. ALL RULE AND BOOKING CODE PROVISIONS ARE MET EXCEPT DAYTIME 8. VALIDATE ADVANCE RES REQUIREMENTS WHEN BOOKING DATE KNOWN 9. ADV RES IS MEASURED FROM ORIGINAL TKT DATE TO DEPARTURE OF PRICING UNIT WHEN CHANGE RESULTS IN LOWER FARE SUBTRACT RESIDUAL FROM THE PENALTY THEN ADD-COLLECT/REFUND—REFUND VIA VOUCHER ENDORSEMENT BOX- HIGHER NON-REF AMT AND NEW ENDORSEMENTS.

The difficulty with ticket purchases starts right at the beginning. Whenever you go to buy an airline ticket, the first question is always, "When do you want to go?" That's not merely a friendly, helpful convenience. Like the paint store, the price of an airline seat varies greatly depending on when you want to go, and how far ahead of time you want to buy the ticket. Right from the start, this transaction goes off track. Buyers want to know how much it costs to get to Orlando, and the airline answers the question with a question, "When do you want to go?" And if you simply say, "I want to go whenever it is cheapest," most airline reservation systems aren't set up to answer that question easily. Internet tools have helped make it easier to find the cheapest prices, but even with powerful search technology, it can be a challenging hunt to find the best deal. It shouldn't be so difficult.

POWER WALLETS

There are lots of ways to beat the airlines at their own game, or at least improve your odds of getting a good deal. We'll explore those in the next chapter. But first, it pays to understand how airlines price their tickets before you match wits with airline pricing computers. Smart ticket-buying has changed in the past few years, as airlines have gotten better at filling all the seats on a plane. When you fly, there's rarely an empty seat. That's not because there is more demand. It's because airlines have gotten a lot better at managing seat inventory.

The root of the Byzantine airline pricing system lies in the wallet biopsy. Different people will pay different prices for the same ticket, and airlines believe they can maximize their revenue if they maximize what they can get out of your wallet. People on business trips are willing to pay more for flights because they're not buying the tickets. Business travelers want conveniences that can cost an airline more, from frequent flights on a route to free first-class upgrades, and they want the airline to hold back seats so that they can get on planes without advance purchase. If a client wants you in Denver tomorrow, you need a seat to get there. The airline likely could have sold that seat to someone at a deep discount in advance, and the airline takes a risk in holding that seat for the business customer. For that risk, the airline collects a reward: a higher fare. The airline makes more money when a business traveler shows up at the last minute to pay ten times what other passengers paid to get on the plane. If the seat flies empty, the airline loses. Figuring out how many seats to sell early at discounts before flights depart and how many to hold back for business travelers who book reservations later and pay a lot more is the whole magic of airline pricing.

Much of the complexity of ticket pricing comes from the airline's desire to segregate customers—load up the cheap tickets with restrictions so that they can't be used by business travelers. Business travelers do self-segregate to some extent when they book tickets through their corporate travel agencies—airlines know those trips are mostly business, mostly paid for by the company, not the individual traveler. But if you simply tried to charge higher rates through one type of agency over another, buyers would switch to the cheapest outlet.

Instead, airlines dreamed up advance-purchase requirements for cheap tickets, along with cumbersome travel conditions. The most-discounted tickets are often not changeable because business travelers like the flexibility to hop on an earlier flight if the meeting wraps up sooner than expected, or leave a day later if the client's schedule changes. Cheap fares have to be bought two or three weeks in advance to get the lowest price, and they often require "minimum stays"—you have to be in your destination for a couple of nights, at least. That weeds out many road warriors who jet around, rarely spending more than one day in the same city. The most powerful segregator of all for airlines is the Saturday night stay requirement. People on vacation often want to be at their destination for a weekend; business travelers typically want to be home for the weekend. To get the lowest fare, you occasionally have to agree that you'll stay out of town for a Saturday night. The gall of it: It's like the paint store telling you that to get the cheapest price, you have to paint on a specific day. What business is it of the airline where I sleep on Saturday night?

The best customers—the road warriors who travel every week on an airline—end up paying the highest prices. Most businesses give their best customers their biggest discounts, but the airline industry does the opposite. I've asked many airline executives over the years to name another business that charges its best customers its highest rates. The only plausible answer I've ever gotten: health care. The sickest patients pay the highest charges—not exactly the model of customer satisfaction to which any other industry should aspire.

Airlines argue that business travelers actually buy a different product from leisure travelers because the seat held in reserve for them has fewer penalties and restrictions. And businesses do get corporate discounts from airlines, so that they don't pay the highest of the highest prices if they buy lots of tickets. Think of it, one airline chief executive suggested to me, as a bakery—the last loaves of bread the baker has for sale before closing for the holiday weekend can command a higher price because people will pay more for what has become scarcer and more urgent. Some call it gouging. Airlines call it "yield management."

Yield management is a science that lots of other industries use, just not as visibly and as annoyingly as airlines. Television and radio stations charge higher rates for advertising at prime time, for example. Renting a beach condo may be a whole lot more expensive on a holiday weekend than midweek in October. The price of a dozen roses is always sky high on Valentine's Day, right? All that pricing is a form of yield management—taking supply and demand and changing prices accordingly.

POWER BUCKETS

In between the two extremes of airline prices—the early discount cheap-fare purchaser and the last-minute whatever-it-takes corporate customer—lies the majority of the passengers on each flight. Some are vacationers who didn't get the cheapest price but did get a discount. Others are business fliers able to book a seat in advance at something less than the highest prices. Typically, airlines have twenty or so different fare categories—or fare "buckets"—and they allocate seats into those different categories. Some percentage of the seats on a flight will be sold forty-five days or more before departure. Some percentage of seats will be sold out of buckets that require fourteen days advance-purchase. Other seats will come from seven-day buckets, or three-day buckets, or unrestricted buckets. Part of the complexity of airline pricing is that not only prices change but so do the buckets. Airline pricing analysts move seats around among different buckets based on demand. If a particular flight is selling heavily early, perhaps because of a convention or special event in the destination city or a large group snapping up seats, some remaining seats may be moved to more expensive buckets. If sales stall after the cheapest seats sell, some cheap buckets may be replenished with more seats.

You don't see all the inventory and price manipulation that goes on at lightning speed inside the "buckets," but it shows up in the price you get offered. If the advertised price for a trip to Florida can't be found on the flights you want, either that bucket sold out or it never had any seats to begin with. (The U.S. government requires airlines to make 10 percent of their seats available at prices they advertise, but it doesn't have to be 10 percent of the seats on every flight. An off-peak flight might have more of the cheapest seats; the Friday evening flight may have no seats at that advertised price.) More maddening, the price offered an hour ago has disappeared. Someone else either emptied the bucket by purchasing seats, or the airline shifted inventory. When you go to buy a car at a dealership, one salesperson may make you one offer while another may tell you something different—and neither one of them can make a deal until the sales manager gets involved as the final authority. Airline tickets can be just as aggravating; one time you go online to price a trip and see one fare, another time you see something different. One day you buy tickets at $350 only to see them fall to $325 the next day. Worse, you balk at the $350 price and the next day they hit $450. How can prices change so much so fast?

What's more, airlines have improved the ways computers allocate seats between connecting customers and local passengers. If you're going from Los Angeles to New York, you're actually competing for seats with people going from Los Angeles to Barcelona, or Los Angeles to Nantucket.

Would it be more profitable for the airline to sell the seat to someone connecting in New York to another flight, or to someone who simply wants to go to New York? The passenger going to Barcelona will pay the airline a lot more than the passenger going to New York, but what if the airline can fill the same seat with a customer going from New York to Barcelona? In that case, the airline sells two tickets instead of one. The Los Angeles passenger headed to Barcelona might be told that the Los Angeles–New York flight has no seats available, when someone looking just for a Los Angeles–New York ticket might see five seats available on the same flight. The airline doesn't want to use one of those last five seats for a Barcelona ticket. It has confidence it can do better in terms of revenue the greater the number of passengers who are buying individual tickets. The airlines try to balance demand for seats from markets all over the world, and price accordingly.

POWER FARES

Discount airlines, those low-cost, low-fare carriers like Southwest, jetBlue and AirTran in the United States and Ryanair and easyJet in Europe, have long used a simpler pricing structure, which has proven popular with the traveling public. Pricing tickets just doesn't have to be so complex to work for airlines. Southwest Airlines Co., the only consistently profitable U.S. airline, uses yield management, but just not to the same, mind-numbing degree as its rivals. Southwest has about four to six different fare buckets for flights. Business travelers seeking last-minute purchases or flexibility in their travels can get discounted business fares or full-priced fares at higher prices than discounted tickets, but these fares are still cheaper than what other airlines would like to charge last-minute buyers. Frugal travelers can get discounts; the earlier they buy, the cheaper the fare. Southwest often isn't the "cheapest" airline on a particular route—other airlines usually offer bigger discounts to at least a few customers. But Southwest's pricing is consistent, and people perceive it as fair. They are willing to pay because they don't feel gouged. And they get consistent service, too. Many aspects of Southwest have been studied and copied by other airlines, but I've long thought that one stealthy reason behind Southwest's success is that the airline makes it easy for people to purchase its product. Shocking, isn't it? And what's more, Southwest ends up with higher average fares—the price people pay to fly, per mile—than its competitors. It has lower average costs, higher average fares, and thus a record of more than thirty years without a quarterly financial loss.

Remember all that fine print covering just one section of American's ticketing rules? Now look at Southwest's rules. Here are the rules and restrictions on Southwest's lowest fare category, which the airline calls "Wanna Get Away?" They are available only on Southwest's Web site and are the airline's most-restrictive fares. These are all the rules—not just one section.

FARES ARE NONREFUNDABLE BUT MAY BE APPLIED TOWARD FUTURE TRAVEL ON SOUTHWEST AIRLINES. STANDBY TRAVEL IS PERMITTED BUT REQUIRES THAT THE CUSTOMER PAY THE DIFFERENCE BETWEEN THE ORIGINAL FARE AND THE "ANYTIME" FARE. FARES DO NOT INCLUDE A FEDERAL EXCISE TAX OF UP TO $3.50 PER TAKEOFF AND LANDING. FARES DO NOT INCLUDE AIRPORT-ASSESSED PASSENGER FACILITY CHARGES (PFC) OF UP TO $9 AND GOVERNMENT-IMPOSED SEPTEMBER 11TH SECURITY FEE OF UP TO $5 ONE-WAY. FARES MAY VARY AS SEATS ARE LIMITED AND MAY NOT BE AVAILABLE ON ALL FLIGHTS AND DATES. LIMITED SEATING, ADVANCE PURCHASE, AND OTHER CONDITIONS MAY APPLY. FARES ARE SUBJECT TO CHANGE UNTIL TICKETS ARE PURCHASED AND MAY BE AVAILABLE FOR A LIMITED TIME ONLY. WHEN COMBINING FARES, ALL RULES AND RESTRICTIONS APPLY.

The limited fine print illustrates the point. Which airline is more interested in making a sale?

In 2004, with big, established airlines under enormous

pressure from growing discounters like Southwest, AirTran Airways, Frontier Airlines, and others, Delta Air Lines Inc. decided to try simplified pricing. The change wasn't out of benevolence. Delta was simply acknowledging reality. Consumers preferred simplified airline pricing and were going to great lengths to use discounters. In Delta's case, lots of people who live in or around Cincinnati, a Delta hub, were driving to other cities in Ohio—Akron, Columbus, Dayton, and Cleveland—to fly on discounters. Delta said it wanted to win customers back, so it eliminated Saturday-night stay restrictions. Penalties to cancel reservations or make changes were reduced, and the number of fare buckets was reduced.

The change didn't last long. Under pressure from higher oil prices, airlines moved back toward making it harder for business travelers to buy cheap tickets. In some markets, Saturday-night restrictions have reappeared. In many markets, airlines have increased one-night stay requirements to three nights as a way of blocking business travelers from discounted fares and forcing them to pay more. Cancellation penalties on domestic tickets have been increased to as much as $150 from $50, plus the difference between a new fare and the original price. Complexity in ticket pricing remains—and probably will until discounters, which handle about 30 percent of domestic air travel now, get closer to a majority of the domestic market. That could well happen over the next decade.

Airlines have also found new ways to pack more people into each airplane, generating more revenue from each flight. Years back, Robert L. Crandall, then the chief executive of American Airlines, told a group of Wall Street analysts that airlines had used better computers and better sales models to drive load factors—the percentage of seats filled—up from 65 percent into the low seventies. It can't go higher than that, Crandall said then. There were just too many flights on Tuesdays and Wednesdays when travel is slower, too many flights in February and slow travel months, too many early morning and late-night flights less attractive to fliers, and too much risk from angering customers and losing big sales if you don't hold back enough seats for business travelers.

That was in 1995. By 2007, airlines were filling more than 80 percent of their seats—about 85 percent in the summer. That means lots and lots of planes flew with every single seat filled with a paying customer or close to it.

How'd they get there? Thanks to powerful computers and algorithms, airlines now track travel patterns down to the hour for each day of the year—what's the demand for a Tuesday 2 P.M. flight to Chicago during the first week of March? They track conventions and special events. They track everything they can to estimate what kind of demand there will be for each flight, and sell accordingly. Predicting business-travel purchases more accurately lets the airline sell more seats at deep discounts with the confidence that no business customers will be locked out. Knowing travel patterns also allows airlines to better parse seats between local customers and connecting passengers as well. When I go to book a ticket online, I almost expect the airline to flash a message on the screen, "We knew you'd be coming."

That change has had an enormous impact on how tickets are sold, and consumers have been slow to catch on. More accuracy into demand models has allowed airlines to avoid many big blow-out sales. Airlines used to offer huge sales when they misjudged the market. Now airlines can fill planes by tweaking buckets and fares, and skipping coast-to-coast sales.

The good news is that means airfares have gotten a bit more predictable. The closer you get to departure, the higher the fare is likely to be. There still may be some last-minute bargains, but they are increasingly rare. Waiting for sales can be a losing game. That could change with changing economic conditions; recessions always force airlines to fill empty seats with fire-sale prices. But the best rule of thumb for finding cheap fares is to start early. As the plane fills, the price only goes up. When people used to ask, Should I buy tickets early or buy them late? I used to answer "Both." Sometimes you get the best deal early. Sometimes better deals could be had late if you had the flexibility, and stomach, to bet on a better outcome. But now the risk of a higher price is too great; chances are good there won't be a sale. Airlines have changed, and you need to change your mind-set, too.

YOUR RIGHTS WITH AIRLINE TICKETS

Airlines have developed ticketing rules and requirements mostly for their benefit and protection. When it comes to airline tickets, travelers have few rights. Here are some of the protections consumers *do* have.

Credit Cards.

If you pay by credit card, you have some rights under federal credit card laws. When a refund is due, the airline must forward a credit to your credit card company within seven business days after receiving a complete refund application. And if the airline goes out of business before you fly, you'll be eligible for a refund from your card company in most cases.

Oops. Change of Plans.

If you change your mind, you don't have great options on non-refundable fares. Most U.S. airlines have committed either to allow customers to hold a reservation for twenty-four hours or to provide refunds if customers cancel within twenty-four hours. Each airline abides by one or the other. After that, you'll pay penalties for changing plans with nonrefundable tickets, plus any fare difference.

Advance Cancellations and Schedule Changes.

If the airline cancels your flight in advance or changes its schedule more than a couple of hours, you can request either a refund or rebooking on another acceptable flight. Airlines don't guarantee their schedules, and changes do happen.

Unexpected Cancellations.

If flights get canceled shortly before departure, your rights hinge on whether the problem was the airline's fault, such as a mechanical breakdown or a crew scheduling problem, or whether the cancellation resulted from bad weather or other circumstances beyond an airline's control.

Airline Problems.

An airline is required to offer you a refund on your ticket (only the unused portion) if you don't want to travel at a later time, or pay for your accommodations if you are stranded somewhere because of a problem caused by the airline. You should expect a hotel room, paid for by the airline, and vouchers for food. Other incidental costs may need to be negotiated with the airline, such as toiletries. The airline is expected to rebook you on the next available flight.

Weather Problems.

For issues outside the airline's control, you're on your own. The airline isn't required to issue a refund, only to rebook you on the next available flight. Some airlines may offer discounted rates at hotels. Some airports provide cots and blankets for sleeping in terminals during major flight disruptions.

Delays.

In the United States, there are no federal requirements for compensation for delayed flights. Airline ticketing contracts promise to provide a seat on the next available flight. The European Union does require some compensation for passengers when subjected to lengthy delays, but the rules don't apply in most situations, due to extensive exceptions to the rules, including weather, air-traffic congestion, and other everyday travel problems.

CHAPTER 4

Hunting That Elusive Low Fare

Armed with the knowledge of how the airlines come up with such crazy pricing schemes, how do you shop for a good deal? Like many complex consumer purchases, you need to develop a good strategy, figure out what price you're willing to pay, and then jump on a deal when you see it.

The first thing to do is comparison shop. There are basically three ways to shop for tickets:

> on your own via the Internet
> on your own via the phone
> through a travel agent

My mother has a fourth option—call your son and get him to do it for you. And maybe that works well for you, too.

If you're not computer savvy, you can research prices over the phone—airlines don't charge to call and ask for prices, but most of them do charge a fee for booking reservations over the phone. Some airlines have gotten better about giving their agents the technology to answer questions like, "When do I have to go to get the cheapest price?" Remember that age-old question "What does it cost to fly to Seattle?" and the answer in the form of a question, "When do you want to go?" It's a bit easier now—a good agent at an airline can search a market over a long time period and find the cheapest seats.

A caution: Good agents at airline reservation centers are getting harder and harder to find, and these days, you often end up with an earnest person in India or elsewhere trying to book tickets for you through what can be a significant language and cultural gulf. I've heard stories of people trying to fly to Dayton, Ohio, and an agent telling them about twenty-two-hour itineraries leading to Africa, confusing Dayton's airport code, DAY, with Dar Es Salaam, Tanzania (DAR).

You can also hire a good travel agent to do the research for you. Travel agents typically charge a fee of twenty-five to fifty dollars or more for booking a ticket, depending on the complexity of the itinerary. A good travel agent can save you that much and a lot more finding an affordable fare. A good travel agent can also be well worth the fee if the agent steers you clear of bad deals, tight connections, or distant airports that might require unexpected ground transportation costs. Good agents can suggest nice hotels and even good restaurants. More important, they can eliminate aggravation and save you time. But travel agencies can have drawbacks, too. You may not get all the information you need. And you may not get the best deal if the travel agency doesn't hunt hard enough. Most airlines make their cheapest fares available in the computer reservation systems that travel agents use. A few have special "Web only" fares that have to be booked directly through the airline.

For do-it-yourselfers, the best way to research prices is over the Internet. Travel Web sites have given consumers access to enormous amounts of information—too much information for many people, but nonetheless copious amounts of useful data. With a few clicks on an airline Web site or on an online travel agency such as Expedia.com, Travelocity.com, or Orbitz.com, or referral Web sites such as Kayak.com, Mobissimo.com, or SideStep.com, which search lots of different places, you can wade through vast amounts of fare data.

On most sites, you can use features to expand the days you want to search, if you can be flexible. Some have boxes to check for searching one, two, or three days on either side of your preferred dates, and even calendars that display the lowest prices over a thirty-day period. Want to go to Paris in the summer? You might look at the entire summer to see the lowest fares, and choose your travel dates accordingly. (Just remember that pricing can change fast.) You can also expand your search by including alternative airports. Web sites have boxes to check if you want to include nearby airports, and some even allow you to specify a radius of twenty-five, fifty, or even a hundred miles.

If you are set on a direct flight and know which airlines serve that route nonstop, shop the airline's own Web site. Airlines now promise that their own Web sites have the lowest prices offered anywhere, and there's really no need to clutter your search if you're not willing to fly on other carriers. But if you can be flexible, there are a couple of different ways to buy online.

In general, the cheapest days and times to fly are Tuesday, Wednesday, and Saturday afternoon—search for those time periods and you will likely find the deepest discounts airlines offer, as those times have the weakest demand for tickets. The timing of when you shop for tickets can affect the price as well. The worst time to shop is on the weekend—which is when many other people are also shopping!

Airlines tend to file price increases on Thursdays to see if competitors will match these increases over the weekend. If rival airlines don't raise their fares, the price hikes can be rolled back by Monday morning before business travelers start buying again. Fare sales typically get announced and loaded into computer reservation systems on Monday, and sales often expire on Friday. So, in general, Monday, Tuesday, and Wednesday are the best days to buy. There's no perfect time to buy, of course, but if you buy over the weekend, you may end up paying for a price increase that will be rolled back on Monday, or missing out on a sale announced that day.

POWER TOOLS

Typically I start a search using Orbitz because I find its pricing matrix the easiest to navigate. Put in your cities and the dates you want to go and Orbitz will show the lowest fares at different airlines, broken down into nonstop, one-stop, and two-stop itineraries. Lots of people like Kayak.com because it searches not only online travel agencies but also airline Web sites themselves, and then offers a one-click link to whichever Web site had the price most appealing to you. Mobissimo.com is another popular site that searches multiple ticket-selling sites at one time, including ticket consolidators and other ultracheap outlets. Mobissimo lists prices, provides the source, such as Orbitz or the airline itself, and provides links to go straight there and buy.

Similarly, CheapoAir.com searches multiple data sources and claims to have negotiated some exclusive deals, casting a wide net for the best deal. Lessno.com (Less money, no hassle) is a new Web site that claims to offer wholesale prices and its own search technology. To me, the best advice is to play around with different sites and find one that you are most comfortable with. It's unlikely one will have prices that differ significantly from the others.

One way to expand your fare search automatically is to install a tool on your computer from SideStep.com. With SideStep, every time you search for airline tickets, either at an online travel agency or an airline itself, a SideStep box opens on your screen and asks if you want SideStep to conduct the same search. SideStep, which has merged with Kayak, goes out and makes an inquiry for you at some two hundred different places—Web sites of discount airlines, for example, that may have cheaper prices. It's a handy way to boost your search power.

Another tool popular with road warriors is ITA Software Inc., a company that created a sophisticated airline search engine. ITA, launched by some veterans of the artificial intelligence lab at the Massachusetts Institute of Technology, provides software to airlines and travel companies. But it also has a Web site available to the public at www.itasoftware .com. ITA can list different flights by many different factors, such as the trip's duration or connection times. It can create its own connections and routings, sometimes producing cheaper prices but with bizarre routings. It may turn out that the cheapest way to get from Los Angeles to Cleveland is to fly to Boston and get on a different airline to Cleveland. ITA can figure that out—but do you really want to connect in Boston?

One handy feature of ITA's search engine is that you can search for multiple destinations just by stringing them together in the "Destination" box. Suppose you want to go to Europe but are indifferent about where you want to land. You can put lots of airport codes or just the city names in the destination box, separated by semicolons, and one search will list loads of flights, with the cheapest listed first. Is it cheaper to start in London, Paris, Rome, Brussels, Amsterdam, Zurich, Frankfurt, or Dusseldorf? You can also expand the search by selecting ITA's feature that adds all airports within three hundred miles. There may be a cheap flight to some airport you hadn't thought of. Start there and then move around Europe, using trains or the many European discount carriers. You may end up saving hundreds of dollars. One example: A flight from New York to Rome in the summer of 2008 was $1,222 if you booked carefully and got a good price. However, a flight from New York to London was priced as low as $610 round-trip, and a flight from London to Rome on either Ryanair or easyJet could cost as little as $200. But be careful—you may have to transfer between airports in London, since the discounters tend to serve outlying airports such as London's Stansted and Luton airports, and discounters generally fly to Ciampino Airport outside of Rome instead of Fiumicino, the city's primary airport. Ciampino does have direct bus service from Rome's main train station for five euros each way while a cab is thirty euros to the center of Rome. Ciampino is far less chaotic than Fiumicino and a bit gritty, but it also has one of my favorite airport codes in the world: CIA.

Remember, ITA isn't a booking site, so when you find something you like, you have to go to the airline's Web site, or a site like Orbitz, which uses ITA Software to drive its searches. (ITA makes its money selling software to airlines and travel companies, not from its consumer Web site.) With complex itineraries, it may be best to use a travel agent. You can e-mail an itinerary to a travel agent right from ITA's site, and it will include all the booking details, such as fare codes. Another way to make the booking is to call the airline and have it reserve for you exactly what you want. The agent will (or at least should) understand the booking codes you have. Then, put that reservation on hold and buy it online to avoid the airline's telephone fees.

POWER CODES

For sophisticated users, there's one other tool to consider: ExpertFlyer.com. Started by an entrepreneur who is a lifelong road warrior, with help from two relatives, one of whom was a Continental Airlines captain, ExpertFlyer lets you peek inside the fare buckets of different airlines—a powerful tool for experienced travelers. If you want to find a particular class of fare that comes with an immediate first-class upgrade, for example, ExpertFlyer can tell you if it's available on a particular flight. It can show how many seats are available for free frequent-flier tickets, or which flights have more empty seats in first class and thus greater odds of an upgrade for an elite-level frequent flier. In short, it can take you inside airline fare buckets. You have to buy a subscription to use ExpertFlyer, either $9.99 for a month of the premium service that includes fare information, or $99.99 for a year. If you think it might be worth your while, try the free trial the company offers and see if it's useful. Just know that to get the most out of ExpertFlyer, you have to step into the netherworld of airline fare codes, a difficult language for a novice to master (though ExpertFlyer does have lists of what the various codes and classes mean). The site does have some easy-to-use menus for searching for available frequent-flier awards—seats or upgrades purchased with frequent-flier miles. Users can also search for trips limiting choices to a specific airline alliance, which can be handy.

Why is ExpertFlyer useful? Because there are lots of options that more pedestrian search sites never show you. Once you know that American lists business-class seats available for purchase with frequent-flier miles under the "U" fare bucket, you can search American's inventory for U-class seats using ExpertFlyer. At American, coach seats are under the "T" code and first-class award seats are under a "Z" code. With the translation key for arcane airline codes, you can find lots of different options on the same airplane. (Codes vary from airline to airline, and they can change. So use ExpertFlyer's translation guides.) It may be worth paying a bit more for a less-restrictive ticket. There may be a fare that comes with an upgrade that you wouldn't have found just using a basic site like Expedia, Travelocity, or Orbitz, which generally offer one choice for each flight in coach, and one in first-class if you ask for it. One example: B-class fares on American are a coach fare that typically costs a few hundred dollars more for international trips but allows you to upgrade to business class for just 10,000 miles. That's a hard fare to find using a general search engine. Most travel sites simply offer up the lowest priced choice, but that's not always the best choice. Serious travelers tend to poke further into airline inventory.

POWER PRICES

There's no one Web site that always has the cheapest prices. Whenever journalists do tests to try and peg where to get

the cheapest prices, the results come up inconclusive—
sometimes one Web site has the cheapest prices on a couple
of routes, and another vendor has the cheapest prices on
different routes. More often than not, all of them have
identical prices because they tend to get their fare data
from the same sources anyway. Remember, the airlines
set prices, not the Web sites that sell tickets. Airlines have
ended the days when some Web sites had exclusive cheap
deals, although a few carriers such as Southwest still offer
Web-only fares. Unless you want to use some of the more
sophisticated sites, stick to something basic.

Here's one comparison I did for a last-minute, week-long
trip from Dallas to Chicago and back. Orbitz, Travelocity,
and Expedia all said the cheapest price was $400 on Conti-
nental Airlines. The same trip could be purchased for $393
at Continental's Web site—without the fees that the other
services charge. Lessno said the cheapest deal was $398
on Continental. Cheaptickets said the best deal was $399
on Continental. Priceline offered $402 on Continental.
Hotwire.com had the only exception—a $349 offer on an
unnamed airline—you'd find out which airline, and what
your itinerary would be, after you purchased the ticket. To
most, it likely would be worth $50 to have some control
over your travel.

POWER KNOWLEDGE

Once you have an idea of the current pricing for an intended trip, you might wonder if that is the best you can do.
Maybe not. Two other Web sites can give you even more
information, and more confidence that you are making the
right choice.

FareCompare.com is one of my favorites for pricing information. It was started by a road-warrior-geek, Rick Seaney, who did technology projects for some travel companies and realized he could create a business offering good fare information to the public. From the first screen, FareCompare.com asks you for your origin and destination, then shows you the cheapest tickets available for the next eleven months, shown by month (airlines put their schedules and fares only eleven months out). Instantly, you can see if the prices on other booking Web sites are good deals or not. (Or start your search on FareCompare and skip the other steps.) FareCompare also includes a star rating on the fares shown—a fare with four stars is one that FareCompare thinks you should jump on. One star means FareCompare thinks you should wait. With FareCompare, you can search just one particular airline if you're looking for direct flights or interested in staying in a particular frequent-flier program. You can also add alternate airports.

If you click on a particular month that looks attractive, the next screen shows a departure calendar with the particular days that fare is available, plus the lowest fare on other days of that month. Pick a day, and a calendar opens for your return flight, showing the lowest fares each day, with the cheapest of the month highlighted. But here's where things get complicated. Click on a return date and FareCompare goes out to search for those particular flights. It may not be able to come up with the "advertised" price on those particular days. FareCompare will find a similar fare—the advertised price may be sold out, or just not available in that particular bucket for that particular day.

One of FareCompare's niftiest features is that you can search for the lowest prices from your departure city worldwide—FareCompare will show you the cheapest prices for all cities in Europe, for example, or in the United States and Canada. There may be times when you are indifferent about your destination—you just want to go to the beach, cheap. If nothing else, the "Compare Destinations" feature gives you a speedy read on the lowest available prices.

As FareCompare is a referral site, not an actual booking site, it will send you to one of its partners, such as Expedia .com, Hotwire.com, Priceline.com, CheapoAir.com, BookingBuddy.com, and others to make the actual reservation. And unless you've specified an airline, you don't actually know what crazy routing FareCompare will offer to you. Stops and longer connections may be included in the cheapest prices, and flight times and routings may not be convenient.

That's why I suggest FareCompare for comparison shopping, and more traditional online travel agencies—Expedia, Travelocity, and Orbitz—for bookings. Or a particular airline's Web site for the most direct bookings. One other caution: FareCompare doesn't include fares from Southwest and jetBlue Airways, two discount carriers that don't file all their fare information in central reservation computers. Southwest and jetBlue prefer passengers to book directly from their Web sites. As part of your comparison shopping, it's always good to check those two airlines if they fly where you want to go.

Farecast.com is another shoppers' tool that can be valuable. Started as an offshoot of a university research project, the company forecasts and predicts when fares might drop and when they might rise. The Web site finds available fares for your particular trip, then makes a prediction whether the price will likely rise or fall. The site also indicates how much confidence Farecast has in any given prediction.

The predictions can be useful, but that's not the main

reason I use Farecast. To make the predictions Farecast keeps a database of historical price information. You can see what the cheapest price was over several weeks. That can be helpful in trying to determine the best price.

Farecast, which was bought in 2008 by Microsoft Corp. (Microsoft has a habit of acquiring travel information companies and owns Expedia.com), asks for your route and the dates when you want to travel. It searches for low prices from several online sources. Like FareCompare, Farecast is a referral site that doesn't do the actual booking. Farecast displays either a list of the cheapest prices, or if you prefer, a grid showing the prices at different times of the day on a specified date. It also shows where it found that particular fare—a booking site or an airline Web site. From its start page, Farecast will also show you a graph of the lowest prices available on that route over the past thirty days.

Alongside those fares, the site lists the Farecast Wait or Buy prediction for what prices will do over the next seven days, along with Farecast's level of confidence. The site also shows whether prices have been rising, falling or, most likely, bouncing up and down for the past two months.

Chasing the cheapest price can be risky. Prices often zip in and zip out, and you have to be quick to catch the bottom. You have to be lucky, too. To me, the best use of Farecast lies in the historical graphs. If you know that the price has never been below $400 during the past two months, you probably shouldn't be hoping to get a price under $400 unless you are certain that fares will fall. If the economy is slowing, oil prices are dropping, or new competition comes into a market, that can happen. But if tickets are selling well, oil prices are high or rising, and airlines are cutting capacity, prices may only go higher.

POWER PICKS

Once you have a good idea of what prices are like, it's time to decide what you are willing to pay. Just like buying a car at an automobile dealer, you'll do much better if you decide what you want to pay before you get caught up in all the complexity.

You also have to decide what you are willing to do to get a certain price. Are you willing to shift your schedule to travel on cheaper days? Are you willing to travel at odd hours, when prices may be cheaper? Are you willing to go to alternate airports maybe farther from your destination? What will that add to the cost and time involved for the trip? If your cruise is sailing from Miami, do you have time to get from Fort Lauderdale to Miami to save some airfare? How much will it cost to get there on the ground? Are you willing to take a connecting flight, or are you only interested in nonstop flights (and if so, is your bottom-line price realistic)? One of the peculiarities of the airline business is that taking two flights can be cheaper than one flight. Go figure. Airlines know they can charge a premium for nonstop service, where there is usually less competition. Since most airlines offer connecting service over lots of different connecting hubs, there is more competition for connecting flights and thus cheaper prices. For the traveler, it's a trade-off. Connecting flights take longer and introduce more risk of travel problems—missed connections and lost bags, to give the two most common examples. Bottom line: The more flexible you are, the more you can save. Just keep in mind that a good night's sleep, or a shorter trip to the hotel, can have a price, too.

And once you make your purchase, there's no looking back, right? Not necessarily. Even with nonrefundable tickets, some airlines will let you change your mind within twenty-four hours of purchase and provide a refund without penalty. Policies vary, so you need to check in each instance. More important, some carriers will make some adjustments to fares if the price changes. They don't voluntarily hand you back cash—you have to pursue it. But there now is an easier way to get something back if the ticket price drops after you buy a ticket.

Yapta.com—Your Amazing Personal Travel Assistant—will track price changes on specific flights or specific routes, and alert you by e-mail to price changes. Yapta is a powerful tool for shopping—if the flights you want are too expensive, set an alert and hope that the price drops. Just be ready to jump on it when—and if—you get that Yapta alert. For already purchased tickets, airlines have different policies on what they'll give you. Yapta spells out the different policies and factors them in before sending you a notice that you might deserve a refund or a voucher. Airlines rarely refund fare differences in cash, but many do offer to give you back the difference in price in the form of a voucher good for a future trip. Some deduct change fees from tickets, and those fees can be as high as $150 on a domestic U.S. ticket. But not all airlines do, and if you can score a voucher when the price drops, your next trip will be a bit cheaper. Just remember you have to call the airline while the lower price is in effect, so that means moving quickly. And the lower price has to be available on your exact itinerary.

Think of Yapta as a bit of a security blanket—something akin to a thirty-day price guarantee at a store, though not as effective or definite because of the many airline rules. The site can help make buying tickets easier if you worry about the price dropping as soon as you hand over your credit card. Of course, many of us don't want to know that we paid more than we had to.

POWER BARGAINS?

Some of the lowest-priced tickets available are found with airline ticket "consolidators"—brokers who take "distressed" inventory from airlines and sell it at deep discounts. Think of them as the outlet mall for airlines. There are flights that airlines know won't fill at published prices, and if they cut the price, they risk an all-out fare war with competitors who slash their prices. Soon the cheaper prices have spread to flights that would have sold without drastic price reductions, and the airline has shot itself in the foot. To avoid that, airlines dump seats with consolidators, who are restricted in how they advertise and identify the airline. It preserves the airline's published fare structure and fills otherwise empty seats.

International ticket consolidators have been around for many, many years. You can see their ads in the travel sections of newspapers, and you may run into them online. In the United States, there's a trade group called the United States Air Consolidators Association that has a Web site, www.usaca.com, that allows you to search for consolidators and narrow choices down to what region you are interested in traveling to and what airline you are interested in flying. That helps you target likely sources of the tickets you want. There are scads of different companies on the Web offering consolidator tickets, including Priceline.com.

While the savings can be substantial—less so as airlines fly full planes and get better at selling tickets themselves at prices they prefer—the trade-offs with consolidators can be significant. With some consolidator tickets, you may not be eligible for frequent-flier miles, or, more important, pre-reserved seat assignment. You often don't get to pick your airline or your route, and there may be a broad time window of when you agree to travel. You pay the cheapest price, and thus, you are on the bottom of the service totem pole.

What's more, you are at a bit more risk when you travel on consolidator tickets for lengthy disruptions if things go wrong. If a flight gets canceled and you have to stand by for another flight, you'll be on the bottom of the standby list with a consolidator ticket. Most airlines won't route customers with consolidator tickets to other airlines either, so you may have to wait a lot longer. Earlier I wrote about one family that lost out on their only two days in Paris because United Airlines had a mechanical problem on a flight from San Francisco to Washington, D.C., and they missed their connection to Paris by minutes. Because they had consolidator tickets, United wouldn't route them to Air France, as it did with other passengers. The low status can ruin a vacation. Is that worth saving $300? A friend of mine was planning a trip to Tanzania for his ten-member family and wanted to put adults in business class and the children in coach on the cheapest tickets he could round up from a consolidator. If he tickets a group two different ways, what happens if the airline decides to bump one of the consolidator seats? Is it worth the aggravation?

Consolidators are good sources of cheap tickets for students and those with lots of flexibility and strong stomachs for stress. But if you have to be somewhere for a cruise or a special event, if you have an expensive hotel room waiting for you, or a date at a nice Paris restaurant, don't play the consolidator game.

For students, by the way, there are two excellent sites

that offer discounted air travel. StudentUniverse.com nego-tiates cheaper prices with airlines, and often has tickets at discounted prices without all the rigorous restrictions air-lines love. You can get discounted one-way tickets, for ex-ample, which are perfect for students who don't know their exam schedule months before they want to return home for Christmas, or may be headed overseas to study abroad and don't know when they'll return. Another site, STAtravel .com, offers similar discounts. Both offer their fares to teachers, as well. And both verify your eligibility. Student-Universe is able to verify online for free using educational e-mail addresses. STA Travel requires an international stu-dent ID card, which costs $22. One example of the savings: A few months before Christmas, a one-way Dallas-Hartford round-trip fare on American Airlines was priced at $1,006; STA Travel had a $242 one-way fare on the same flights.

POWER PACKAGES

Another option to consider is buying a package tour, which may or may not include a consolidator's ticket. Online agen-cies such as Expedia, Travelocity, and Orbitz have gotten quite skilled at putting together packages. These pack-ages can save you money—and time and stress. The magic comes mostly in the price of hotel rooms (something we'll explore separately in a later chapter). While airlines take care to provide all published fares to all outlets, hotels are a different story. Each travel vendor can negotiate its own rates with chains of hotels, and even with individual hotels. Expedia may have special rates to offer on fifteen rooms at a boutique hotel in New York while Orbitz may have a special deal with a similar hotel down the street. These days, all of the big agencies have deals with many, many hotels. Sometimes the travel vendor negotiates special rates with the hotel, but more often than not, the travel agency buys the hotel room at a discounted rate and then sells it for whatever it can get. The hotel gets something for a room that might otherwise go empty; the travel agency gets the opportunity to make a lot more money on the booking than the small booking fee the customer pays and a booking commission on the hotel. The travel agency takes on more risk but can get more reward.

Even with good markups, those rooms can still be a deal. They can be booked separately from one of the popular Web sites, or bundled in packages with airfares. You can't tell when you shop what rooms are under what program, but you may notice that one site says a particular hotel is sold out, while a competing site still has inventory, or the two sites offer different rates. If you're on a budget, it's worth checking to see if a package might save you some money.

Here's an example: Expedia.com offered a three-night summer weekend in 2008 at the Ritz-Carlton in San Francisco, plus a car and round-trip airfare for one person from New York, for $1,803. The same elements bought individually—the cheapest airfare at the time on AirTran Airways plus the same hotel bought directly from Ritz-Carlton and the same economy car rental from Hertz—cost $2,128, or $325 more than the package. Expedia negotiated better rates than you likely could get individually.

The package power, however, doesn't always work in your favor. For a trip for two people to San Jose, California, on the same summer weekend, Expedia offered a room at the Hawthorne Suites Hotel plus airfare on American Airlines and a Hertz economy car for $1,456. But you could have bought the same reservations individually for $1,273, or $183 less than the package. Bottom line: There are no guarantees that a package can save some money, but a little sleuthing online can help you determine the best option.

Remember, with a package you give up flexibility, such as selecting the exact airline flights you want, and there's no real booking advantage to packaging travel components unless you can save some money. It can be more convenient and save you a bit of shopping time, but the more companies involved in a booking, the more potential for confusion, disappointment, and finger-pointing. If you book a rental car through an airline and the reservation gets messed up, whose fault is it, the airline or the rental car company? One will blame the other, leaving you caught in the middle. It's no fun to show up at a hotel and be told your reservation doesn't exist; always reconfirm your reservation with a hotel when booking through a package. It may be a bit more secure to book directly with the service provider—it minimizes the chance of a reservation mix-up.

Price is one consideration; safety is another. If you want to check on the safety record of an airline, there are a couple of sources. First, the European Union began publishing in 2006 its "blacklist" of airlines barred from flying to the E.U. due to safety concerns. You can find it at http://ec.europa .eu/transport/air-ban/list_en.htm. The list is long and filled with airlines you've never heard of, but if you are flying to a remote part of the world and using a local airline, it may be worth your while to check. Another safety check you can make is to see if an airline you are considering has under- gone an "operational safety audit" by the International Air Transport Association. This trade group has an extensive program to audit airlines to make sure they meet basic in- ternational safety standards. At this writing, there were 203 airlines around the world that had invited IATA in and received passing grades. You can find the registry of airlines that have passed the safety audit at http://www.iata.org/ps/certification/iosa/registry.htm.

Someday airline pricing won't be as crazy, confusing, and confounding. More simplified pricing will take effect, and maybe airlines will realize that if they make it easier to use their product, people will be more willing to buy. Until then, we do what we must to work the system in our favor as much as we can.

Happy hunting. May you always pay less than the person sitting next to you.

CHAPTER 5

Up-Sells, First-Class Bargains, and Enhancements

At the point of sale, airlines and travel companies now try to "up-sell" you on all kinds of add-ons, short of full-blown package deals. The add-ons range from tickets to sightseeing tours and Broadway shows to travel insurance, ground transportation, and even better reserved seating. As cash-pressed airlines concoct more ways to dig into traveler wallets, expect to see more offered add-ons, and once-free items, like meals and exit-row seating, coming with a price tag. It helps to know what you want or what you need before you get bombarded with choices to click.

The up-sell effort began years ago when airlines realized they had a captive audience of travel buyers and they could sell more than just airline seats. Airlines realized that when they had you on the phone, they could do what travel agents do: book a car rental reservation, for example, and earn a small commission from the car rental company. Car rental companies pay airlines to be the "preferred" choice offered to flyers. Hotels do the same thing. There was a time in the airline business when carriers thought they could be "vertical" sellers and offer one-stop shopping for all travel. The parent of United Airlines bought Westin Hotels and Hertz and renamed itself Alegis Corp. The theory was that even if airlines lose money, profits from the other businesses would smooth over the losses, but airlines proved no better at managing hotel chains or car rental companies than they were at running airlines, and the "vertical" conglomerate idea lost favor as airlines had to sell off noncore assets when they hit rough times.

Still, travelers are willing to buy other things from airlines besides a seat on a plane and the opportunity for lost luggage. In recent years, with airlines under enormous financial pressure, the ancillary selling has become a frenzy at some carriers—a Turkish bizarre thrown onto your computer screen with all kinds of opportunity to spend more money. Booking sites like Travelocity, Expedia, and Orbitz do it, too. Many of the add-ons can be a good deal, and there's plenty of time to be saved with one-stop shopping rather than chasing down tour tickets, museum passes, and other things you'd buy anyway. It pays to compare all your options first before you buy.

Trying to squeeze every last penny out of customers, airlines now charge fees for amenities and services that used to go to early bookers, savvy travelers, and elite-level frequent fliers, like sections of coach seating with a few extra inches of legroom. Paying for a bit more legroom can make flying a lot more enjoyable, especially if you are a large person or get irritated when people in front of you recline into your lap. The opportunities are numerous. JetBlue Airways now has extra legroom in the first six rows of its cabins, and charges $10 to $30 extra for each flight to sit there. Northwest Airlines charges extra for prime coach seats like exit rows and bulkhead seating. Price: $5 to $35. United Airlines has the most extensive offering—"Economy Plus" seating in coach. Economy Plus gives you four or five extra inches of space—it's quite generous for domestic coach service these days—and costs $14 to $109 each flight, varying by distance and how much demand United thinks there will be for the roomier seats on that particular flight. "Economy Plus" is free to elite-level frequent fliers but offered at check-in to others if seats are available. One other option if you fly United a lot but don't have elite status: You can buy an annual pass to "Economy Plus" for $349. This pass makes a cool gift, too, for a frequent traveler.

Some airlines are trying to charge extra for what they consider "premium seating" without any extra legroom. US Airways, for example, sells aisle and window seats at the front of its planes for a few extra dollars if you aren't an elite-level member of that airline's frequent-flier program, or one of its airline partners. The seats don't have extra space like jetBlue or United's front-cabin, higher-priced seats. US Airways just figures many people like to be up front in the airplane, and they will pay extra for the privilege. Other airlines are moving quickly to offer "preferred seating" at the time you buy a ticket. The holdup has been changing the giant central reservation system computers that drive airline bookings for travel agencies and online vendors so that they can accommodate things like selling specific seats. As the software changes, more carriers will try to sell preferred seating to more customers.

Air Canada has been a pioneer in this "à la carte" selling. When you book online at Air Canada's Web site, you can buy a bare-bones ticket without any perks—you can't even reserve a seat. It may cost thirty-five dollars or so a ticket to move up to a reserved seat; something families may feel compelled to do so they can sit together. Getting full credit for your frequent-flier miles on your trip requires moving up to a higher fare category. The ability to change your ticket without penalty costs more, of course. An exit-row seat costs more, too. You can buy meals and pay baggage fees online. You can also knock a few dollars off the cheapest fares if you agree not to check any bags. As Air Canada says in its promotions: "Pay for what you want. Don't pay for what you don't. It's a whole new way to fly." Indeed, airlines in the United States have been watching Air Canada and have been surprised at how customers have adapted to à la carte pricing. More and more, that is the way we will fly.

Is it worth paying extra for better seating? It can be if you can get extra legroom, such as in an exit row or some "bulkhead" seats at the front of a cabin. (Be careful with bulkheads—some seats are now pushed so close to the bulkhead that you get less legroom than in standard seating, though you don't have to worry about the traveler in front of you reclining a seat into your lap. SeatGuru.com warns, for example, that the middle section of Continental's Boeing 767s in coach have bulkhead seating where "many find legroom to be restricted.") Check SeatGuru.com and the airline Web sites themselves for accurate information on what you get from different seats on different airplanes and various airlines. In the case of the US Airways offering, it's not worth extra money, since there is no extra legroom or better service involved. Being up front does mean you'll get off the plane quicker, and I find that to be an advantage only at airports where I'm going to be racing to a taxi stand or rental car bus when I have no luggage checked, particularly late at night. But is it worth it to pay twenty-five dollars just to get off the airplane three minutes faster? Probably not. Some people find the ride a bit smoother at the front of the airplane because some people feel a slight sway in the tail of an airplane, particularly a long airplane like the Boeing 757.

POWER CLASS

Some of us are willing to pay more for more comfort. For most of us, the true differentiator between coach and comfort is getting into the front cabins of the airplane—business class and first class. There are tricks to getting into those wide leather seats without breaking the bank.

Road warriors have lots of tactics for getting upgrades, and we'll explore those in the next chapter about frequent-flier program benefits (and busts). But even if you aren't a platinum premier flier, you can buy your way up front at a discount.

Airlines have long looked at first-class cabins more as a driver of loyalty than a revenue generator. They priced seats so high—thousands of dollars for short domestic trips—that few customers ever paid for a first-class seat. Most seats served upgrading frequent fliers and off-duty pilots, traveling airline executives, and other "nonrevenue" passengers flying for free. The first-class cabin won airlines business from those road warriors who would buy unrestricted, expensive coach tickets—and expect their upgrades. International flying is different. Many companies will pay for business-class tickets costing upward of $10,000 per trip, even if their cost-conscious travel policies forbid buying domestic first-class tickets.

In recent years, airlines have explored ways to raise additional revenue with the first-class cabin; a change that makes it harder for frequent fliers to get "free" upgrades. A new class of coach fare was created that included an "instant upgrade." Called "Y-Up" fares, they are coach prices—Y class—that conform to corporate travel policies requiring employees to travel in coach, yet the instant upgrade provides passengers a first-class seat.

Some airline Web sites now make it easier to find these kinds of fares. American's Web site, aa.com, has a function that allows you to search by "Fare and Schedule," for example, and then returns a matrix of fare and schedule choices that includes coach fares with first-class upgrades, along with regular first-class fares. You may find that a later flight gets you an upgrade, maybe for a slightly higher fare or maybe even at a lower price than the morning flight you looked at as your first choice. US Airways has also been a strong seller of Y-Up fares. You might find that a connecting flight in first class is actually cheaper, and perhaps more enjoyable, than a nonstop coach ticket for your vacation.

The quickest way to find Y-Up fares, however, is to use FareCompare.com. FareCompare has a Y-Up button to click on its opening screen: "First Class Airfare Yup." Clicking on that leads to a list of first-class fares for different cities from your home base, along with a comparison to the unrestricted coach price. If you have to pay $609 round-trip on Delta for a New York–Orlando ticket, why not pay $769 for first-class seats, round-trip?

Most booking sites don't automatically check for these kinds of deals, so you have to do the hunting on your own. ExpertFlyer is another way to search for these sneaky fares. Finding them, and using them, can make your travel far more enjoyable.

Besides Y-Up fares, airlines have also been experimenting with selling last-minute first-class upgrades. US Airways has been a pioneer in this regard. When checking in at an airline kiosk, or with an airline agent, travelers sometimes will be asked if they'd like to purchase an upgrade. The cost is $50 one-way for short flights, $100 for longer trips, and $150 one way for cross-country flights. If you can afford it, and find yourself otherwise stuck in a middle seat, the splurge on an upgrade can take some pain out of your business trip, or get a vacation off to a comfortable start.

On international flights, upgrades are harder to score, though US Airways and some other airlines sell them for about $500 on the day of departure if there are empty seats. There aren't overseas Y-Up fares, but there are ways to get a seat you can sleep in at a discount.

For vacationers, airlines have started selling deeply discounted business-class seats with long advance-purchase requirements—forty-five days or more. These limitations make them unusable by most corporate customers who can't plan that far ahead—and likely have employers or clients willing to pay higher rates anyway. For a trip to London, for example, there are business-class fares around $3,000 or so, compared with full-fare business-class tickets in the neighborhood of $10,000 round-trip. The reason: yield management. By more precisely pegging demand, airlines have learned that they are better off selling some seats for $3,000 that likely would not sell, and might otherwise go to frequent fliers upgraded for free. It's worth checking an airline's marketing partner for those kinds of discounts, too. Airlines form "code-sharing agreements" with other carriers and put their own flight code on a partner's flight, then sell seats on each other's planes. Delta might have a seat to sell on an Air France flight that it prices a lot less than Air France, or vice versa. The inventory that Air France has might sell faster than seats offered by Delta. Even though they are selling seats on the same airplane, two partners often price the seats differently. Use those discrepancies to your advantage.

There's another reason why airlines have been discounting their international business-class seats: new competition. New airlines, and some existing carriers, have started all-business-class flights across the Atlantic and the Pacific. A few start-ups such as Eos Airlines, Maxjet, Silverjet, and L'Avion shook up the market but disappeared under competitive pressure from established rivals and high fuel prices. Big carriers such as British Airways and Lufthansa have gotten into the all-business-class business. Lufthansa has been hiring a charter operator called PrivatAir to fly all-business-class airplanes on several routes between the United States and Europe. The service is uncrowded, high-quality, and appealing to many corporate fliers. It's attractive, too, for vacationers who can afford it. You can find discounted tickets, especially at off-peak periods. (Interestingly, "off-peak" for business class is summertime, when many business executives vacation and aren't making business trips. So some of the best times to find discounted business-class seats is exactly when vacationers want them—summer.)

British Airways launched its own carrier dubbed "Open Skies" that offers business-class and some coach-class seats on routes from continental Europe to the United States, and jump-started its expansion by acquiring Paris-based L'Avion in 2008. Until a new "Open Skies" treaty was signed between the United States and the European Union in 2007, carriers were only allowed to fly from their native home country to the United States. Now with the liberalization, British Airways can fly to the United States from anywhere in Europe.

If business class is out of reach, a new alternative has been popping up at international airlines around the world (though not yet with U.S. airlines). Carriers are offering "Premium Economy" cabins that have extra legroom, better meal service, and other perks that make it more comfortable than coach, but a lot cheaper than full-blown business class. British Airways and Virgin Atlantic have pioneered Premium Economy. Some Asian airlines are joining in—Qantas introduced Premium Economy service in late 2008 with about six to ten more inches of legroom, a steeper seat recline, and a wider seat than coach. It's a nice alternative for business travelers whose companies or clients won't pony up for business class, or for vacationers who just can't cope with being cramped in coach but can't bring themselves to spend thousands of dollars for a ten-hour luxury. If "Premium Economy" proves popular, U.S. airlines may have to follow suit someday.

POWER FLIGHTS

There are many other factors besides price to consider when shopping for tickets. You might want to research the dependability of a flight before you buy it—is it prone to long delays or cancellation? You might want to compare available seats on a couple of possible flights before you buy. With unfamiliar international carriers, you may want to check the airline's safety record before making a purchase. Or perhaps you need to take into account some seasonal factors when booking a trip, such as booking a connection during the winter in a city prone to snow storms.

Start with seasonal considerations. If it is winter and you are traveling in northern climates, plan extra time for flights, consider flying later in the day, and avoid connections in snow-plagued airports such as Chicago and Cleveland. Flying later in the day can pay off because it can take time for airports to move snow that accumulates overnight. Runways have to be plowed, to be sure, but the bigger contributors to delays are often the ramp areas, which don't get as much attention from plows. Airlines are often responsible for snow removal around their terminals, and they may not be as swift as airport plows. Early morning operations can get stuck in the snow—planes can't get in and out of gates, baggage is slow to load. Unplowed local roads can affect operations, too, if pilots or flight attendants can't get to the airport. In winter, afternoon is a better time to travel.

In summer, the opposite is true: Travel in the morning if you can. The scourge of air travel in the summer is "convective" weather—better known as thunderstorms. Those typically build with the heat of the day, so afternoons and evenings can be more prone to storms. It's also wise to avoid connections at southern airports in the summertime. Atlanta, Dallas, and Houston, for example, are notorious for summer storm bursts.

The best source for reliability of different flights is at FlightStats.com where you can check the history of a particular flight, a particular airline, a certain city, and a specific route. The flight history is useful because some flights are more prone to long delays and disruption than others. When bad weather hits, for example, airline operations planners look for lightly booked flights they can cancel because those flights leave fewer people to rebook. They also look for flights that make a complete "turn"—they return to the same hub airport from which they left. If a plane is scheduled to go from Atlanta to Chicago and back to Atlanta, both trips can be canceled and the aircraft itself, plus its crew, never gets out of place. In addition, flights can frequently be canceled because of crew issues—the pilots working that trip come to it at the end of a long day, for example, and just a small slip in the schedule means they won't be able to make the trip under federal limits on how long pilots can be on duty. So that flight gets canceled far more often than others. At the same time, some trips may routinely get delayed—they get stuck at the end of a long line of airplanes, for example, or the airplane used for the trip comes out of New York and is always two hours late. Sometimes flights struggle with operational issues that the airline hasn't fixed—it takes too long for baggage to get loaded, or the fuel truck always runs late, or it gets blocked in an alleyway at the terminal on most days. The result is that in any airline schedule, some flights get canceled more than others. Better to take a flight that runs on time 90 percent of the time than a flight that is on time only 20 percent of the time, especially if you are using that flight to make a connection. Of course, past performance is no guarantee of future results, but at least you've tried to minimize the damage.

You can check the reliability of European airlines through the Association of European Airlines, a group of thirty-three carriers in Europe (http://www.aea.be/research/performance/index.html). The AEA offers rankings of airlines both by baggage performance and punctuality. Like the U.S. Department of Transportation, which publishes a consumer report on airlines every month available on its Web site that shows on-time performance, baggage handling, bumped passengers, and consumer complaints, the AEA data just show totals for each airline, not specific track records for individual flights. But it can be worthwhile to know that British Airways is having lots of trouble getting baggage delivered to passengers on time, for example.

In general, flights that leave in the morning tend to have better on-time performance than evening flights. Airlines make a big push to get aircraft off to a good start each day—once delays occur, a plane may never catch up. There are exceptions, to be sure, but early flights may prove more reliable than later flights.

POWER SEATS

Savvy travelers also check the seating chart before booking a ticket. You can do that from an airline Web site, or from most travel booking sites. If only middle seats remain, then check other flights. Is it worth paying fifty dollars more to get an aisle seat? It may be, especially if it's a long flight on a crowded plane. To hunt for the best seats, use SeatGuru .com. SeatGuru has an extensive database of information about particular seats on particular aircraft at most big airlines. It flags "undesirable" seats—seats that don't recline, for example, or don't have good under-seat storage because of boxes of equipment for entertainment systems. Some seats don't recline as much as others; some windows are misaligned, particularly on wide-body jets. The site also marks desirable seats—extra legroom or width, power plugs, and other amenities. SeatGuru can warn you that the last two rows on a United Airlines A320 feel tighter because of the curvature of the airplane, or that the first row in the first-class cabin of a US Airways A320 has restricted legroom—not the roomier seating found in the bulkhead row of many other planes. Seats 17A and 17K on British Airways 777s don't have a window, even though they are "window seats," so if you want a view, sit elsewhere. Every plane has oddities and annoyances, and SeatGuru can steer you to more comfort.

CHAPTER 6

Frequent-Flier Rewards and Rip-offs

I pasted S&H Green Stamps for my mother when I was a kid. They were the frequent-flier miles of my childhood. In the 1960s, the rewards catalog printed by Sperry and Hutchison Co. was said to be the largest publication in the United States, and more Green Stamps were issued than postage stamps. Merchants handed out the Green Stamps as rewards, and consumers wet the gummed backing and pasted them into books. Filled books could be redeemed for goodies like toasters at an S&H Green Stamps store. Sperry and Hutchison got paid by merchants who needed to offer the reward to build customer loyalty, and the company provided prizes. One big benefit to S&H was that many stamps were never redeemed, either lost, trashed, or left in books that never filled.

In the early 1980s, the airline industry was facing a huge customer loyalty test, and Green Stamps became the model for salvation. Before 1978, the airline industry in the United States was regulated—the government, through the Civil Aeronautics Board, decided which companies could fly which routes and set the price for tickets. In 1978, the government deregulated the airline industry, over the protests of incumbent airlines, so that new airlines and lots more competition could be created. The domestic United States had "Open Skies"—anyone could fly anywhere, once you had a license. Prices, naturally, took top billing. PeopleExpress came along offering transportation at cheap prices. People loved it. Why should they pay more to fly American or United or Eastern?

Faced with a sudden and severe need to engender brand loyalty, American Airlines under then-President Robert L. Crandall introduced the notion of a frequent-flier mile in early 1981. Customers would be given one "mile" for every mile they flew, and those miles could be cashed in for free trips. The idea was brilliant—like the Green Stamp, only better. Miles would accumulate electronically—cheaper than issuing stamps or certificates. And American could limit the real cost of redemptions. Many miles would be forgotten or never reach required levels for awards, just like the Green Stamps, and by limiting the number of seats on a particular flight that could be "bought" with miles, American could limit the "damage" from redemptions. Seats that otherwise would be empty would go to frequent fliers. The actual cost would be only the small cost of handling a reservation, a bit more fuel to burn, a couple more bags to load and unload, and any meal that the passenger might consume. Sure, some awards might go for trips for which customers would otherwise pay, so revenue would be lost, but the gain from customer loyalty would be far greater. With a much bigger network of flights, American could offer something PeopleExpress couldn't: the chance to earn miles whether you were going to Dallas or Des Moines or Detroit, and the chance to redeem them for free trips to anywhere in the world.

"The mile is simply what evolved out of discussions about devising the optimum retention and customer-motivation tool," said Crandall. "We thought that we could come up with an equivalent to the S&H Green Stamp—only better." Crandall and his management team were right— the frequent-flier mile proved to be an even more powerful marketing incentive than the Green Stamp. Miles opened the world for many people. The lure of a possible ticket to Paris or Hawaii proved powerful, even for people who had no chance of ever having enough miles for those destinations. Customers began limiting their flying to one airline to build miles faster, even taking indirect and inconvenient routes just for the miles. By the end of 1981, one million people had signed up for American's AAdvantage program. The program became a tactical weapon—airlines offered triple miles to combat competitors and all kinds of specials to beat back discounters. Travelers, especially business fliers who weren't buying tickets out of their own pocket, began paying higher fares to fly their airline of choice for the miles. The airline seat was no longer just a fungible commodity.

POWER CURRENCY

Today, there are more than 50 million AAdvantage members, and most every airline has some form of frequent-flier rewards program or another—180 million accounts worldwide. An estimated ten trillion frequent-flier miles are in those accounts around the globe, according to Randy Petersen, the guru of frequent-flier miles who publishes *InsideFlyer* magazine. The mile has become a global currency. Through airline partnerships, you can earn miles in just about any corner of the world or redeem them on any continent.

And you don't have to fly to earn miles, either. Credit card companies buy miles from airlines for about one penny per mile to reward customers. So do charities, roofers, florists, hotels—you name it. You can earn miles on your mortgage payments. Consumers buy groceries, pay college tuition, and lease cars with credit cards, just to get the miles.

In 2007, American, the largest frequent-flier program in the world, issued 200 billion frequent-flier miles. About half of them were given out by the one thousand merchants and other "participants" in the AAdvantage program who buy miles from the airline. At about one penny per mile, American took in $1 billion in revenue from frequent-flier mile sales. That's real money to a company that had about $23 billion in total revenue in 2007. And the miles are so important now to merchants that some will go to extreme lengths to prop up airlines financially just to protect their mileage partnerships. When Delta Air Lines had to reorganize in U.S. bankruptcy court in 2005, American Express helped bail Delta out by "prebuying" $500 million worth of Delta SkyMiles.

More miles are now earned on the ground than in the air. Strategies for earning and burning miles can dominate our consumer lives, affecting where we buy and how, and where we vacation and how. Miles have become the Green Stamp of the go-go age. But as with any big program, the miles business has become far more complex, and strategies for maximizing your frequent-flier bonuses need more attention. Like any oversupplied currency, the value of the frequent-flier mile has been devalued, and inflation is rampant. There are two reasons. One is saturation—so many miles in circulation chasing an ever-more limited supply of reward seats. Airlines have not increased the number of seats available for rewards at the same pace that they have issued miles, so supply has tightened. The other reason is that airlines have been raising the price of those awards, weakening the buying power of each mile. In some cases, the actual price of a ticket or an upgrade, in miles, has been raised. What you could once get for 60,000 miles may now cost 80,000 miles. In other cases airlines have simply pushed customers into higher-cost mileage buckets to raise the price of a trip. You may find it impossible to get a 25,000 coach seat, but the airline offers plenty at 50,000 miles. The airline hasn't raised the sticker price of awards—but it has effectively doubled the cost by forcing you into a different award category. It used to be that if travelers could redeem miles for about two cents per mile, they were doing well. Spend 35,000 miles on a $700 ticket to Hawaii, and you have yourself a good deal. But these days, many awards get redeemed a lot closer to one penny per mile. That $700 ticket to Hawaii may cost you 70,000 miles—if you can find a seat.

There is some solace for mileage junkies—as the price of regular tickets goes up, mileage awards become more valuable. If the ticket to Hawaii now is priced at $850, spending 70,000 miles may look like a slightly better deal. But overall, frequent-flier miles don't have the buying power they used to have. You need to be smarter about how you use them.

POWER LEVELS

As miles themselves have been devalued, and road warriors have found themselves sitting on more miles than they will ever redeem, airlines have created other ways to engender customer loyalty through their frequent-flier programs. The biggest driver of buying preference now is elite-level status in a frequent-flier program. Reaching a "gold" level, or better yet one of the tip-top levels like "platinum" at various airlines, brings all kinds of perks that just plain "members" don't get. Premium frequent fliers get to reserve seats up front at some airlines, and get first crack at better seating like exit rows or, at United Airlines, the "Economy Plus" section. They get separate lanes to reach security checkpoints at many airports, and often have separate lanes at airline check-in counters. Elite-level fliers get to board first at most airlines, letting them fill up overhead bins before others. Some carriers give their elite-level fliers priority on standby lists. And they get the biggest perk of all, the most powerful driver of customer loyalty: the first-class upgrade. The top levels of frequent fliers typically get offered upgrades about three days before departure; the lowest levels of elite fliers get offered any seats available twenty-four hours before departure. Some airlines give elites free upgrades; some have a payment system in coupons or "stickers" earned by flying or bought by travelers. If you are a road warrior and top-level flier on a particular airline, you may enjoy first class fairly routinely. Why fly any other carrier?

Elite levels typically begin at 25,000 miles per year, and reach up to 100,000 miles per year for the top levels. Programs differ on what they count to get there—airlines invented the concept of "elite-qualifying miles" to say that some miles are better than others. Miles earned flying the airline almost always are "elite-qualifying miles," though some airlines have decided that miles earned on the cheapest fares aren't. Credit card miles often don't count toward your annual elite qualification. Policies vary on whether miles earned on other airlines—partners within an alliance—count toward elite qualification. Like everything else associated with miles, airlines have tightened rules and made it harder to qualify for elite status. Most used to have a 500-mile minimum for each trip, for example. If your flight was 300 miles, you still would earn 500 miles for the flight. But several airlines have dropped that minimum, paying 300 miles for a 300 mile trip. Even so, the lowest levels aren't out of reach for occasional fliers: five trips a year between New York and Los Angeles will get you 24,750 miles. If you go abroad a couple of times and do some domestic flying, you'll hit the gold mark.

POWER OF CONCENTRATION

The first rule for earning miles is to concentrate your efforts on one program, even if you travel only eight or ten times a year for business and pleasure. You can fly different airlines as long as you keep your travels within one airline partnership.

If you live near the hub of a big airline, the choice is obvious. Houston means Continental Airlines (unless you do all your flying domestically on Southwest). Minneapolis, Detroit, and Atlanta mean Delta Air Lines—there aren't a lot of other choices. Alliance partnerships can open up choices for some people. If you are a member of US Airways' Dividend Miles frequent-flier program, there's no need to join United's program. You can earn US Airways miles on United and, better yet, you can redeem your US Airways miles on United. The alliances spread internationally—Air Canada, All Nippon Airlines, Lufthansa, Singapore, South African, Asiana, Austrian, Scandinavian, LOT Polish, and others, are part of the same Star Alliance as United and US Airways. The same holds true for Delta and Air France in SkyTeam, and American and British Airways in the One-world alliance. Elite status at any one of those airlines gets you better handling at its partner airlines, as many benefits are reciprocal.

If you can't pick one frequent-flier program, the best alternative may be to join Alaska Airline's program, even if you don't live in a major city Alaska serves. Alaska's program has long been a favorite of frequent-flier aficionados because it can be more generous than others. Alaska is a bit like the Switzerland of the airline world—it has maintained nonallied status. Alaska hasn't joined one of the big alliances, but it has forged partnerships with four of the biggest U.S. airlines (American, Delta, Continental, and Northwest) and their international partners. You can fly any of those airlines and earn Alaska miles, concentrating your flying even when you spread it out over several different airlines.

POWER PROVIDERS

Which programs offer the most seats? That's always hard to tell, since airlines guard the number of seats they make available to frequent fliers. We do know from airline disclosures that on average, 3 percent to 9 percent of an airline's capacity goes to frequent-flier award redemptions. In 2007, for example, American Airlines carried 2.6 million passengers on frequent-flier award tickets, about 7.5 percent of all boarded, according to the company. Another 843,894 passengers used upgrade awards. It's worth noting, too, that 419,317 American customers used miles for product redemptions, such as vacation packages, magazines, tickets to concerts, or new barbecue grills. And nearly one million American customers redeemed mileage awards on other airlines in partnership with American. At Southwest Airlines, frequent fliers redeemed 2.8 million award tickets in 2007. That was 6.2 percent of all paying passengers Southwest carried that year.

Randy Petersen's WebFlyer site for mileage addicts keeps an unscientific running tally of the successes travelers have at redeeming frequent-flier awards and upgrades. Among airlines, US Airways ranks first with readers reporting success at getting what they wanted 68 percent of the time. Midwest Airlines was second in the ranking at 65 percent success, followed by Qantas Airways from Australia and Virgin Atlantic Airways from the United Kingdom at 63 percent. Among U.S. airlines, the rest of the big carriers fall this way, in order of greatest redemption success: Southwest, American, United, Alaska, Delta, Continental, and Northwest. Choice Hotels was top among hotel programs at 100 percent success, and Starwood was second at 89 percent. Just looking at upgrades, US Airways and United had the best success rates, followed by Alaska and Northwest.

POWER CARDS

After picking a program, the next most important step toward free travel is to pick a credit card that complements it. For millions of people, most of their miles will be earned on the ground. An estimated forty-five million credit cards issued by U.S. banks give airline miles as rewards. Credit cards present the biggest mileage opportunity for you to enjoy cheaper travels. As you might imagine, the credit card market can be confusing because the options are varied, often within the same credit card company.

Most airlines have an affinity charge card that earns you miles from the airline. American's partner is Citibank, which offers both Visa and American Express cards earning AAdvantage Miles. Continental Airlines is tied to Chase, Delta to American Express. You want a card that can deliver miles on your airline of choice. Some cards allow you to use miles earned on purchases toward elite-level status (most don't). But the miles gained on a credit card can make it easier to earn free tickets or first-class upgrades (one of the most popular ways to use frequent-flier miles is toward first-class upgrades).

In recent years, however, savvy frequent fliers have switched to hotel-connected credit cards that allow you to convert points into airline miles, sometimes at favorable rates. Hotels can be a bigger portion of the cost of your trip than airfare, and using your miles toward hotel awards can save you lots of money. One of the most popular of this breed of card is the Starwood American Express card, which earns one point in Starwood's hotel program for every dollar you charge on your credit card. With those points, you can get free and discounted rooms at Starwood hotels anywhere in the world, including the Sheraton, Westin, W, Le Méridien and Four Points chains. You can also easily convert your Starwood points into airline miles at dozens of airlines around the world. The points convert at various rates, some beneficial to you and some not. For example, send 20,000 Starwood points to American's program and you get 25,000 AAdvantage miles. Redeeming points at Continental is not nearly so attractive—20,000 Starwood points become only 10,000 Continental miles.

But you may never want to convert those points to miles. Instead of fighting with airlines for free seats with limited availability, blackout dates, and other restrictions, use your points for the cost of hotels on your trip, and buy airline tickets. You may get more savings from your points that way.

The Starwood program has no blackout dates for hotel redemptions, and you save hotel taxes when you stay in a free room. The Sheraton Manhattan, for example, sells rooms booked far in advance in the summer for about $300, or 12,000 Starwood points per night. That's about 2.5 cents per dollar spent on the credit card—far better than the 1.0 to 1.5 cents per mile typically awarded by airline programs. If I use 24,000 points for two nights at the hotel, I save about $200 over using 25,000 miles for a $400 airline ticket.

There are also credit cards that can earn you free tickets on any airline, not just one tied to the card. The Capital One "No Hassle" card may be the best known in this category. Capital One lets you pick from several different options, and one of the company's most popular cards offers 1.25 miles for every dollar you spend. A "standard" airline ticket award costs 35,000 miles at Capital One—that gets you an airline ticket costing between $150 and $350. You book the ticket you want and buy it, and Capital One reimburses your account after deducting the miles. A ticket that costs $350 to $600 costs 60,000 miles. Is it a good deal? To get a $350 airline ticket, you'd have to spend $28,000 on the credit card. That's about 1.25 cents per dollar spent. If you can get that ticket for only 25,000 miles through an airline program, you would be better off with the airline program. But remember that the airline program has all kinds of restrictions and blackout dates—a frequent-flier award seat may not be available on the day you want, or the time you want, or the price you want. If you have to spend 50,000 miles on that $350 ticket, you're better off at Capital One. And if the freedom not to have to worry about airline availability is important, then the Capital One card is a better deal. (By comparison, a cash-back card generally pays you only about one cent back for every dollar you charge.) On the other hand, the Capital One conversion gets worse if you have to spend more than $350 on your airline ticket, and pay 60,000 miles.

Another consideration with credit cards and frequent-flier programs is to select a card that gives you a specific perk. The American Express Platinum card has many perks travelers like, including free access to airport clubs operated by American, Delta, Continental, or Northwest. For frequent travelers, lounges are valuable places to work, sleep, shower, unwind or just drink through long delays. At times, the Platinum card has offered you a free coach-class domestic companion ticket on any of six U.S. airlines if your fare is $299 or more and you meet certain restrictions, like booking a week in advance, and a free companion ticket for international first-class or business-class if you buy one full-fare first- or business-class ticket. Just remember that you have to qualify, and you have to pay a $450 annual fee.

POWER RUNS

If you've maximized your mileage earning and still you come up short for some trips or elite-level qualification, what do you do? You go on a "mileage run."

The mileage run—taking a flight just to rack up the miles—is a favorite gambit of hard-core frequent fliers who covet the perks of premium levels more than air and water. Toward the end of the year, it's worthwhile to look at how close you are to an elite-level threshold. If it looks like you are going to come up a bit short, find a cheap, long trip for a mileage run. Time on a plane can seem like punishment to many, but if spending a Saturday flying to Los Angeles and back means that for the next year you'll be able to use premium lanes at airport security, board early, get better seating, and qualify for upgrades, it may be worth it. One wasted day—Seattle to São Paulo and turn around and come right back—will yield more comfort for your travels all year.

The key to a mileage run is to maximize distance and minimize cost. Devotees of the scheme have a forum on FlyerTalk.com, an online community for road warriors, where they share ideas and post good fares that make for productive mileage runs. Mileage junkie Joe Lin found a special deal American was offering one time on flights between Boston and Tokyo—a route American was trying to build up. He paid $439 for a trip and ended up with 41,000 miles for his thirty-six hours of flying—about 16,000 miles he earned on the round-trip flights, plus various bonuses. With a second low-priced mileage run, he ended up with enough miles for a business-class international ticket—a seat worth $7,000 to $10,000 that he got for less than a $1,000 investment.

Those kinds of windfalls are hard to find, especially as fares rise and mileage promotions become rarer and rarer for airlines. It pays to watch for special deals in your frequent-flier statements and e-mail advertisements from an airline. Another source of bonus mile promotions: www.MilesMaven.com, a site that lists promotions and will tell you what you can find on specific routes. MilesMaven also lists promotions on a particular airline if you just want to hunt for a productive mileage run and can also show you hotel promotions that can generate more miles or points. (Note: Airlines now sometimes require you to register in advance for promotions, so check the rules carefully.) One major factor to remember is that when airlines launch new routes, they typically start with low introductory prices and often throw in incentives like double mileage.

POWER AWARDS

And now that you've loaded up your account, what is the best way to cash in the miles? That depends on your travel preferences. There are two basic mileage redemption strategies—use them for upgrades or use them for tickets. For many road warriors, another trip is no vacation, and they have far more miles than they can ever use. Sure, they can give tickets to relatives and use miles for a Caribbean vacation once in a blue moon, but the real value of the miles lies in upgrades—moving from coach to business class on international trips, for example, or business class to first class. For many business travelers, international coach is downright painful. Yet some companies and some clients may balk at paying many thousands of dollars extra for a business-class ticket. The path to getting a couple of hours of sleep is in your mileage account. Fly to Europe or Japan on United, for example, and you can upgrade one class of service for just 15,000 miles one way if you bought a full-fare ticket. The cost to upgrade one class is 30,000 miles one-way if you bought a discounted ticket, though some discounted tickets may not be eligible. (Prices are subject to change and airlines have been raising the price of awards. United will add cash co-payments in mid-2009.) Upgrade awards can be used one-way. Maximize your miles by upgrading on overnight flights when sleeping accommodations are most valuable, and suffer eight hours in coach on the daylight return flight from Europe without spending the miles on an upgrade.

Buying business-class tickets themselves with miles is one of the most highly prized awards—and one of the most difficult to get. At United, you can get a business-class ticket to Europe for only 80,000 miles round-trip if you book far in advance, or 180,000 miles if you don't. The math on an 80,000-mile business-class ticket is impressive. Assume that an advance tickets cost $5,000 round-trip. That works out to 6.25 cents per mile—excellent value for your miles. And from the airline's perspective, if you got your 80,000 miles flying and through your credit card, the airline likely collected $800 or so—probably a little bit better than one penny per mile from the credit card company, and close to nothing per mile on the miles you earned in the air. All things being equal, the airline would certainly rather sell that ticket for $5,000 or more than give it to you for your 80,000 miles. Consequently, those seats are hard to get.

Many travelers call up airlines and say they want to go to Rome on a business-class ticket—anytime, any way. The airline tells them there are no seats available. There may be one seat here or there (but you want two, right?), and maybe to Brussels instead of Rome because it's not as popular a destination. It can be enormously frustrating. Seats at double the price—160,000 miles each in this case—may be available, but that may be a lot more than you are able to pay in miles.

How do you improve your odds of landing valuable seats? By shopping early and often. Most airlines open flights up for booking 330 days before departure—basically eleven months. That can vary airline to airline, as some airlines open up day by day and others month by month. You can check with your airline and inquire when a particular flight goes on sale. There is an online tool to help you with this: www.AwardGrabber.com. Put in your flight date and click on how far in advance your airline releases seats, and AwardGrabber will tell you what day seats will be released. Want July 9? Better call on August 13 of the preceding year.

POWER STRATEGIES

To be first in line, you may need to call or go online to book at midnight—whatever hour the airline opens up booking for new dates. With many frequent-flier tickets, you may not need to buy the reservation if you can get one, but instead put it on hold for however long the airline gives you. And being first in line is no guarantee that seats will be available. Some flights just don't have seats available for the cheapest frequent-flier awards. That's a separate bucket, and the bucket for the flight you want may have been empty from the start. It is worth your time to keep checking for the flights you want over the coming month, as inventory can and does change. Airlines may loosen frequent-flier seat inventory if flights aren't selling well. Check connecting flights and alternate cities as well as nonstop flights. If you can work your itinerary so that it includes a city with a flight that may have less demand than others, your chances improve.

Years back, I took my family to Hawaii on first-class frequent-flier tickets because American had started a new flight from San Jose, California, to Honolulu. New routes take time to build traffic, and even though all seats to Hawaii from American's other hubs were sold out or blocked from frequent-flier awards, the San Jose flight had lots of seats. Making the connection was a trade-off worth the cost of four tickets. Another trick to getting prized awards is to make sure you check an airline's code-sharing partners. Some carriers make this process seamless now, offering code-sharing flights online as part of their regular inventory. For others, it may be better to go to the Web site of the particular airline and see what's available, or call the partner airline directly. In some cases, business-class seats may be more plentiful, and you can book using your miles.

Airlines don't release much information about their frequent-flier programs, including how many seats they make available for award redemption or even what the most popular routes are for redemption. InsideFlyer.com, one of Petersen's Web sites, does estimate routes that get the most award traffic. Los Angeles–New York tops the list as the most popular city pair, but that might be expected, since that is the busiest long-haul route in the United States, There's a lesson in that, however, for all of us. The Los Angeles–New York route is quite competitive with lots of airlines, including a couple of discounters, linking the two biggest cities in the country nonstop. Fares are often quite low on that route—people might get more mileage out of their miles by using them for more expensive trips.

New York is at one end or the other of the top three most frequently traveled routes using award tickets—New York–San Francisco and New York–Orlando are number two and number three, respectively, in the list. The large population of New York is sure to put it at the top of a list of award tickets used, but I do think the city pairs show that people end up using frequent-flier awards where they can most easily find an available seat. Markets with lots of service tend to have seats available. Other popular routes: Honolulu–Los Angeles, Boston–San Francisco, and Chicago–New York. On the whole, we think of Hawaii as the top destination for frequent-flier award tickets, but airline limits on available seats crimp customers' ability to get there on miles.

POWER TRAPS

One important trap to remember with frequent-flier awards: Dormant accounts disappear. Airlines aggressively cancel accounts that don't have activity for a few years. Miles earned now carry a time limit and they can expire. The limits vary. AirTran Airways and jetBlue Airways delete credits one year after they are earned if they haven't been redeemed. Miles at United, US Airways, and American expire after just eighteen months of inactivity—not adding or redeeming miles. Delta zaps your miles after two years of inactivity. For most, you are safe, as long as you take a flight within that time window or otherwise keep your account active—redeeming an award counts. Some customers have been surprised—outraged, really—to discover that their account balances were reset to zero by the airline and the miles saved for that trip to Tahiti vanished. Some airlines do allow you to reactivate expired miles, but it can be expensive. At American, it's fifty dollars to for every 5,000 miles reinstated, plus a thirty-dollar processing fee for each transaction. Ouch!

Other issues: It may not seem fair, but airlines can change the rules on their frequent-flier programs as they see fit. The "terms and conditions" that you agree to when you join announce that the company can change the rules, and while some customers years ago did sue, protesting changes, the airlines prevailed in court. That's why the price of awards changes, why the rules on how miles expire change, and why you have to be up-to-date on policies.

Airline bankruptcies and mergers also can result in changes to programs, or even losing miles altogether. In a bankruptcy, miles are treated as a liability the airline owes, just like its debt. You become a creditor, in a legal sense, and the bankruptcy court could eliminate the obligation the airline owes you on your miles. In reality, however, airlines need their frequent fliers, whether the airline is in bankruptcy reorganization or not. To cancel all the accounts would infuriate the airline's best customers and undermine any reason for loyalty. It would be like pouring gasoline on a fire—a sure end to the airline's business. Carriers have protected their frequent-flier programs in bankruptcy court and preserved mileage in accounts. You need not worry if your airline files for bankruptcy protection.

On the other hand, if your airline goes out of business, your miles may go down with it. Unless another carrier steps in to win over customers by acquiring their frequent-flier accounts, you could be out of luck. This has happened with some small airlines, but not with a big carrier. When American bought the assets of bankrupt Trans World Airlines in 2000, for example, it bought TWA's frequent-flier program and merged its members into American's program, giving AAdvantage miles in place of TWA miles. American wanted TWA's customers to fly American. But when ATA Airlines, Aloha Airlines, and Maxjet Airways all went out of business in 2008, no carrier stepped in to rescue those frequent-flier miles. If you are worried about the health of your carrier, you might want to spend miles sooner rather than later so you don't get left with worthless assets.

POWER REDEMPTION

For many of us, the hunt for free tickets to Honolulu at Christmas or Paris in July is a quixotic quest—you may never get what you want. It just may not exist. You can either be furious with your airline—"They lure me in and take my money and give me something I can never use!"— or you can adopt a better strategy. Consider yourself a scavenger. Persistence can pay off.

Sometimes. On the whole, however, I think it's foolish to be hell-bent on using frequent-fliers miles for a summer trip to Europe or a winter trip to Hawaii or some other peak-time trip to a popular destination. First of all, if you can plan in advance, you can often get cheap fares. If you're going to Orlando or Las Vegas, for example, there are almost always cheap tickets available. Never waste miles on trips like that.

Instead, use miles first and foremost for the expensive, unexpected trips that are part of life. Sooner or later, you may have to go to a funeral or rush off to take care of an ill relative, bring an older child home for the weekend, or go see your best friend's new baby. Having frequent-flier miles in the account makes those last-minute trips possible without breaking a budget. Consider the miles as a form of freedom. Buying tickets at the last minute can be expensive, but at many airlines, "full-fare" frequent-flier tickets are available even at the last minute on routes that don't get a lot of free-ticket demand. Let's say you're in Boston and you need to make a sudden trip to Houston, leaving on a Friday and returning on a Monday. Continental's price recently for a next-day departure was $1,195 round-trip. But Continental also had "SaverPass" awards available on the same flights—not much demand for frequent-flier tickets to Houston! The cost: 25,000 miles plus a $50 service fee. That's an efficient, money-saving use of miles. Better yet, take $500 that you might have been willing to pay for the Houston trip, or even the full $1,195, and put it in a "travel kitty"—a fund for expensive vacations. When it's time to go to Europe, buy your $1,000 coach ticket with money you set aside in your fund, and go without worrying about the availability of frequent-flier awards to Paris. That's how to get to Paris for only 25,000 miles, anytime you want to go.

Another smart idea: Use the miles for more expensive holiday trips, because many routes will have frequent-flier seats available even after the cheapest tickets have sold out. Getting children home from college at the holidays is often a good use of frequent-flier miles—exam schedules and other complications may keep you from buying tickets to get your son or daughter home at Christmas, for example. You may have to bump up to the "full fare" of frequent-flier awards—generally about 50,000 miles for a domestic ticket—but if the best airfare you can find is $600 or $700, it may be worth spending the miles rather than cash at the holidays. Spend the cash on yourself later.

However you choose to use miles, think of them as currency. They have value; they are an asset that can help you better manage your household and your lifestyle. Frequent-flier trips aren't "free"—the airline most likely got paid for many of those miles, and you were paid in miles instead of cash back or other rewards. Earn your miles smartly and spend your miles wisely. Travel will be far more exciting and enjoyable.

FREQUENT-FLIER PROGRAM WARNINGS

It's best to think of frequent-flier miles as short-term holdings rather than long-term hoardings. Bad things can happen to those who wait a long time to use their miles.

Rules Change:
When you agree to the "terms and conditions" of the frequent-flier program, you agree that the airline can change the rules on you. Many airlines that used to pay 500-mile minimums on short trips, for example, changed the rules to pay actual mileage flown, reducing the miles you get. Another airline trick: making more discounted fares not eligible for upgrades using frequent-flier miles.

Prices Change:

As ticket prices go up, airlines also raise the price of mileage awards. That European trip you thought would cost you 60,000 miles may now cost 100,000 miles.

Inventory Changes:

It's darn near impossible to figure out how many seats airlines make available to frequent-flier awards, but to most travelers, it's not enough. Some popular flights have no mileage seats open for redemption.

Airlines Change:

Typically when airlines merge, one frequent-flier program is folded into another, and accounts aren't impacted. But sometimes when airlines go out of business, miles become worthless.

Accounts Change:

This is the most insidious problem that catches people off guard—miles expire at most airlines after a few years, and some accounts are wiped out if they have been inactive for a certain period of time. Pay attention to expiration dates—put them on a calendar. And if you are in danger of losing miles, call the airline and try to work out a plan to keep your account current.

CHAPTER 7

Preparing for Takeoff

Before any flight, pilots and crews go through careful preparations. How much fuel the plane will burn is calculated, along with the maximum weight the plane can carry given the wind and temperature and length of the takeoff runway. Alternate airports are selected in case the weather is bad when the flight arrives, and fuel is included on board to make sure the plane can fly there, make an approach, and still have at least forty-five minutes extra fuel to spare. Flight attendants get briefed on unusual passengers or possible problems. It may not always seem like it to the casual flyer, who may see airline operations as unorganized and sloppy, but many lists are checked and many preparations are taken before every flight.

Travelers should be no different than pilots. Not that you need a checklist for every trip you take—though that may help you avoid forgetting items to pack. Beyond that, how you prepare can go a long way to improving your trip.

Here's my sample checklist:

Power Buying

✔ Where do I want to go, and when?

✔ Are there alternate dates that might be cheaper?

✔ Are there alternate airports that might be cheaper?

✔ If I'm planning a multicity trip, will the order I visit cities affect the price? Example: For a London, Paris, Rome, Madrid tour, can I find better airfare or better seats by starting in London or in Rome? (Usually London).

✔ Have I checked the reliability of the possible flights?

✔ What hotels do I want? Price them out on travel Web sites as well as going directly to the hotel.

✔ Will I need a car?

✔ Can I save money by buying air tickets, hotels, and cars together in a package?

✔ Do I have seat assignments on any flight I buy? If reserved seats aren't available, should I consider buying a different flight? (It often helps to hold the reservation, call the airline, and beg for assigned seats. Change it, if they refuse to help you.)

✔ Do I want some sort of travel insurance or overseas medical protection?

Power Planning

✔ Do I need museum, dinner, train, or tour reservations? If preparing for a cruise, do I want to prearrange shore excursions or use the boat's offerings?

✔ Print out directions for places I know I will be visiting. Even if you are using taxis, you might want MapQuest or Google maps showing the route, so you know if your driver is taking you astray.

✔ Do I need to make plans with friends, relatives, or business associates?

✔ Do I need vaccinations for my trip, or need to obtain extra prescription medicine or prescriptions themselves for traveling?

Power Packing

✔ Check the anticipated weather for all destinations. Chilly nights? Scorching days?

✔ Plan a minimal number of outfits. When can I use a hotel or local laundry, allowing me to take less clothing? What will I wear on the plane to save space in my bag? (Suit jackets are the place to start.) With baggage fees adding up to significant expenses and airline reliability at handling bags diminishing, it really pays to travel light. More on that in Chapter 8.

✔ Pack an extra fold-up bag so I have room to carry home purchases.

✔ Consider shipping bags or business materials ahead to your hotel.

✔ Weigh your bags. Don't have any airport surprises that can slow you up.

Power Predeparture

✔ Check the weather along your route. If storms await you, can your airline reroute you? Check airport statuses at www.fly.faa.gov.

✔ Sign up for flight-status alerts from your airline or a service like FlightStats.com.

✔ Collect phone numbers for hotels near any airport where you'll be making a connection—just in case you get stranded.

✔ Consider a car service or taxi rather than leaving a car parked at the airport. It can be cheaper than high airport parking rates.

✔ Check your documents. Are passports current? (Some countries won't let you in if your passport will expire in the next six months.) Do you have the visas you need?

If you run down those items, you'll be good to go when it comes time to head to the airport.

POWER INSURANCE?

One of the preparations most difficult to evaluate is travel insurance, and that is one of the services that airlines most frequently hawk now. Travel insurers will pay for the un-reimbursable parts of a trip (such as airline tickets and hotel deposits) if a policyholder has to delay or cancel a trip, or help cover the cost of meals and hotel rooms if you get stranded. Policies often cover medical care if you get sick overseas as well as medical evacuation. That's potentially important, since your medical insurance may not be accepted by hospitals overseas. Insurance is plenty popular with travelers—more than seventeen million policies are sold each year in the United States, according to U.S. Travel Insurance Association, and sales have doubled since the September 11, 2001, terrorist attacks.

Do people know what they are buying? The programs are filled with exclusions. The irony is that bad events—hurricanes, terrorism, airline bankruptcies—drive up sales of travel insurance. But once those events happen, you can't insure against them. The policy you buy often excludes the coverage you want.

The offerings come in different forms. Airlines and

online travel sellers offer basic trip protection at modest cost, often less than twenty dollars per ticket. The insurance offers some protection if you have to cancel a nonrefundable ticket (cancellation insurance), or if you get stranded somewhere during your trip (called delay protection), or if you have to head home early because of an emergency (trip interruption protection, which usually only pays up to the cost of your original ticket, likely far short of what it will cost to get home on short notice). The catch is that only "covered reasons" trigger the insurance, and many of the most common travel problems aren't covered. If you have to cancel the ticket, for example, the insurance may only kick in if you canceled for a medical illness or death in the family—covered reasons. Some policies include unforeseen emergencies like a fire at your house. But the policies don't help you, typically, if you have to change plans because your boss needed your help with a project, or you decided that February would be a better time for skiing than January. Even the medical coverage can be tricky—any sort of preexisting medical condition may not be covered, for example. And the delay coverage may have limits that render it unlikely to help you in typical situations.

Seven of the eight biggest U.S. airlines sell "Ticket Protector" insurance from Access America, a unit of World Access Service Corp. Airlines usually offer policies (and prompt travelers to click a little box) right before they ask fliers to push the "buy" button on their tickets. Even though the policies are all from the same company and are all called Ticket Protector, they differ in the coverage they offer, says Mark Cipolletti, vice president of marketing at Access America.

Not all the policies provide protection for weather delays and other events outside of an airline's control, for example.

Continental adds travel-delay insurance and a concierge benefit—a phone number to call for help—to its policies, he says. American Airlines offers both basic trip coverage and a more comprehensive plan.

On a $345 ticket for a June 2008 trip, Northwest's Web site offered Trip Protector at just $15.52. That included trip cancellation and interruption insurance, but no delay protection. American's basic Trip Protector costs more—$18.97 on a $345 ticket, but includes a $500 travel delay benefit and $500 baggage-delay benefit.

Beyond the basic airline offerings, there are more comprehensive, and expensive, travel policies out there. A couple of Web sites, including SquareMouth.com, TotalTravelInsurance.com, and InsureMyTrip.com, search policies and compare both quotes and the conditions and coverage offered, and can be useful if you are interested in travel insurance. Just as with the airline-sold policies, watch out for the fine print exclusions.

Many people buy travel insurance for Caribbean cruises during hurricane season, but you have to buy the policy when you book the cruise for it to be effective. Once a storm forms and is named by hurricane trackers, you can't buy coverage for that storm. (The company may still sell you the insurance, but it won't cover for any "preexisting" storm.) And even if you did buy the insurance early, long before hurricanes begin forming, you may not have coverage unless a storm makes it impossible for you to get to your destination, there's a mandatory evacuation order, or your destination is uninhabitable. Not wanting to go because of minor storm damage doesn't count. If you're simply worried that a hurricane might hit during your vacation and you cancel to avoid hassle, you'll get reimbursed only if the storm devastates your particular vacation spot. "Travel insurance doesn't cover state of mind. A specific event has to happen," says Dan McGinnity, a spokesman for Travel Guard, a unit of American International Group Inc.

Another reason people seek out travel insurance is concern about future terrorist attacks. There again, the coverage limits can render it useless. Many insurance policies only refund canceled trips if the terrorist event you were worried about happened in a city on your itinerary and within thirty days of your trip. If a bombing in London makes you afraid to go to Paris, or even Manchester, England, your travel insurance won't help. Many countries are excluded from terrorism coverage, too, particularly countries where the U.S. State Department has issued any kind of warning. Once the warning goes up, the insurance you buy will exclude that country from coverage. Some policies exclude terrorism coverage altogether, forcing worried consumers to choose carefully. Only six of twenty-four Travel Guard International policies in a recent sampling had any terrorism protection, for example. The comprehensive policies that do have it account for 80 percent of sales, notes Travel Guard, one of the biggest travel insurers. Another catch: Some insurance companies may declare a terrorism event as an "act of war," which is excluded from coverage on almost every policy. The fighting between Israel and Hezbollah across the border of Lebanon was excluded from terrorism coverage by some insurance companies, including one of the biggest, Allianz AG's Access America, even though the United States and others consider Hezbollah a terrorist organization.

The reality: There's little coverage for fear.

Coverage for airline bankruptcies, shutdowns, and labor strikes may be limited as well. A suddenly defunct carrier may be excluded from the coverage. Some insurance companies issue a list in their fine print of only a dozen or so air-lines that they will cover in the event of a shutdown. Others list lots of airlines they exclude—any carrier with any past or foreseeable financial trouble, essentially. You may buy the insurance because it promises coverage for airline shut-downs, but your carrier may not be covered. And once a union sets a strike date—usually long before travelers and reporters take strike threats seriously—insurance coverage for that strike is invalid.

It's the "theory of the burning building," insurance com-panies say. If your house is on fire, you can't call up and buy fire insurance. Once terrorists strike, or tropical storms get names, or war breaks out, or airlines run into financial trouble, you can't insure yourself against those specific and all too real perils.

Insurance regulators say they don't get a lot of com-plaints about travel insurance, but when they do, the most frequent complaint is claim denial. "It just seems to be that people are not reading the policy and understanding what they are buying," says Nina Banister, a spokeswoman for Florida Department of Financial Services.

One way to beat many of the restrictions is to buy "cancel for any reason" policies offered by at least two travel-insurance companies, M. H. Ross and TravelSafe. Those are more expensive—typically about 40 percent more than stan-dard policies—but less hassle. Those policies let you cancel up to about a week or so before departure for any reason— hurricanes, or terrorism, or your Aunt Millie. The policies typically have a large deductible or may only reimburse you for 75 percent of the cost of the trip. Though they only cover what you can't get back from airlines, hotels, and tour com-panies, "cancel for any reason" gives you more flexibility and will likely pay you back something if plans do go awry.

INSURANCE COMPLAINTS

If you have a dispute or complaint about travel insurance and are unable to resolve it with the company, try your state insurance commissioner. Each has a Web site with a complaint form, or a telephone number to call for a consumer advocate.

Some tips

Document every call and letter with the insurance company, and make sure you get the names of individuals you talk to.

Be patient. The insurance commissioner's office will likely send the complaint to the insurance company and allow time for the insurance company to respond.

Find out if there are others who have had similar complaints. Large numbers can bolster your cause. You might check other states for problems related to your policy.

Remember, the state can't act as your attorney, so you might want your own. But because states do license insurance companies, an effective insurance commissioner can often pressure a company into a resolution that may be acceptable to you.

POWER PROTECTION

The latest trend in travel insurance is to offer "delay protection." Capitalizing on all the concern travelers have about airline delays, missed connections, and overbooked flights that can leave travelers stuck at airport hubs for several days, insurance companies highlight delay benefits. Low-cost policies that include "delay insurance," pay for hotel rooms and meals if you get stuck. Delay insurance is included in some policies that offer protection such as refunds if you fall ill. These policies usually cost less than fifty dollars when flying on inexpensive domestic routes.

Airlines, too, are getting into the protection game, making money off the disruption they sometimes create. Air Canada, often a pricing scheme innovator, launched a new "travel assistance" service that provides hotel rooms and even airfare on rival carriers if you pay twenty-five to thirty-five dollars extra per one-way flight when you buy a ticket. With delays and disruptions increasing, Air Canada says customers suggested to the airline that they'd be willing to pay extra for some assurance that the airline would take care of them. The "On My Way" service, which began in 2008, comes with a phone number to call specially trained Air Canada agents who can book and pay for hotels, find seats on other Air Canada flights, or book competing airlines if Air Canada doesn't have an option to offer within two hours. Air Canada, a unit of ACE Aviation Holdings Inc., will pay for rental cars if driving is faster and even make prepaid meal reservations. Other airlines have been observing Air Canada's solution and will likely follow suit if there's revenue to be earned.

Remember, most airlines won't pay for hotels and meals if the problem stems from factors out of an airline's control—only if the airline had a breakdown. That bifurcation has led to battles between passengers and airlines over whether problems were caused by the airline or not, and surprises for passengers with unexpected hotel bills. Part of the murk is that it's not always clear what led to passengers getting stranded. Delayed passengers on a

morning flight with a mechanical problem that gets canceled due to afternoon storms should receive accommodations, for example, even though some airline agents might
blame bad weather. And airline operational issues can ex-
acerbate disruptions. Scheduling crews or airplanes too
tightly can lead to cancellations when bad weather strikes,
for example. Comair Inc., a Delta subsidiary, had a massive crew-scheduling computer meltdown on Christmas
Eve 2004. There was a bad snowstorm at the time, and
Comair, citing bad weather, refused to pay to accommodate passengers. The U.S. Department of Transportation
investigated and found Comair had cheated passengers.
The airline was fined $75,000.

To avoid arguments with airlines, some people may
prefer insurance. With delay-insurance coverage, you have
to file a claim and document your spending, just as with
any other insurance. Coverage is often limited to a daily
cap of $100 or $200, depending on the policy. Policies generally cover hotels, food, and expenses such as toiletries.
Travel Insured International started offering a new policy
for budget travelers in 2008 called Worldwide Trip Protector Lite that will cover $100 a day in expenses, up to $500,
if you are delayed more than six hours. It's priced based on
your age and how much your ticket cost: On a $500 ticket,
the "Lite" insurance costs $15 for people thirty years old
and younger, up to $32 for people over sixty-one years old.
Another option: American Express Co. offers delay insurance to card members for $9.95 per trip if they enroll in a
service that automatically charges the premium when they
buy tickets on their credit card. The insurance covers $200
a day for up to two days if you are stuck overnight because
of a delayed or canceled flight or missed connection.

POWER INFORMATION

Preparations and protections for your travels don't end with insurance decisions. You can protect yourself and ensure a great trip if you do some destination research before you go. There's a world of travel information on the Web that's ripe for the surfing.

The Internet has changed the travel guidebook business. You can not only access much of the research and writing online from Fodor's to Frommer's to Lonely Planet to Rick Steves, but also reviews and information posted and shared by fellow travelers. It's like listening to your neighbor describe a fantastic vacation—likes and dislikes—with a slide show to boot.

Often some of the best, most up-to-date information on destinations can be found online from locals. Local newspapers are a good source, especially for entertainment listings and restaurant reviews. Many newspapers have their travel sections online. *The Wall Street Journal* has a travel section on its Web site with lots of offerings, including a Middle Seat blog called "The Terminal" with the latest travel information. Simply using Google to search for information about a particular destination or attraction can yield lots of information from locals. Some of that may be canned info—Web sites sponsored by local tourism boards, for example. But some can be far more honest assessments from residents and visitors.

The travel review business has been booming as well. Most Web sites that sell travel have sections where customers can post reviews of hotels and attractions. To be useful and trustworthy, you need lots of comments and ratings. Avoid being swayed too much by a particularly aggrieved visitor (though more than one or two bad reports shouldn't

necessarily be discounted), or by an enterprising hotel manager who gets his friends and colleagues to post favorable
reviews.

Different kinds of stand-alone sites may also be useful.
Lonely Planet has a site called Thorn Tree Travel Forum
(accessible from LonelyPlanet.com) where you can post
questions (How much to get to Manaus from La Paz?),
offer up a planned itinerary for review, and comment and
get feedback on all kinds of travel questions. VirtualTourist
.com is another site that claims one million members posting on their travel experiences. IgoUgo.com is another
review site, now owned by Travelocity.com. (I find IgoUgo,
in particular, has heavy ad content that can be distract-
ing). The biggest of the travel review sites is TripAdvisor
.com, which is owned by Expedia.com. (Expedia also owns
SeatGuru.com and about ten other specialized travel Web
sites). TripAdvisor, like others, offers a subscription service
that will e-mail you information and specials on a destination of interest as they develop. TripAdvisor's bread and
butter is hotel reviews. Major properties in big cities have
hundreds of reviews, and you can sort hotels by both price
and popularity. TripAdvisor also has restaurant reviews and
a forum for posting questions.

Here's one little comparison: I checked a company called
Tuscany Bike Tours A.S.D. that is based in Florence and
offers guided single-day bike tours through the wine country with van support and meals for about sixty euros each
day. I figured that fun activities in Tuscany would be an
appropriate sampling of the merits of different sites, just to
compare some of the breadth of their information. Tuscany
Bike Tours (www.tuscany-biketours.com) didn't show up
on VirtualTourist.com or IgoUgo.com—the most popular
activity listed on IgoUgo had only five reviews. On TripAd-

visor, Tuscany Bike Tours had fifty-three different reviews, among a host of other activities for Florence and Tuscany.

For business travelers in particular, a handy resource for trip planning is the online community at FlyerTalk.com, where registered members can post questions about travel strategies and destinations. Wondering what to do during a six-hour layover in Amsterdam? The road warriors who use FlyerTalk can tell you all about the airport's casino, its museum, and its extensive shopping, or how to take a train for a quick tour of the city. If you're looking for a good restaurant for a business meeting or the best hotel in London for a wheelchair-bound executive, FlyerTalk can help.

POWER ALERTS

Once you've done your search, there are some other important preparations to make before you get around to packing and heading to the airport. A top priority: Set up flight status alerts so you can get early warning of delays and cancellations.

Airlines offer flight alert notifications for your cell phone, either as voice, text, or e-mail. The alerts give gate information for departures—handy to know where to park—and gate and baggage claim information for destinations. They also have the scheduled time, and at least in theory, any changes to that schedule.

In most cases, the alerts can be helpful. I've found myself sitting at a gate waiting for a flight, for example, and then receiving an alert that the gate has changed. The alert comes in long before the gate agent gets around to announcing a gate change, if there is a gate agent around to alert customers. Along these same lines, I was sitting on a long-delayed flight waiting to take off for New York and my flight alert gave me far better information on our expected departure than the plane's captain. It was kind of fun passing around the new posted departure time of an hour later to fellow passengers, only to have the captain announce thirty minutes later that we were still thirty minutes from departure.

More significantly, early warning of a canceled flight can help you be first in line for rebooking or first on the phone with the airline to snag a seat on another flight. Flight alerts keep you up-to-date on how much time you'll have between connections—how often do you find yourself on one plane wondering if your connecting flight will also be delayed, or not? One other great use for flight alerts: picking up people at the airport. A change in gate or terminal or arrival time could leave you parking in the wrong place or even waiting in the wrong area unless you get the word.

Airlines vary in their flight alert prowess. I did a Bake-Off of flight alert systems, signing up for dozens of flights at different airlines and comparing both how timely the updates were as well as how accurate they were. Delta, Continental, and American were the best. They gave me timely updates, good gate information, and updates as flights progressed or were delayed. Only Continental, however, sent alerts when flights took off. Once a plane is in the air, you have a much more accurate estimate of when it will actually land, so knowing when the wheels leave the ground is a big help. United's system was utilitarian—the Joe Friday "just the facts" flight alert system. It offered no updates unless something changed, while the other systems let you know when the plane was airborne or landed. Southwest's flight alerts were Spartan, as might be expected. Southwest didn't offer gate or baggage claim information, and was slow with updates. In my test, a Southwest flight left Chicago's Midway Airport seventy-three minutes late, but

Southwest's departure alerts never notified people of the delay. Alerts sent for the flight's arrival at Omaha did pick up the delay, but not until an hour before landing.

Northwest's flight alerts were downright troublesome: Some of the information was inaccurate, and only frequent fliers of Northwest had access to updates. One Northwest flight in my test arrived four hours late at Detroit, but the flight status notification service told me it arrived twelve minutes early. Imagine the anger of someone who drove to the airport to meet someone based on the alert.

The most useful source of more information was at FlightStats.com, a fabulous resource for travelers that collects data not only from airline computers, but also from airports and the Federal Aviation Administration. I prefer FlightStats over any of the airline services. FlightStats sends frequent updates, including notices when planes take off and when they land. On some flights in my test, I received eight different updates from FlightStats, compared with only one or two from an airline. I routinely use FlightStats when I travel.

If you're sitting at a computer and wondering where a particular flight is, FlightStats will give you a graphical image on a map, too. There are other flight-tracking services useful for watching particular airplanes, including corporate jets if you know the tail number. FlightExplorer.com, FlyteComm .com, FlightView.com, and FlightArrivals.com tell you where the flight is, often placing it on a map and sometimes overlaying weather radar, and what time it should arrive. Those services get their data from the FAA and often have a hard time finding a flight until it is active in the FAA's system. That means flights may not show up if they are suffering long delays or if they have been canceled. That's another reason why FlightStat's use of multiple data sources pays off.

POWER WARNINGS

Other preparations on your own checklist? Collect phone numbers for hotel chains, and maybe some specific properties at a hub airport where you are going to make connections. If you get stranded, you'll be glad you have them. Sometimes there's a line to use the hotel phone at a baggage claim area; sometimes the last few rooms available go to those who call quickest. I always keep the phone number for the hotel I'm headed to handy and call when I'm delayed or arriving late to tell the front desk that I am coming and not to give my room away to another guest.

If you are traveling overseas, it's worthwhile to check the State Department's Web site (www.state.gov) for any advisories and any requirements for visas in countries you plan to visit. (India often trips up some travelers; U.S. citizens are required to have a visa to enter India.) The State Department lists travel warnings about various countries, long-term issues, as well as travel advisories about temporary or immediate situations. Also, check the Centers for Disease Control for health concerns and vaccination requirements (www.cdc.gov or 1–800-CDC-INFO). Some countries still require yellow fever vaccines, for example, and the CDC recommends yellow fever vaccines for travel to certain provinces of countries that don't require it. The CDC Web site has a wealth of good information, from particular health concerns in countries to tips for preventing disease while traveling.

Gather up all your documents—confirmation numbers and the like—and keep them separate from your checked luggage. One organizing tool I've grown fond of is a Web site called TripIt.com. You register your e-mail address with TripIt, and when you get confirmations by e-mail from airlines, hotels, car rental agencies, or other travel-related vendors, such as Broadway shows or sporting events, you can forward the confirmations to plans@tripit .com. TripIt, which is a free service, automatically builds an elaborate, chronologically correct itinerary for you. It's fast and easy. (I've sent confirmations from multiple trips at the same time and TripIt sorted them out correctly.) The TripIt itinerary includes phone numbers and confirmation numbers, and it adds directions to hotels or appointments you might want to add to the itinerary. The itinerary has a link to SeatGuru.com that will help evaluate your assigned seats; you can add weather forecasts or restaurant suggestions, too. Instead of a folder full of confirmations (though you might want the originals in case there is a dispute over a booking), you can carry your TripIt itinerary on a couple sheets of paper or load it electronically into your calendar and have what you need. (One caution: Some people may not feel comfortable having personal travel information at a third-party Web site. TripIt assures privacy, but some people may not want to expose their comings and goings to outsiders. Also, TripIt's user agreement lets it send you marketing messages based on your itinerary unless you opt out.)

A day or two before you leave, check the weather for your departure city, your destination, and any connecting points on your trip. (Weather.com has good maps and travel forecasts.) If storms are expected, you can sometimes get your airline to reroute your itinerary, or move you to an earlier or later flight, before you ever leave for the airport. For current airport conditions and travel slowdowns, check www .fly.faa.gov. That site has good information on any air-traffic-control programs in place to slow down or stop takeoffs for major airports. It's worthwhile to check wait times at Transportation Security Administration checkpoints at www.tsa.gov. TSA doesn't offer current conditions, but the historical averages can suggest what you may be up against. Knowing that the wait at Phoenix Sky Harbor Airport's Terminal Four at 8 A.M. on Saturday mornings can be as long as twenty-seven minutes, according to TSA, can help you plan. (Waits may in fact be longer than the TSA's Web site indicates. I waited forty-five minutes at Terminal Four and just barely made my flight.)

POWER PACKING

Some people focus on minimizing wrinkles when they pack, and these days, as the cost of checking baggage escalates, minimizing baggage fees can be a major driver of packing strategy. For me, the focus is on minimizing the chances that my luggage will be lost. There are some important steps to take.

In terms of minimizing wrinkles, most seasoned travelers have figured out what works for them—what kind of baggage they like to travel with, whether they have more success at folding clothes, or rolling them up, or whether they prefer hanging bags. Most hotel rooms have an iron and ironing board. Wrinkle-free packing is a bit like worry-free travel—it doesn't exist.

The luggage you use can make a difference. The Holy Grail is lightweight but durable. When you have to carry bags, you want them to be as light as possible. When you turn the bag over to an airline, which will shoot it down a conveyor belt, slam it a few times with pneumatically driven metal arms, throw it on a cart and pile hundreds of pounds of material on top of it and maybe even drop it a time or two on airport pavement, you want something tough. Baggage manufacturers try to balance those two design concerns, and in general, superstrong lightweight materials are more expensive than heavier or weaker materials. That's why good luggage is worth the investment.

With that, you've done all you can do to prepare. Now it's up to the airline. In other words, here comes the scary part.

CRITICAL PACKING RULES

✔ Never put valuables in checked luggage—no jewelry, no electronics, nothing a baggage clerk or security screener with sticky fingers could sell at a pawnshop. There are too many thefts from luggage to take the chance, and airline rules exempt anything of significant value from the airline's responsibility. Sweet, huh? Your diamond necklace gets stolen and the airline says it is not responsible. (Other insurance such as baggage coverage from a credit card company or your homeowner's policy might cover you, however.)

✔ Never check prescription medicine in your luggage— always carry that on board with you because it may be difficult to replace, especially in a timely fashion. It's a good idea when traveling abroad to take an extra prescription with you for each of your necessary medicines. A U.S. consulate can help you get them filled in an emergency. It helps to have the generic name of the medicine, since brand names aren't used universally in different countries.

✔ Keep an inventory of what you have packed so you know exactly what needs replacing if the bag goes missing. It will help with a claim if a lost bag is never found. Better yet, keep receipts for your purchases, then you have an easier time documenting value should an airline need to replace items.

✔ Note exactly what your bag looks like—write down a description. If the bag doesn't show up at your destination, the first question the airline will ask is, what does it look like? Having the brand, the size, a description, and other identifying characteristics will greatly improve the chances that you and your bag will be reunited.

✔ Weigh your bags before heading to the airport. Most airlines start charging extra for any bag over fifty pounds. You can hit fifty pounds easily—and some airlines will hit you for an extra $125 each way. Avoid expensive surprises, or the pain of repacking on the airport lobby floor.

✔ Check the dimensions of your bags. I have a large suitcase, dubbed by the family the "rolling coffin," that is now considered "oversize" by airlines. If the bag is too big, it'll cost you a bundle—$150 each way on many airlines. These days, if a bag's length, width, and height added together exceed sixty-two inches, you'll pay. Check your airline and measure your bag if it's large.

CHAPTER 8

Baggage Woes

A comedian from Wales named Rhod Gilbert has a hysterical video (search YouTube.com for Rhod Gilbert and you'll find it) about his airline experience on a trip to Australia. For the first time in his life, he gives up a backpack for his travels and buys a nice new suitcase. He purchases new clothes for the journey. Upon arrival at baggage claim, a single metal handle comes down the conveyor belt for delivery to customers, obviously the remnants of someone's luggage.

"I'll admit, I'll admit if I'm completely honest, the first three times this went around the baggage carousel, I laughed as well," Gilbert said. "And then everybody else, they went home." It turns out the handle came from his suitcase—it had the identifying name tag still affixed to the handle, even if the bag itself was long gone, and it had an airline warning tag for baggage handlers: BEND YOUR KNEES. HEAVY. Gilbert marched the forsaken handle over to the airline baggage office, where an employee asked, "What seems to be the problem?"

"I'm pretty sure I packed more than this," he said. Then the typical airline questions started so that forms could be filled out.

"Could anybody have interfered with it?" the baggage clerk asked.

"We probably shouldn't rule that out," Gilbert said.

"Did you leave it unattended at any point?"

"I suppose I must have."

"Did you pack it yourself?"

By the time the clerk got to "Does your luggage have any distinguishing features?" and he responded with "It's got a long black handle," the audience was in stitches.

Airline baggage handling has long been a staple for comedians, maybe even more so now that airline food has been removed from the menu of classic stand-up fodder. It works time and time again for two reasons: Airlines do bad things to luggage, and we can all relate one way or another. Even if you haven't been through the misery of lost luggage, you probably fear it.

In the United States, airline baggage service has gotten worse every year since 2002. It's a creaky old system, plagued by arthritic equipment, ill-conceived plans, lack of new technology, and a dearth of baggage handlers. The rate at which bags get mishandled in 2008 was almost twice as high as it was in 2002. Complaints about baggage service that travelers filed with the Department of Transportation have been skyrocketing—stolen items, broken items, lost garments, soaking wet belongings, and ruined vacations are among the many gripes. Worst among the major airlines over the most recent five-year period reported by the government: US Airways has been at the bottom, followed by Delta and American. (AirTran, jetBlue, and Continental were the best among major carriers.)

FIVE YEARS' WORTH OF LOST LUGGAGE

	Total Mishandled Baggage Reports (Domestic Only)	Domestic Passengers	Reports Per 1,000 Passengers
AirTran	328,063	87,722,660	3.74
jetBlue	313,731	76,092,204	4.12
Continental	751,929	177,752,929	4.23
Northwest	1,023,604	231,277,043	4.43
Southwest	2,058,381	453,252,125	4.54
United	1,413,433	300,330,014	4.71
Alaska	354,727	75,267,335	4.71
American	2,251,783	391,250,631	5.76
Delta	2,262,893	376,162,534	6.02
US Airways	1,814,146	283,165,412	6.41

Source: U.S. Depart. of Transportation, 2003–2007

POWER FEES

Even as reliability declines, airlines have aggressively added charges for baggage service, making it expensive to travel with some bags (and you don't get a refund on your baggage fees if the airline doesn't deliver the bag, either). The baggage fee barrage started after the September 11 terrorist attacks when airlines were reeling financially and half the U.S. industry was operating under protection from creditors from U.S. bankruptcy court. Airlines need skycaps to help keep lines inside terminals smaller and to provide the customer service that many people want. Airlines couldn't afford the skycaps, who make most of their money from tips. (Some skycaps at busy airports haul in six-figure incomes from tips. It's a closely guarded secret in the skycap fraternity. If you're a regular customer at an airport, you'll notice there is little turnover among skycaps and the skycap workforce is typically senior. Few people give up those kinds of jobs.)

The solution: Start charging two dollars a bag for skycap services. That allowed airlines to continue providing the service without paying for it. Skycaps hated the fee because it cut into their tips, and skycaps in Boston even sued American and other airlines over the two-dollar charge. To the surprise of airline executives, the public adapted to the two-dollar charge. Many people avoided it by toting their bags inside a terminal for checking. Deploying the new technology of self-service kiosks helped reduce long lines. Lots of customers still wanted to use skycaps and were willing to pay for the service. So far, so good. (A similar pattern followed with eliminating free meals on domestic flights and offering "buy on board" sandwiches, snacks, and salads. It turns out that customers were willing to pay for something tastier in terms of food than horrendous free airline meals.

When the oil-price shock of 2008 rolled around, airlines had to find new revenue to offset higher fuel prices. Fees became the order of the day. Everything an airline did besides fly your fanny from one city to another was offered "à la carte" as an extra service available for a price. That included baggage service.

We don't fly naked (though there are flights for nudists in Europe). You have to bring *something* with you when you travel. You buy a ticket and the airline promises to transport you and your bag to another city. Baggage service was like the bed and the shower at the hotel room—a necessity, not an add-on like room service, laundry, premium movies, or Internet access. Or is it?

United Airlines took the first step in 2008 by instituting a $25 one-way charge for checking a *second* piece of luggage. United decided that one piece of luggage came with the cost of a ticket, but more than that should be paid for separately, according to head marketer, Dennis Cary. While travelers moaned and groaned, they adapted. Many understood the plight airlines were in because of high fuel prices. And the $50 round-trip second bag fee didn't look onerous when compared to other baggage fees airlines charge: A third bag costs $200 to $300 round-trip at most U.S. airlines. Overweight bags (more than fifty pounds) can cost $300 round-trip, as can oversize bags. The fees accumulate: A third bag that is overweight and oversize can cost hundreds of dollars. Some airlines charge hefty fees for sports equipment, though most consider golf clubs standard-size baggage. If you aren't careful, you can easily equal your fare with baggage fees.

Other airlines matched United's second bag initiative, and when travelers adapted to that, a few months later American Airlines announced it would start charging $15 each way for the first checked bag, or $30 round-trip. As with other baggage fees, lots of travelers are exempt, such as elite-level frequent fliers or international travelers. One by one, other airlines matched American's first-bag fee. At the same time, airlines also started cracking down on excess carry-on baggage, figuring that many people will overstuff their carry-on bags to avoid paying the fees. Indeed, in the first full month the fees were in place, July 2008, American customers checked one million fewer pieces of luggage than they did in July 2007. The whole mess makes the traveling experience more difficult and less enjoyable. And it hasn't done anything to improve baggage handling, either.

Delta took a different tack—temporarily. Delta decided

that passengers are entitled to check one bag as part of
the transportation we buy when we purchase a ticket. But
Delta doubled the second bag fee to $50 one-way or $100
round-trip. Delta's CEO, Richard Anderson, said that in
essence, he believes two pieces of carry-on luggage and one
checked suitcase ought to be enough for anyone—more
than that and you are using the airline for cargo service.
The people who have more than one bag ought to pay. It's
a fairer setup than many of the other airline strategies, but
like many fees and fares in the airline world, it didn't have
a long life. Eventually, every airline will charge for any sort
of baggage service. And in late 2008, Delta had a change
of heart and imposed a $15 one-way first bag fee and
dropped its second bag fee to $25 each way, putting it in
line with American, United, Continental, US Airways, and
others.

HEAVY LIFTING

Baggage fees are changing all the time at airlines. Here's a sample of
different airlines in late 2008, based on one-way domestic travel.

Make sure you check the fee schedule of the airline you're flying
before packing.

And remember, you'll pay double for round-trip travel.

Airline	First Bag	Second Bag	Third Bag	Overweight (51–70 lbs)
AirTran	$15	$10–$20	$50	$29
Alaska	Free	$25	$125	$50
American	$15	$25	$100	$50
Continental	$15	$25	$100	$50
Delta	$15	$25	$125	$90

Airline	First Bag	Second Bag	Third Bag	Overweight (51–70 lbs)
jetBlue	Free	$20	$75	$50
Northwest	$15	$25	$100	$50
Southwest	Free	Free	$25	$25
United	$15	$25	$125	$125
US Airways	$15	$25	$100	$50

A host of culprits lie behind the baggage woes: poorer on-time performance that leads to misconnected bags; staffing cutbacks, which mean fewer baggage handlers; and a lack of investment in equipment and technology. There have been lots of innovations in logistics and shipping, but airlines have been slow adopters. They are moving bags the same way they have for the past twenty years or so—not efficiently or productively. What's more, stricter security standards such as limits on the volume of liquids in airplane cabins has forced more people to check bags. As airlines push toward smaller planes, shifting more and more traffic to regional airlines with smaller jets, more bags are left behind. Smaller planes don't have as much capacity for luggage, and the transfer of bags from one airline to another doesn't work well. Both airlines point fingers at each other when bag handling gets bollixed.

U.S. airlines now lose between four million and five million bags a year—more than twelve thousand each day—and that's just in domestic air service. (The Department of Transportation doesn't count mishandled baggage on international trips.) Most of those bags catch up to their owners within several hours; but many—airlines don't disclose exactly how many—are never recovered.

POWER LOSSES

Some of the baggage nightmares people encounter can be gut wrenching. National Public Radio host Scott Simon contacted me once out of absolute desperation over a lost bag. He and his wife had gone to China to adopt a second child, and United Airlines lost one of his suitcases. It happened to be the one with the white dress the child was wearing at the orphanage when Mr. Simon and his wife arrived, and other irreplaceable mementoes. United gave Mr. Simon a phone number for the baggage office in San Francisco, but the phone was never answered. Either the baggage office didn't want to talk to customers or the staff was out looking for luggage at all hours. United went on a worldwide search for Mr. Simon's bag after *The Wall Street Journal* included his story in a litany of summer travel woes, and the bag was found—in Maui. Go figure. Then there are the poor souls—many of them—whose bags were snared in a British Airways meltdown in London that stretched for more than a year. Thousands of bags piled up at Heathrow Airport. Left outdoors, they were rained on and piled into metal baggage containers where they fermented, literally. When people did get baggage delivered to them, many found the contents covered with mold.

Luckily, those kinds of nightmares happen to only a small percentage of travelers. On average, a bit more than 99 percent of all airline passengers in the United States get to their destinations without any luggage problems—a statistic that airline executives trumpet. (Of course, more than half of passengers never check baggage to begin with, so the percentage of people who check bags and don't get them back on schedule is significantly higher.)

More than 99 percent seems like a pretty good track

record until you delve into it deeper. On average, airlines lose a bag or two for one passenger out of every 150 people or so. That means one person on your flight, typically, will arrive without luggage. Take a look around the next flight you are on—which of you will be the unlikely flier? If you're on a wide-body jet, of course, there will be more unhappy customers on average. It seems to me that the unlucky baggage owners will undoubtedly be the people who most need their luggage—the ones heading to a family wedding with a bridesmaid's dress in a bag, or the couple about to board a cruise for whom there will be little chance that their luggage will catch up to their stateroom. Indeed, one of the big reasons that airline baggage is such an important issue is that the penalty to the passenger when things go awry is severe—you are left without necessary items, you don't know when your belongings may be returned to you, and you don't know what you can or need to replace right away, or whether the airline will pay for it. For those four million to five million U.S. travelers a year who end up with lost luggage, each will remember the experience for a long time.

IMPROVING YOUR BAG'S CHANCES

✔ Always mark your bags distinctly, but not with long ribbons that could get caught in machinery. Use tape, or tightly tied package ribbon, directly on the bag. And don't rely on big luggage tags—they can get torn off. Baggage has become uniformly boring black these days, and there's nothing worse than seeing fifty similar black bags on a carousel. Colorful identifying marks not only make it easier for you to spot your bag, but also keep other people from picking up the wrong bag—unless, of course, eight people on your flight all had black bags with yellow ribbons.

✔ Don't bother locking your bag. Companies sell "TSA approved" locks for luggage, but time after time TSA officials simply break the locks to search bags and may even be more likely to search a bag if you try to lock it. It's not worth it. A luggage lock won't keep TSA or thieves out of your suitcase. Don't waste the time or money on a lock.

✔ Watch the agent tag your bag. Make sure the code is right—is your bag going to SAN (San Diego) or SAT (San Antonio)? Just remember the old Henny Youngman line: "I told the ticket lady, 'Send one of my bags to New York, send one to Los Angeles and send one to Miami.' She said, 'We can't do that!' I told her, 'Why not? You did it last week.'"

✔ Pack an itinerary and cell phone number inside your bag. If the bag loses its destination tag (they get torn off by machinery sometimes), airline workers will open it and look for ways to contact you. I always throw in a business card. (You may want to avoid personal information like your home address, especially if you include an itinerary showing how long you will be gone.)

Package shippers such as FedEx and United Parcel Service would likely be out of the overnight delivery business if they mishandled one package of every 150 customers. At both, the rate of mishandled packages is far closer to 0 percent than airlines can claim. In some respects, the shippers have an easier job because they have more time to move cargo. Customers expect delivery overnight, not on the spot within twenty or thirty minutes of landing. Yet the package shipping firms pick up your package and have to deliver it. At airlines, customers bring the cargo to the airport and claim it at the airport.

The package shippers can also tell you where your belongings are at most any given moment because they scan the package number at various stops along the journey. At airlines, one of the most aggravating aspects of baggage service is that often the airline has no clue where the wayward bag is, or when it might arrive at its destination.

Why is that? Both the luggage and the package have a unique serial number attached. The airline puts a luggage tag on your bag; the shipper has a waybill. Both airlines and shippers employ bar code scanning—there's a bar code on the tag that can be scanned over and over to keep track of the shipment's progress. The difference is that shipping companies scan that bar code all along the way while most airlines do not. At airlines, the bar code affixed to your tag helps sort bags at the airport of your departure. Rarely do airlines use those bar codes to track bags, until after they are lost. You drop the bag off and the airline puts the tag on. It goes through TSA screening and then, at most airports, into the dark netherworld of baggage belts, carts, and storage rooms. Some airports have automatic sorting systems that can scan tags automatically and route bags through a maze of motorized belts and bumpers, hitting the bag onto a specific belt or raising a gate to block it to steer it to the right drop spot. The sorting system dumps bags bound for Chicago at one spot, bags headed to Los Angeles at another spot. Baggage handlers load them onto carts and drive them out to jets.

Those systems are crude and brutish. Big bludgeons

called "pushers" whack at bags to move them to the proper conveyer belt. Baggage rooms are hidden from passengers underneath your feet in airline terminals (passengers typically board from the second floor of a terminal). Down below, airline employees inhabit a different world—crew rooms and baggage apparatus for the most part. The baggage sorting room for United Airlines at Chicago's O'Hare International Airport has miles and miles of conveyor belts and sounds as if workers are fabricating steel. You can get into the room through a door beside the underground moving sidewalk connecting two parts of the terminal. On the passenger side, George Gershwin's "Rhapsody in Blue" soothes customers, with colored lights timed with the music. On the baggage side, there's just grinding and clanging. Baggage areas are noisy, with lots of clunky machinery and carts darting about honking horns. If passengers ever saw the beating their bags take just getting to the airplane, they might never check a bag again.

The system can break down just about everywhere. Tags can be torn or crumpled or rendered unreadable by the machinery, and then dumped into a pile for manual sorting. That takes time, and some of those bags end up missing their flight. Bags can be routed to the wrong pile and sent off to a flight to San Antonio instead of Miami. At some airlines, the mistake may get caught only if a baggage handler happens to check the tag and notice the mistake. What's more, hot weather makes the air thinner, and so aircraft wings don't generate as much lift as they do in colder climates, so some flights, particularly in hot summer months, may not have the cargo capacity to take everyone's bag. (High-altitude cities are more prone to this conundrum than others.)

Some airlines—United and Continental were early adopters— try to scan bag tags before the bags are loaded into jets at their big hub airports. If the bag is about to go into the wrong airplane, the handheld scanner alerts the baggage handler. The scanners also tell the airline if the bag made it onto the plane. That information can help narrow the search for a missing bag. But scanning technology has never been adopted widely by airlines. In 2008, Delta started to use handheld scanners. American, the world's biggest airline, wasn't using them and had no immediate plans to start using them. The handheld scanners take time, and manpower, and thus money. Having extra baggage handlers or allowing more time for loading airplanes is a lot more expensive than paying the costs of mishandled bags, so airlines don't invest in such accuracy. Airlines have tried to devise ways to scan—mounting a dozen scanners in one place to scan a bag from all different angles and hoping to read the tag as a bag moves down a belt. Some systems read 80 percent of the bags successfully, but that leaves many, many bags that end up in an unread pile to be sorted manually.

And God forbid your bag needs to make a connection somewhere. Many bags end up as statistics when they get incorrectly sorted at a hub airport, perhaps tossed on a cart of bags connecting to California flights when the bag should be bound for Boston. Bags fall off carts or get left in cargo holds of jets themselves. Late flights often may mean short time connections between flights. While passengers run to their next gate, bags don't move there as quickly. At some airports, the distances between jets are so extreme that there may not be time to drive the bag to its connecting flight. That's a particular problem with bags from regional airlines connecting to mainline partners. (Regional airlines have the worst baggage handling records in the airline business, but some of that may be because their bigger partners blame them anytime a handoff goes astray.) When regional jets park at remote loading and unloading areas, the bags have a long way to go. And it's rare these days that an airline will hold up a departure for luggage, unless there's lots of it coming from connecting flights. Delays are expensive; delayed luggage is not.

Delta admitted to a particular problem in Atlanta, its biggest hub, in 2008. Connecting bags that arrive more than two hours before their next flight get stashed in a holding room. But like most of the Atlanta baggage operation, the system was manual until recently. Many bags never got fished out of the holding room in time for the flight. This problem grew as Delta put more and more flights through Atlanta, and customers booked more trips with longer connections. What irony: You book a lengthy connection to make sure you and your bags will make the connection, which ends up increasing the odds your bags will end up lost. To fix the problem, Delta invested in new technology to flag bags that need to move out of the holding room at the proper time. The airline also invested in conveyor belts in Atlanta because most of the Delta terminals weren't linked by underground baggage-moving equipment, requiring driven carts to speed around the airport. Indeed, the head of operations at Delta said that until the airline launched a $100 million capital spending program, the baggage facilities in Atlanta were designed to handle only one-fifth of the actual luggage volume.

POWER POUTING

Just what does the airline owe you when it loses your bag? For travelers, the cost of a mishandled bag can be severe.

Not so for the airline, really. And therein lies one of the fundamental reasons why we don't have better baggage handling in the airline industry.

Here's your recourse. If your bag doesn't turn up with the luggage delivered from your flight, head to the airline's baggage office, usually near the carousels. Don't leave without filing a lost bag claim, even if they tell you your bag is on the next flight and not to worry. And here's the most important thing: Get a local phone number for baggage service. A central baggage service toll-free number can sometimes be helpful (though often not useful at all). But when it comes down to whether your suitcase has arrived in Tulsa or not, you need to talk to someone in Tulsa, at the airport, with the airline.

If you are going to be without your bag for some time, ask the airline for help with incidental expenses and discuss the policy on replacement clothes and other needs. Policies vary. You may think the airline will reimburse you for clothes for a big presentation the next day, but some offer only a bathroom-amenity kit with a small tube of toothpaste and other creature comforts for the first twenty-four luggage-less hours, then $25 a day for three or four days. Don't be surprised if the airline tells you it has run out of the amenity kits as well. That happens frequently. If so, demand at least $25 for your first-day needs.

Among the more generous airlines, Northwest and Southwest offer an amenity kit plus $50 on the first day of a lost bag. Continental offers up to $250 for emergency purchases if a bag is lost for more than a day; Northwest goes up to $150. At the other end, Frontier offers a kit for the first twenty-four hours then pays up to $25 a day for four days of temporary needs. US Airways and AirTran have a limit of $25 a day for three days.

Clothing is a tougher issue than toiletries. If you think you're going to get an airline to buy you a new Armani suit for your meeting in the morning, forget it. Some carriers will pay only half the cost of replacement clothes, and most consider only "reasonable" purchases (read: "cheap suits"). "If people go out and replace a wardrobe without prior approval," said a spokesman for American, "that's going to create problems." Some airlines suggest renting clothes. (Some tuxedo-rental stores will rent business suits.) And while Alaska Airlines is often quite forward in its thinking about customer service, it has one major blind spot when it comes to lost luggage. Alaska won't give cash to buy temporary items if your bag was lost due to weather—somehow bad weather absolves the airline from misplacing your bag.

If your bag doesn't turn up, the airline may wait several weeks before it declares it officially "lost." Once that happens, the airline expects you to file a claim for the lost property. Here's the bad news: Regardless of how much you paid for the handmade shirts, Italian shoes, or English-tailored suits, the federal cap on airline liability for lost baggage on domestic flights is about $3,000 per passenger, not per bag. That's right, the federal government sets a *cap* on how much the airline can be held responsible. Keep that in mind when packing, and remember, it's per passenger, not per bag. Also, beware that airline ticket rules have lots of exceptions: Jewelry, cameras, business papers, cash, and other valuables aren't covered at all, so never pack valuables in checked luggage.

More bad news: Liability for international trips is even lower. Most trips overseas are governed by a treaty known as the "Montreal Convention," which caps airline liability at about $1,500 per passenger (the limit fluctuates with currency-conversion rates). But if you travel to or from nations that haven't fully ratified the 1999 Montreal Convention, including Argentina, Australia, Bahamas, Bolivia, Honduras, Israel, Singapore, and others, then the 1929 "Warsaw Convention" applies at some airlines and liability is capped at $9.07 per pound, or $453 for a fifty-pound bag. (Tip: If the Warsaw Convention covers your trip, it pays to pack multiple small bags rather than one big one, since liability is per bag.)

When you file a claim, receipts are typically required for items valued at more than $250. AirTran wants a receipt for anything worth more than $100. Then "depreciation" kicks in. Airlines reimburse the actual value of the item, not replacement or original cost. And the airline gets to decide what the present value of an item was when it lost it. There's no real appeal process either, other than arguing back and forth with nameless airline customer service agents, unless you want to take the airline to "small claims" court (which some people do).

In a newspaper story on the perils of lost luggage, I profiled Andrew Shipman, a mutual-fund portfolio manager whose five-year-old Tumi leather rolling bag was lost by Delta. Even though he had receipts for recently purchased clothing and the Tumi bag itself costs more than $600 to replace, Delta still chopped $645 off his $2,258 claim and paid $1,613, citing "depreciation for prior use." Seeking more explanation, he called Delta and was told he couldn't talk to the person who processed his claim, only fax questions to her. (A spokeswoman for Delta said claims agents talk to customers all the time.) Mr. Shipman faxed a letter, and the claims agent replied that Delta was sorry he wasn't happy but considered the case closed. "I'm amazed that the airlines can get away with operating with such little regard for their customers, especially when fault ultimately lies with the airline," Mr. Shipman said.

POWER ALTERNATIVES

Package shippers such as FedEx Corp. or United Parcel Service Inc. or luggage shippers such as Luggage Forward Inc. or Sports Express LLC may now be an attractive alternative, especially considering how expensive airline fees have gotten on checked luggage. Here's one small Bake-Off: With FedEx, you can ship three bags—two forty-pounders and one sixty-pound bag, from Dallas to Boston and back for about $250 if you use the three-business-day service, and the price might be a lot less if you have access to a corporate account with discounts at FedEx. Put the bags in shipping boxes or just use tags that shippers now have for luggage. (FedEx and other shipping firms do handle lots of luggage for airline-leery travelers.) Package shippers will track the bags, too. On United, those same three bags would cost you $450 round-trip if traveling alone. Luggage services are more expensive, but you get the convenience of pickup and delivery. The same three bags on a Dallas–Boston round-trip cost $628 for Luggage Forward to handle, and take several days each way.

The Holy Grail for baggage handling may be found in new technology—radio frequency identification tags. Instead of trying to read bar codes printed on tags, RFID baggage tags can transmit information about a bag to sensors, much like a toll-road pass transmits information about your car and account when you use a tunnel, bridge, or toll road. RFID, experts say, can reduce lost luggage by 20 percent. RFID systems are 99 percent accurate in reading tags, a significant improvement over the 80 to 90 percent accuracy that airports get with bar-coded tags read by optical scanners.

RFID is already being extensively used to track inventory and improve warehouses—Wal-Mart Stores Inc. is a big proponent. Consumers are already using it. The technology is proven, and effective.

So what's the problem for airlines? Money. RFID tags are more expensive than cheap printed bar-code tags, and the equipment is pricey, so airlines have been reluctant to invest in better technology. As the price comes down, however, and the cost of replacing and returning bags goes up, RFID may find its way into the airline business. RFID baggage tags once cost more than one dollar apiece. By comparison, the current bar-code tags cost only about four cents apiece or less. But the price of RFID tags has fallen in recent times to fifteen cents apiece or less. If the price gets down to ten cents apiece, the International Air Transport Association projects that airlines worldwide would save $760 million annually by adopting them and reducing lost luggage.

Already, the price has gotten so low that several airports, including Las Vegas and Hong Kong, have already invested in RFID themselves and are using RFID baggage tags for customers leaving their airports. Las Vegas handles more than 70,000 outbound bags per day, so 7,000 bags or more had to be manually sorted when bar-coded tags were used. RFID has reduced that to only about 700 bags a day that.

To get the full benefit of the technology, airlines would have to deploy RFID antennas at different parts of their operations, such as on belts that move bags up into the belly of airplanes. The system could alert baggage handlers to a bag about to be loaded onto the wrong flight. Another benefit: Handheld receivers can help find a bag in the cargo hold when a passenger's bag has to be removed. It works like a Geiger counter, beeping more loudly as it gets closer to the hunted bag.

RFID isn't a cure-all for lost baggage—luggage will still fall off carts, be removed from flights too heavy for takeoff, get left behind by inattentive baggage handlers, or end up stolen. But given how bad the problem has gotten, and how much airlines are charging for their baggage service, the time is ripe for system improvements. If we're paying for baggage service, we should to be able to expect better service.

IF YOUR BAG IS LOST

Insist on temporary help, such as toiletries or an allowance for clothes. Some airlines won't offer unless asked.

Get a phone number for a local baggage office, not the call center in India.

Keep copies of the baggage claim form you fill out, and hold on to your bag-tag claim checks you were given when you checked in.

If you bag is permanently lost, file a claim well documented with receipts if possible, and know that the airline may reduce the value you set on items, and only pay your claim up to government minimum requirements. For domestic U.S. flights, the government sets the minimum liability per passenger at $3,000. International liability is lower, at roughly $1,400 per passenger, depending on currency fluctuations.

Remember, airlines won't pay for jewelry, electronics, photos, papers, or most any other valuables. And if you've worn your Armani suit, the airline will depreciate the value.

You may have more insurance than you realize. Many homeowners' policies offer some coverage for household goods away from home. Your credit card may also offer some protection. When you buy airfare on many credit cards, some travel insurance is included for baggage that is permanently lost, stolen, or damaged. If that's not enough, most travel-insurance policies carry baggage coverage.

CHAPTER 9

Hassle-Free Security (Hah!)

From the beginning, airplane travel adopted the nomenclature and many of the customs of sea travel. That's why we call the commander of the airplane the "captain." (He or she would be the "engineer" on a train or the "driver" of a motor vehicle.) The captain's assistant is the "first officer." Many airlines call the chief flight attendant on international flights the "purser." Passengers ride in the cabin and buy tickets for different classes of the vessel. The uniforms airlines employ, at least for pilots, are often nautical in style. When air travel first took off, what travelers knew was voyages by sea, and so aviation adopted what was familiar and comforting.

And just as maritime ventures have battled with pirates from early days of sailing, so, too, have airlines had to battle air pirates—hijackers. Like pirates on the high seas, some skyjackers have seen airplanes as a vehicle for theft. But right from the start, bandits realized that airplanes could be far more valuable targets than a way to steal bounty. They could be used to travel to forbidden places. They could be used to further political agendas. They could be used to disrupt commerce and create fear in the general public. Eventually, terrorists realized that the planes themselves could be used as weapons—guided missiles packed with tremendous fuel and force.

The first recorded hijacking was, perhaps not surprisingly, for political purposes. On February 21, 1931, a group of rebel soldiers hijacked a Pan American mail delivery plane with two American pilots at the city of Arequipa, Peru, and tried to force them to drop propaganda leaflets over Lima. The pilots refused and the rebels ended their seizure on March 2, without any damages to the plane. Between the end of World War II and 1958, there were twenty-three hijackings recorded worldwide, according to a review of aviation security prepared by the U.S. Centennial of Flight Commission. Most were committed by Eastern Europeans seeking political asylum. One resulted in the world's first fatal hijacking, when three Romanians killed an aircrew member in July 1947.

The first hijacking in the United States occurred on May 1, 1961, when a man forced a commercial airliner headed on a short hop from Miami to Key West, Florida, to detour to Cuba. Fidel Castro had come to power in Cuba in 1959, and for a time, several flights were hijacked from Cuba to the United States by people seeking to escape the Cuban dictator's regime. Then the pattern changed. Since travel to Cuba was banned from the United States, some people hell-bent on getting there resorted to hijacking airliners for the ninety-mile flight to the island. In 1961, there were four hijacked flights diverted to Cuba.

Hijackings, of course, prompted security changes. The first step was for the government to provide armed guards on commercial planes when requested by the airlines or by the Federal Bureau of Investigation. In September 1961,

President John F. Kennedy signed legislation that prescribed the death penalty or at least twenty years' imprisonment for air piracy. That wasn't enough of a deterrent, however. Between 1968 and 1972, Cuban hijackings became almost epidemic. The U.S. Department of Transportation counted 364 hijackings to Cuba in that four-year period, including boats and private aircraft. Some were fugitives trying to outrun U.S. police by seeking asylum in Cuba.

In January 1969 alone, eight airliners were hijacked to Cuba. That spurred the Federal Aviation Administration to create a task force to figure out how to deal with air piracy. (Interestingly, it was called the "Task Force on Deterrence of Air Piracy," not the Task Force on Eliminating Air Piracy. From the beginning, airline and airport security has been focused more on lessening the crime, recognizing that eliminating it could probably happen only if all airplanes were forever grounded.) The task force recommended the use of metal detectors to screen passengers, and in October 1969, Eastern Air Lines began using magnetometers. Hijackings continued, of course, mostly by targeting other airlines.

In September 1970, Arab terrorists from the Popular Front for the Liberation of Palestine (PFLP) hijacked three jets all bound for New York—Trans World Airlines Flight 741 from Frankfurt, Swissair Flight 100 from Zurich, and Pan American Airways Flight 93 from Amsterdam—and ordered them flown to the Middle East. A fourth hijacking had been attempted that day, El Al Flight 219, but the two hijackers on board the Israeli Boeing 707 were subdued by passengers and a sky marshal when the captain put the plane into a steep dive. The attempt was thwarted. Two terrorists who had been denied boarding on the El Al flight by security bought first-class tickets for the Pan Am flight instead. The TWA 707 and the Swissair DC–8 were flown to a remote airfield in Jordan and one—the Pan Am 747 jumbo jet—went to Cairo, Egypt. Three days later, on September 9, a British Airways Overseas Corp. VC–10 jet was hijacked and flown to the same airstrip in Jordan.

Terrorists blew up the empty jets on September 12 when they feared a rescue raid was coming, and the horrific sight was captured by a British television crew. Some hostages had been released early on; remaining hostages were released at the end of September after intense fighting between Jordanian troops and the PFLP.

The brazen terrorism captivated the world's attention, nearly touched off a Middle Eastern war by itself, and forced the United Nations Security Council into an emergency session. It also triggered far more concern about air safety. On September 11, 1970, President Richard Nixon announced that the United States would deploy a hundred air marshals to ride aboard jets and begin using X-ray equipment along with metal detectors to prevent weapons from being smuggled aboard aircraft. He also said the United States would consult with other countries that had been successful at thwarting hijackings. "Piracy is not a new challenge for the community of nations. Most countries, including the United States, found effective means of dealing with piracy on the high seas a century and a half ago. We can—and we will—deal effectively with piracy in the skies today," Nixon said, according to a White House statement. Hijackings continued, however. It wasn't until 1973 that the FAA made inspection of carry-on baggage and scanning of all passengers by airlines mandatory.

From the beginning, the government directed airlines to do the security screening in the United States. Instead of police or military or federal employees, airlines would be responsible for conducting the security checks. Most airlines hired companies to handle the screening, just as they hire caterers to provide food or fuel companies to gas up airplanes. And over the years, the attention to security rose and fell with various terrorism events. After long periods of relative calm, security issues received little attention, and passenger convenience was the paramount concern. An attack would bring calls for improvements—always an initial call for more sky marshals, followed by tighter security and new technology. Inevitably a period of relaxed security would follow, then an attack and heightened security, and then more relaxing of screening and security measures.

The 1985 hijacking of a TWA plane in Beirut by Lebanese terrorists, who shot and killed a U.S. Marine and held a gun to the head of the captain while TV cameras caught his grimace, led to more changes, including making the air marshal program "permanent" on U.S. international flights. And then things relaxed. The Christmastime 1988 bombing of Pan Am Flight 103 over Lockerbie, Scotland, killed all 259 aboard the London–New York flight as well as eleven people on the ground, and led to requirements for U.S. carriers to X-ray or search all checked baggage at European and Middle Eastern airports and to match passengers to their baggage to make sure no one checks a bag aboard a flight and then doesn't fly.

POWER BALANCING

Each time security measures are studied, airlines and government officials have a trade-off to balance: deterring attacks without deterring travel. Air travel would be much safer if every passenger were subjected to a personal search and interview by trained inquisitors, but no one would fly.

The volume of passengers would overwhelm security capabilities—or make flying wildly expensive. To the other extreme, simply walking onto a jet without any screening might be considered most convenient for travelers (though many would balk at the lack of security), but inept at catching bad guys. Each time authorities try to find the right balance, the costs to airlines of heavy security measures were weighed, as were passenger inconveniences, and each time government made it clear that passenger screening was an airline function, not a government function. Congress even joined in the micromanaging of the skies. One law prompted by concerns from the many Americans who like to carry pocketknives, for example, allowed knives aboard airplanes as long as the blades were no longer than four inches.

And then came September 11. A group of Al Qaeda terrorists boarded four different jets armed with weapons that wouldn't detect security scrutiny, even if spotted by screeners, then hijacked the jets and flew two into the World Trade Center twin towers in New York and one into the Pentagon in Washington, killing more than three thousand people. The box cutters and knives they used complied with the four-inch-blade rule. Mace was used to subdue passengers. While technically not allowed by FAA rules, there wasn't much process to detect mace or pepper spray, and in reality, many people, women in particular, carried it for personal protection on key chains and in purses. The commission appointed to study the September 11 attacks found that several of the hijackers at Washington's Dulles Airport set off metal detectors. But surveillance-camera tapes show that the screeners waved handheld metal detectors around but never resolved what had set off the metal detectors. What's more, the commission's report noted that ten of the nineteen hijackers were selected for added screening by the airline's profiling system and by alert ticket-counter agents who thought they seemed suspicious. At the time, that only meant an extra check of their checked baggage—no special screening of them or their carry-on bags.

The terrorists had studied the vulnerabilities of a lax security system, where low-paid contract workers handled the monotonous work of watching X-ray machine images and herding people through metal detectors, often paying little attention even to the passengers who set off the metal detectors. A once-over with a hand wand—"Must be my car keys" or "I have a metal joint"—and you were on your way. Government investigators had periodically written reports about weak security at airports, journalists wrote stories about how fast-food workers inside airports were higher paid than security screeners, and security experts sometimes tried to sound an alarm—all to no avail.

EMPOWERING SCREENING

After September 11, the government took over airport security screening, creating the Transportation Security Administration, a new federal agency to hire and train screeners and run airport checkpoints. Knives were banned, as were disposable razor blades for a time. For the first time in the United States, Congress ordered that checked bags be scanned for bombs. And each time there was a new threat, there was a new change in security procedures. After another terrorist tried to blow up an American Airlines jet with plastic explosives in his shoes, all shoes were ordered to be sent through the X-ray machine. After Chechen rebels blew up jets with explosives hidden in their coats, all coats were ordered to be sent through X-ray machines. After an alleged plot was uncovered in the United Kingdom to blow up planes with liquid explosives, all liquids were banned at checkpoints, and then rules were modified to allow for small quantities of liquids, pastes, and gels for toiletries.

And so today's sometimes heavy-handed, sometimes infuriating, often inconsistent airport security regime was born, breeding long lines, bewildering rules, and what has become the largest bureaucracy in the U.S. federal government.

To say the least, TSA had a difficult infancy. The agency had a massive job to hire tens of thousands of airport screeners—few of the low-paid contractors made the transfer to federal employee—and at the same time come up with a better security regime. TSA was plagued by overspending: More than $1 million was spent to outfit its headquarters with art and fineries, for example. Overstaffed, under-utilized checkpoints led to a new nickname for TSA—"Thousands Standing Around." Worse, travelers grew outraged with inconsistent enforcement of rules, unpredictable and often long lines at airports, and the general rudeness of TSA employees. For a time, the agency seemed slaphappy, tagging road warriors, elderly travelers, and even U.S. senators for "secondary screening"—the pat-down, paw-through-your-bag examination performed after you went through metal detectors and X-ray machines. Some 10 percent to 20 percent of travelers, were subjected to a secondary screening, an absurdity that was eventually curbed.

Early in TSA's reign, rules were confusing to travelers, and especially to screeners. Shoe removal was intensely enforced at some airports and seemingly optional at others, until TSA made it mandatory nationwide. As expensive luggage-scanning machines were deployed over several years, TSA relied on various screening techniques—some airports used bomb-sniffing dogs, while others had a work-force to open bags and search, ensuring that carefully packed clothes would be askew and sometimes leading to the disappearance of valuables into the pockets of opportunistic TSA thieves. (After several indictments, TSA had to install surveillance cameras to keep its own employees from stealing.)

After the alleged liquid-explosive bombing plot, TSA initially banned all liquids from the airplane cabin, forcing many travelers to check their luggage. But TSA didn't have the baggage-checking staff, so bags piled up. Airlines didn't have enough baggage-handling staff either, so bags were often delivered late, and complaints about lost baggage soared. Scrambling to find a smarter way, TSA did extensive testing with the FBI on liquid explosives and decided that small quantities could be allowed in airplane cabins. Small quantities made it hard—some say impossible—to mix a liquid bomb inside an airport or an airplane. The exact results of FBI testing are classified, but the government decided that limiting liquids to no more than three ounces per bottle, and limiting the number of bottles to what you can fit in a quart-size plastic bag, kept planes safe from liquid-explosive bombs.

And in classic bureaucratic befuddlement, they were ever so strictly enforced. If you had one tube of lip gloss, it wasn't allowed if it wasn't placed in a quart-size plastic bag. If you had a five-ounce tube of toothpaste that was half full, that wouldn't be allowed, even though the amount of material complied with the three-ounce rule. If your quart-size bag had a fold-over top instead of the prescribed zip-top, it didn't meet TSA standards. And so it went, catch-22 after catch-22. One day at the Dallas–Fort Worth International Airport, I asked about a huge plastic tub at a TSA checkpoint filled with small cans of shaving cream and tiny tubes of toothpaste. Were they contraband items that ran afoul of safety rules?

"No, people didn't have quart-size plastic bags," the TSA official said. And TSA, of course, couldn't provide a quart-size plastic bag, or waive the "rule" for a single tube of toothpaste. Eventually, TSA and airports realized they could help themselves, and their customers, by having a stash of conforming plastic bags at security checkpoints for the convenience of travelers—both those without bags and the people in line behind the scofflaw who had to wait while the inevitable rule explanation and subsequent argument over absurdity ensued.

Another rule was fodder for a Seinfeld routine: TSA initially banned empty water bottles. You couldn't carry a water bottle through security and then fill it up at an airport water fountain, but you could buy a full water bottle inside an airport shop. TSA claimed there was a classified security reason that related to the characteristics of liquid explosives. In addition, the initial X-ray machines TSA had could detect containers, just not what's inside. So getting all containers out of carry-on bags would speed up security screening. "As stupid as we may look, we didn't miss that one," the head of TSA, Kip Hawley, told me in a 2006 interview. Eventually, however, TSA relented and allowed empty water bottles. But the decision was never well communicated—to TSA staff or to travelers. Search TSA's Web site for rules on water bottles, and you'll come up dry.

How crazy was it? Just consider Ann Persoon, who tried to board a flight in Cedar Rapids, Iowa, with "unmarked" bottles of shampoo and cream rinse. Her favorite brands didn't come in sizes of three ounces or less, so she made a special trip to a store to buy small, leak-proof clear travel bottles and filled them with hair-care products. A TSA screener incorrectly told her the rules allowed only bottles with manufacturer's labels on them, and he promptly threw them out. "Most travelers want to cooperate with airport security because they realize that their own safety depends on the TSA officers being vigilant. But sometimes it gets frustrating," said Mrs. Persoon.

POWER DOUBTS

Low morale among screeners has been a constant problem for the TSA and has contributed to a high turnover rate, according to the Department of Homeland Security's inspector general (IG). That makes screening all the more inconsistent. In a 2008 report, the IG found a screener attrition rate of 17 percent—nearly one-fifth of the workforce turns over every year. That's higher than at other federal agencies, the inspector general found. The number of complaints from TSA screeners was also higher than at other similarly sized federal agencies. Screeners have many of the same complaints as travelers: "inconsistent" work rules, insufficient staffing at checkpoints, a "lack of trust" of management, and favoritism by local managers.

At the heart of all the issues, from the overspending to the stealing to the barking at people standing in lines to the long lines themselves, the public didn't have a lot more confidence in the TSA's prowess at catching bad guys than it had in the private contractors hired by airlines.

In many ways, the long lines themselves were the biggest threat, both to the safety of passengers and to the financial health of airlines themselves. From a security standpoint, queues stuffed with people make tempting targets for terrorists—several times overseas, terrorists have attacked airport lobbies. It has the double-attraction for terrorists of offering lots of people in a vulnerable situation, creating fear, and disrupting commerce. People won't fly if they are reluctant to go to the airport. And for airlines, long lines at the airport became a financial disaster. Sometimes travelers waltzed through security screening in five minutes; sometimes it took fifty minutes. The problem was you didn't know, so to make sure you'd get on your flight, you had to get to the airport an hour early or more to get through screening. That made flying for small trips far less efficient, and many travelers opted to drive rather than fly for short journeys. Driving didn't take as long—it might even be faster, once airline delays are added in. And it didn't include the hassle of stripping down for the TSA. Short-haul air travel fell dramatically, creating a serious problem for airlines.

Over several years, TSA has improved its lines. It has standardized some procedures—shoes, for example. It has learned a lot about how to move people through security lines. Next time you go through, take note that instead of one X-ray machine for every metal detector, TSA has switched to two X-ray machines feeding into one metal detector. The X-ray process for carry-on baggage takes longer than stepping through the metal detector—you have to unpack, essentially, depositing your laptop computer in one plastic bin, then electronics like cell phones, keys, coins, liquids in a plastic bag, coats, and shoes. Removing some of the metal detectors, which weren't getting constant use, opened up more space for more X-ray machines and helped move people through quicker.

In 2008, TSA decided it needed to retrain its entire workforce to make sure that its screeners knew its rules and procedures. The agency also hoped to calm down checkpoints by reducing the barking screeners did at passengers. Complaints about screeners had poured into the agency, and it took note. (In one classic TSA moment, I inquired why the rate of complaints lodged against TSA had taken a sharp jump in May of 2007, and TSA's answer was an admission that up until that point, TSA had been losing many complaints travelers filed and hadn't been counting all the complaints it did receive. It was underreporting the problem significantly.) Whether the result of underreporting or declining service, TSA service complaints skyrocketed some 80 percent in the summer of 2007 over the previous summer. Complaints to TSA far outnumber complaints that travelers file with the Department of Transportation about airlines. The agency decided it better make some improvements.

Often screeners yell at customers about holding on to their boarding passes as they go through the lines, or removing shoes and laptops. Most travelers know the rules—often better than the screeners themselves. But TSA also learned that from a security perspective, a calm area is far better for screening. If travelers are calmer and quieter, a terrorist who might be nervous may stand out more, security experts say. TSA even trained about 20 percent of its workforce in behavior detection methods, and sent some of them patrolling other parts of the airport, such as check-in desks and gate areas, trying to spot suspicious people worthy of closer inspection.

The agency has tried lots of methods to improve airport security. In an effort to ease traveler anxiety and perhaps even improve safety, TSA began rolling out a new setup at its security lanes where fliers are asked to self-segregate into different screening lanes depending on their security prowess. There are "Black Diamond" lanes for "Expert Travelers," who know the drill cold; "Casual Travelers," who run the airport gauntlet infrequently; and people with small children or special needs, who move slowly through screening.

The idea, akin to how ski resorts divide skiers by ability, was suggested to TSA by focus groups of fliers. The agency didn't think it would work, said Mr. Hawley, the director of TSA at the time. But a test showed travelers liked the idea, and it had some benefits for security screening. TSA began rolling it out in 2008 where it could—not all airports have enough volume or enough floor space at checkpoints to make it work. The program started in Denver and Salt Lake City, and spread to Orlando, Boston, Atlanta, and other major airports. Some travelers initially found the regime confusing—which category do they really fall in? Is it voluntary or mandatory? It's voluntary, actually. Many people say they simply cut to whatever looks like the shortest lane, ignoring the TSA's request to segregate. (TSA is OK with that—it evens out lines.) But most of the time people, perhaps surprisingly, sort themselves into the appropriate lane.

The different setup improves traveler throughput—how many people get through screening in an hour—because people who can get through quickly don't get stuck behind slow-moving folks as much. And it helps calm people down, especially slow-movers who get anxious when road warriors start bumping into them or sighing loudly from behind. It worked so well that in late 2008, TSA added "family" lanes to every checkpoint nationwide.

TSA POWER!

From its early inflexibility, the TSA is now trying new ideas, deploying new equipment, and giving screeners new training. As a small step toward laptop relaxation, TSA decided to allow "security friendly" notebook carrying cases that can go through X-ray machines without removing the computer from the bag. Most have a butterfly design where they unzip and lie flat, so nothing but the carrying case is on top of the computer itself, giving the X-ray machine a clear shot at the object. Some are simply envelope-type carrying cases that the laptop slides into, with nothing else to obscure the X-ray view. The bags can save you some hassle at checkpoints, unless you end up arguing with an uninformed TSA screener over whether your bag is "legal" or not. And of course, you have to like the bag for all the other, more important purposes the bag serves. Does it work as a briefcase, for example?

Technology ultimately has the most promise both to speed up and improve security. Already, more accurate X-ray machines are in use at some airports that take multiple scans of the contents of a bag, much like a medical CT scan, and can accurately evaluate what's inside a laptop computer, for example, without having to remove everything around the device. In London, where the United Kingdom is already using that technology, there are no laptop-removal requirements—no matter what kind of bag the computer is in. New software for the new generation of X-ray machines will let TSA relax the three-ounce rule as well, Mr. Hawley told me in late 2008. The machines will be able to identify liquid explosives, letting passengers carry shampoo, soft drinks, and other liquids through security checkpoints. TSA hoped to relax the liquids rule in 2009.

Other technology is being rolled out. "Puffer" machines that blow short bursts of air on you help with detecting any sort of explosives that someone might be hiding under clothes. The machine analyzes the air collected for traces of chemicals. The puff itself can be startling the first time you go through. And no, it doesn't blow air up women's skirts to reveal all, Marilyn Monroe–style.

Full-body scanners in use at several airports in place of metal detectors also have a much better chance of detecting bombs strapped to bodies. These machines may be the future we all face at security—they can detect metal objects, liquid and chemical explosives, and just about anything hidden under clothes. Some people may be a bit queasy about the full-body scanners, however. A TSA officer in a cubicle out of sight from the scanner gets to see an outline of your body in all its naked glory. The image is far from titillating, but it doesn't leave much to the imagination, either. For that reason, TSA has made those types of scanners optional—you don't have to do it if you don't want to. But it certainly can save you from an unpleasant patdown where a screener frisks you with gloved hands.

In the end, making improvements in security screening should speed up checkpoints. It's all a matter of money, technology development, and TSA management. All three have been lacking in the past.

Airlines have also tried to make security easier for travelers, realizing that the hassle was hurting their bottom line. Airlines have given up terminal space to expand TSA checkpoints, and most have tried to create express lanes for their first-class passengers and elite-level frequent fliers—their best customers, in other words. These accelerated lines can be a huge help to frequent fliers.

Indeed, the availability of the premium lanes is so unpredictable that airlines don't bother to tell their customers where the lines are available. Some list some cities on Web sites that have premium-customer lines, but airlines admit that not all cities are included and the availability is subject to change. And no airline bothers to try to list specific checkpoints with premium lanes. Of course, to road warriors it might matter greatly if you know a premium line would be available, cutting how early you might need to arrive at the airport. Show up at an airport lobby and a check-in kiosk offers you the chance to catch an earlier flight. Can you make it? That may depend on how long it takes you to get through security. Unless you eyeball the checkpoint, airlines don't give you a clue.

POWER CUTTING

Another security line aggravation for many travelers: Airline and airport employees cutting in line. After standing thirty-five minutes in a security-screening line one day, road warrior Peter Hughes was miffed when an American Airlines pilot cut in front of him in line. When the pilot sat down in the first-class seat next to him, off duty and returning home, Mr. Hughes was fuming. "He said he was entitled to it, and he wasn't ashamed about it," said the investment banker, who has accumulated five million miles on American. "This is the only industry that lets employees cut in front of customers."

Airlines control airport lobbies and the security lines until you present your identification to a TSA official, and then the TSA takes over. It's a silly distinction in some ways, but it means that airlines can provide special lines for elite-level frequent fliers—and airline crews.

Flight crews cut in line if they don't have a separate screening area. The airline industry says there's a good reason that pilots and flight attendants can jump to the front of the line—airplanes need to get out on time, and they can't do so without crews. Most travelers don't seem bothered by on-duty flight crews walking to the front of the line, but off-duty crews are seen as abusing the system by some travelers. Airports and airlines also allow concession workers to cut to the front of the line at many airports—though some airports, including Washington's Reagan National and Dulles International, say they try to forbid it. In Atlanta, complaints from travelers about crews and airport employees cutting in line prompted the airport to set up a separate employees-only line.

Another way to jump the line: pay to enroll in a "Registered Traveler" program. After years of study and foot dragging, TSA now allows private companies to sell speedier lines. The cost is $100 to $200 a year, in general, and you have to turn over lots of information about yourself, along with fingerprints. In return, you get to skip to the front of the line at airports where the program is in place, and its availability is growing. If you don't have elite status on an airline that moves you to the front of security lines, you should consider joining the Registered Traveler program, especially if you are the type of person who hates TSA hassles. The separate line, and someone to help you with your plastic tubs and belongings, may be worth the price of admission.

POWER CLEARANCE

The largest of the Registered Traveler programs is called "Clear," offered by a company called Verified Identity Pass Inc. Verified Identity was started by entrepreneur Steven Brill, who launched *American Lawyer* magazine, Court TV, and other media projects. Mr. Brill became frustrated with the delay and absurdity of airport security screening after September 11, so he set off to create a better way. Once you sign up for Clear, pay your annual fee and a one-time fee to get your security check, you receive a biometric identity card. Go to the Clear lines at airports where the program exists (Clear had twenty-one by late 2008), or Registered Traveler lines from any other company, for that matter, since a requirement of the program is that all vendors' cards work at every Registered Traveler access point, and you move straight to the bins by the X-ray machines. Clear has blue-shirted workers to help you carry things and butt their way into the queue at lanes, if need be. The card also exempts you from being selected for secondary screening, unless you do something to trigger closer scrutiny, like set off a metal detector.

Why does the government allow the line cutting? Because Registered Traveler vendors help pay for airport security screeners. Is it worth it? To many people, moving to the front of the line is worth $150 a year or so, especially if it is available at an airport you use frequently. Yet others find they get much of the same benefit by being an elite-level frequent flier and having access to premium lines at many airports. Besides, many security lines aren't that oppressive. Ultimately, it depends on your own travel pattern and your tolerance for uncertainty and lines. If you worry about getting trapped in long lines, then it may be worthwhile to try a Registered Traveler card. Another growing population of likely candidates for registered Traveler programs: people with metal hips, knees, and limbs. Security screening can be a major hassle if you have an artificial body part, and a special screening card may help.

POWER ROUTINES

Whether you have a Registered Traveler card or not, you can get through security without hassle. It's relatively easy:

Adopt a routine. Before you leave for the airport, check security wait-times for your departure airport at www.tsa.gov. Long waits are still common at many crowded airports, such as the more congested terminals at Los Angeles International Airport on a Friday afternoon, or international departures at New York's Kennedy International Airport, or Fort Lauderdale, Florida, after several cruise ships unload. Many airports that are heavy with originating traffic, rather than connecting passengers who don't have to pass through security again, still suffer long lines in the early morning hours, when travelers start queuing up sometimes before TSA staff appear.

The average and supposed maximum wait times measured in a recent time period are broken down on TSA's Web site both by individual checkpoint and by hour of the day. You can see if one particular checkpoint always has longer waits than another and plan accordingly. At some airports such as Dallas–Fort Worth and Kansas City, curved concourses have multiple checkpoints; for many people, it's worth a five-minute walk to save twenty minutes waiting in line, or more. At Delta's JFK terminal in New York, there are two screening areas for international flights, and one always has a shorter line than the other. Some airports have trains or walkways inside security that allow you to shuttle between terminals—go through security at a less-crowded terminal and avoid long lines. (You may find better parking at those lower-volume terminals, too.) Many airports, including big ones with centralized checkpoints like Denver International Airport and Atlanta's Hartsfield-Jackson International Airport, often have a second screening area. If you know that, on average, lines are shorter there, head to the shorter line. Stress-less travel is based on well-developed line-avoidance.

TSA is supposed to measure wait times at regular intervals on a set schedule, but many think that TSA officials check wait times when they are smallest to make their performance look better. As a rule of thumb, you may want to add 50 percent to TSA's version of a typical wait time. The TSA says the wait at Phoenix Sky Harbor Airport's Terminal Four at 8 A.M. on Saturday mornings, for example, can be as long as twenty-seven minutes. I waited forty-five minutes at Terminal Four one Saturday morning and just barely made my flight. Still, the relative performance of various checkpoints should give you an advantage in finding the shortest line.

Once you get to your preferred checkpoint, have a routine for how to handle all the tasks of getting through the lane. Avoid anything that will slow you up, or worse, subject you to secondary screening. Have your driver's license or passport ready when it is needed, and put it back in a safe place every time. Make sure that you shed all metal before you go through the metal detector and you have your boarding pass. Do it the same way every time, and you'll move through security quicker and easier.

Here's my routine. Before I enter the line, I get rid of my metal. My watch usually goes in a zipped-up pocket inside my briefcase, or carry-on bag, along with my cell phone, BlackBerry, and any pens I have stuffed in my pockets. I leave the change in my pocket for the time being. When my license comes out of the wallet, it goes wherever I have my boarding pass—usually a breast pocket on my shirt if I have one; otherwise I put it in my left-hand pants pocket.

Once I get past the document check, the boarding pass goes back in the pocket because I'll need it soon. The driver's license goes back in the wallet—always—even if it means taking a few seconds before rushing to one of the screening lanes. Until the rules change again (and they may someday), you only need your identification that one time.

When it's time to unload, I grab two plastic tubs—one for the laptop computer (which can't have anything else in the tub, per TSA regulations) and another for shoes, coat, keys, toiletries, and other stuff. Usually I carry my laptop and my quart-size plastic bag stuffed with toiletries in the outer pocket of my rolling bag for easy access. I dump coins from my pockets into a shoe so it will be easy to get out on the other end. I send my rolling bag and briefcase through the X-ray screener first, followed by laptop and shoes. That way I can repack easily in reverse order on the other side. You don't want the laptop to walk off without you if you get delayed somewhere along the way. When I get to the metal detector, I've got my boarding pass in my hand. If I do it right, I've avoided any chance of setting off the metal detector or breaking one of TSA's minuscule rules that will lead to more screening.

SECURITY FAQS

And what if you run into problems? Here are some tips on special circumstances and common security issues.

✔ **What if you're running late?** If you're within thirty minutes of departure and there's a long line, beg at the premium line. Or ask passengers for a break. Many people will let you in. Don't stand in line while your flight pushes back.

✔ **What if you really need to carry on three bags?** I don't recommend it, but there is an out: Declare medicine in your bags. If you get stopped by an airline worker or even TSA and told you can't take three bags on a flight, declare that one contains prescription medicine. It will exempt you from the two-bag limit.

✔ **Are prescription drugs exempt from the three-ounce limit? What about contact lens solutions?** Medications, baby formula and food, breast milk and juice, and contact lens solutions are allowed in reasonable quantities exceeding three ounces, TSA says, and are not required to be in the zip-top bag. If they are bigger than three ounces and outside your zip-top bag, you must declare these items for inspection at the checkpoint so they don't catch you trying to slip items through. There's an extensive list of prohibited items on TSA's Web site, www.tsa.gov.

✔ **What if I have wrapped Christmas presents and the TSA wants to open them?** TSA can do that. Don't ever pack wrapped presents, even in checked luggage. Either take the gifts unwrapped, along with some wrapping paper, or ship wrapped gifts through the U.S. mail or a package shipping company such as UPS.

✔ **What are your rights?** Not many, really. TSA has trained its workers to be intolerant of belligerent behavior and inappropriate jokes. A man with a T-Shirt saying KIP HAWLEY IS AN IDIOT, expressing his view of the TSA chief, was once detained by TSA and police. When dealing with TSA, it is best to take the high road and be helpful and compliant. If TSA wants to search you, you have the right to have the search performed by an officer of the same sex. You certainly have the right to write down names and badge numbers of TSA officials, and local police, if you feel as though you are being mistreated and want to raise an issue later. But one thing is likely about dealing with TSA: Arguing will make you late for your flight.

✔ **How do I complain?** The most frequently registered complaint against TSA is improper handling of personal property, or loss or damage. Second on the complaint list: courtesy. If you feel like you have been wronged, there is a value in registering a complaint. It's a way of holding the feet to the fire. Congress, journalists, and others track the complaint numbers—and that's most of the value. Don't expect satisfaction when you complain to the TSA. Many people report never getting a response, and those that do find it hollow. Sometimes TSA will apologize and say, "Gee, that doesn't sound good." Sometimes the agency even says it will take action if you provide the identity of the screeners involved. Unlike airlines, TSA doesn't offer any sort of vouchers or frequent-flier miles for compensation. Rarely does TSA pay for baggage damage or loss claim. The agency tends to blame the airline involved, and you'll have better success seeking recompense from the airline.

That said, here's how to register a TSA complaint. Provide as many details as you can, but keep the description of the episode succinct and send it by e-mail to: TSA-ContactCenter@ dhs.gov or call 1–866–289–9673.

If you believe you have been unlawfully discriminated against at a TSA checkpoint, you can contact the External Compliance Division in the Office of Civil Rights at TSA. OCR-ExternalCompliance@dhs.gov or 1–877-EEO–4-TSA (1–877–336–4872).

✔ **What if I think my name is on a TSA watch list because I continually get tagged for secondary screening or have even been detained by police at an airport?** This is actually a more frequent conundrum than you might think. The problem: common names.

The Department of Homeland Security works with other agencies to maintain a list of possible terrorism suspects. There's a "no fly" list for suspected terrorists who just aren't allowed aboard airplanes in or bound for the United

States. But it's the watch list that causes so much trouble—it has some 700,000 names on it, and many of them are as common John Thompson and James Wilson.

Government lists cast a wide net and include all kinds of spellings of names and aliases used by terrorism suspects. Some common American names end up on the list because they are similar to names used by Irish Republican Army bombers, for example. But the main culprit appears to be those crafty terrorists who think using a common name as an alias will render them invisible to law enforcement. If one suspect uses John Thompson as an alias, many people named John Thompson will end up getting a grilling every time they fly.

Officials familiar with security procedures say much of the problem with misidentifying people comes from imperfect data in airline reservation systems trying to match up with imperfect data on government watch lists. Airline computers, for example, often don't include middle names or even middle initials, and they certainly don't have other identifying information such as birth dates, age, or even gender.

Homeland Security has a program to try and clear people from the watch list, called Traveler Redress Inquiry Program, or TRIP. It was launched in February 2007 after years of complaints from multitudes of travelers who inexplicably turned up on terrorism watch lists. Famously, even Senator Edward Kennedy (D., Mass.) was tagged for extra screening, along with young children, military veterans with security clearances, and many others. Even more frustrating for many is that removing their names from terrorism lists seemed impossible.

So far at least, travelers say TRIP has done little to ease their security hassles. They complain that government officials have been unresponsive and offer little information even when they do answer inquiries. Travelers who have been told they have been placed on a "cleared" list still find themselves subjected to added security procedures and unable to preprint boarding passes for airline flights or use kiosks at airports. Then, after waiting in line to check in, they find themselves trapped in a catch-22 while supervisors probe their identity and status on the "cleared" list so that they can avoid the delay of being selected for additional screening at checkpoints.

What do you do if it happens to you? First, work with your most frequently used airline to see if it can remove you from scrutiny based on your frequent-flier number. The airline's computer system makes the first match for a flagging. This approach works better, of course, if you actually go through the TRIP process and have a letter from TSA saying you are indeed cleared. To use Homeland Security's TRIP process, you apply online at www.tsa.gov and follow the prompts to the DHS TRIP program. There's a form to fill out, and you'll be asked to provide lots of information like your passport, driver's license, and birth certificate numbers as well as information about your travels when you were detained. You can file the completed form electronically, e-mail it to TRIP@dhs.gov, or mail it to DHS Traveler Redress Inquiry Program (TRIP), 601 South Twelfth Street, TSA–901, Arlington, VA 22202–4220.

An easier solution is to try flying under your middle name to see if that will let you escape scrutiny. While John Thompson may be suspicious to the watch list (I've heard from three John Thompsons over the years, including one who traced the origins back to a jailed Irish bomber), Marvin Thompson may not.

In the end, perfection in security isn't possible. The single biggest improvement in air safety from a security standpoint wasn't all the hoo-ha that goes on in airport lobbies but the installation of hardened cockpit doors, and the instructions for pilots never to open them if a disruption arises on board. The doors mean you can't get into the cockpit with a knife or sharp object, so those are no longer a hijacking threat anymore. In reality, it's now much more difficult to hijack an airplane. From an aviation security perspective, the real threat now is a bombing. That's a significant threat, and one on which we probably are not yet focusing enough attention.

The goal of airport security isn't, as some people assume, catching all possible weapons. It is to make terrorists think there's a credible chance they will get caught before they get airborne. As the September 11 Commission noted, the whole game is to provide an effective deterrent so the bad guys will go elsewhere. "Terrorists should perceive that potential targets are defended," the commission said. "They may be deterred by a significant chance of failure."

So take heart—despite whatever hassles and incompetence you see with TSA, flying is safer than it was in 2001. It doesn't matter if the screeners miss pocketknives or the three-ounce bottle you forgot to pull out of your bag.

CHAPTER 10

Bumping, Upgrades, and Boarding

You have a ticket—nonrefundable, unchangeable. You studied fares and you guessed which flights would be most convenient. You asked your spouse, Will these flights work? "Maybe" was the response. But there are no maybes with airlines. With most tickets you are locked in unless you want to pay a penalty and a higher price. You made the best guess and pushed the "buy" button. Then, when you wanted to push the trip a day back, or a day earlier, or switch to a morning flight, the airline said, "No way."

You showed up at the airport an hour before departure to get a boarding pass. That will be assigned at the gate, you are told. At the gate, the agent says, just take a seat. We'll have seats for you in a few minutes. Then the agent starts asking for volunteers to give up their seats and fly to-morrow afternoon. Now you're sweating. They don't have seats for you, the guy who bought those tickets six months ago. Come on, where are the volunteers? The flight starts boarding. And then you are called to the front. "Sorry, we're switching you to a flight tomorrow," the agent says. What the airline agent doesn't say is, "Ha-ha! We sold your seat to someone else—that guy in the Gucci loafers. We got lots more money than the piddling amount you paid us. So we don't have a seat for you until tomorrow."

POWER BUMPS

Officially, you have been "involuntarily denied boarding," a euphemism for "bumped." In the auction world of airline tickets, your seat went to the highest bidder, even though you had, at least from your perspective and your options, an iron-clad, unchangeable-without-penalty contract. Can a grocery store sell more bananas than it has in stock? Can a car dealer sell you a car—and then after collecting your money tell you it doesn't have the car you just bought? Can a business sell the same piece of merchandise to two different customers? No!

But denying a traveler a prepurchased seat is legal. When you buy an airline ticket, you have a contract with terms spelled out in an airline's "Contract of Carriage." You fulfilled your part of the bargain, but all the restrictions are against you. The airline reneged on the deal. Where is Ralph Nader when you really need him? Mr. Nader, alas, once took on the consumer unfriendly world of airline overbooking and bumping to court years ago. And Mr. Nader lost.

Airline overbooking dates back all the way to 1967, when the Civil Aeronautics Board, which regulated the airline industry at the time, decided to allow airlines to overbook to cover no-shows. The board figured that the extra revenue allowed airlines to offer lower fares, and that overbooking benefited consumers who otherwise couldn't buy a ticket on a flight that would have empty seats. Overbooking was seen as a benefit to consumers as well as to airlines.

Of course, in 1967, airlines sold tickets much differently

from the way they do today. The government set ticket prices, and flying was expensive, regulated by the Civil Aeronautics Board. There was no competition to speak of in the airline industry. Yet because tickets weren't saddled down with pages and pages of fine-print rules, customers had flexibility. If you couldn't make the flight, you could take another. And thus there were no-shows. The airline industry, of course, has changed dramatically. But the overbooking rules stayed in place.

In the early 1970s, Mr. Nader found himself bumped from an Allegheny Airlines flight. (Allegheny became part of what is now US Airways.) The airline most surely regretted that decision. Mr. Nader sued, claiming the practice was illegal. The case went to the Supreme Court, which ruled in 1976 that airlines could legally bump people from flights, but they first had to ask for volunteers to give up their seats, and they had to compensate customers for the inconvenience. Because of Mr. Nader, gate agents ask for volunteers to give up seats in exchange for free tickets or travel vouchers.

"It was a spectacular success," Mr. Nader says now. (He hasn't been bumped off a flight since, to no one's surprise). Other travel lawyers don't agree. While it increased the benefits for bumped passengers, it gave airlines solid legal clearance to an anticonsumer practice. Aviation attorney Mark Pestronk, who often represents travel agencies and travel companies, says the current system is flawed because airlines defraud bumped customers out of their tickets. A fairer system, he says, might be to allow transfers between passengers—like theater tickets. If you can't go, you can work a swap with someone, sell the tickets or give them to a friend. But that doesn't happen because of security hurdles, and because airlines don't want companies buying lots of cheap tickets and then doling them out to last-minute travelers just by changing names.

POWER BOOKING

Airlines claim they have to overbook because some tickets are refundable and some customers don't show up. Curbing overbooking would hurt revenue, possibly push ticket prices higher, and make it harder for business travelers to find seats for last-minute trips. An airline seat is a perishable product—you can't put it back in inventory and sell it another day. Airlines need to sell that seat. Besides, some travelers like getting bumped in order to score vouchers for free or discounted future trips.

There is a lot of science behind the practice. Airlines use reams of historical data and sophisticated modeling to predict, flight by flight, how many no-shows there will likely be. They also weigh the popularity of flights and the available options to rebook people. For instance, a 5 P.M. flight on a Friday might be open to more overbooking because an 8 P.M. flight on the same route on the same day typically doesn't fill up. All told, on average, about thirteen passengers among every ten thousand are denied a seat on a flight, and 91 percent of those people chose to give up their seats voluntarily and take different flights.

There are some obvious problems. First and foremost, because the overwhelming majority of airline tickets are nonrefundable, it's increasingly difficult for airlines to argue that they haven't sold the seat. Even if you don't show up, you don't get your money back. You can pay a penalty plus any increase in fare and rebook to another time, but the penalty protects the airline. Why does the airline also need the added protection of overbooking?

Perhaps airlines should only be allowed to bump passenger with refundable tickets.

Second, despite the preponderance of nonrefundable tickets, airlines have been increasing their overbooking and involuntary bumping practices. In 2007, nearly 64,000 passengers were involuntarily denied boarding on domestic U.S. flights, nearly double the number bumped against their will five years earlier. Under financial pressure, airlines have pushed harder to fill every seat, and the "load factor"—the percentage of seats filled—has risen dramatically at U.S. airlines. The by-product: more bumping. Fewer passengers are taking vouchers to give up seats than five years ago as airlines have gotten stingier with their offers, enticing fewer volunteers.

POWER CHITS

More likely, vouchers have declined in popularity as savvy travelers have come to realize they have lots of restrictions and can be difficult to use. Another issue: It's harder for airlines to get them to their destinations after giving up a seat on a flight. It's one thing to offer $200 to take a flight three hours later. It's something else altogether to accept $300 to move to a flight thirty-six hours later. What's more, some vouchers can't be used with the least-expensive fares or are restricted from holiday travel periods, and some airlines make you go to the airport to buy tickets with vouchers.

One saving grace is that many vouchers are transferable—you can give them to friends and relatives who might be able to get better use out of them. Or you can sell them. A colleague of mine was given a $400 voucher by Delta for a horror trip, and since he doesn't fly Delta much, he offered the voucher for sale on the Atlanta Craigslist Web site. (Since Atlanta is Delta's biggest hub, he figured he'd find the most demand there.) Sure enough, he ended up with $275 for his $400 voucher—about sixty-nine cents on the dollar, which he rightly considered a good value.

A major problem with the compensation system for involuntary bumping—people denied a seat when they have a ticket— is that the penalty for many years was too soft. Until 2008, the penalty for involuntarily denying boarding to a passenger was a maximum of $400. The airline also has to fly you to your destination on the next *available* flight. That penalty was set in 1978, soon after the Nader ruling as the industry was being deregulated. It hadn't been raised in thirty years. Had the maximum amount been adjusted for inflation, it would have run up to more than $1,200 by 2008. But since it was locked in, the only thing that increased was the airline's incentive to overbook. If you can sell someone a $1,000 ticket and bump a cheap-fare passenger for a $400 penalty, why not? In a sense, an airline can always keep flights open for booking for people who will pay premium prices at the last minute because you can just eject some poor soul who paid a lot less. What's more, the airline had no reason to offer volunteers more than $400. (Involuntarily bumped passengers can demand cash for the penalty on the spot, but most don't know that and settle for the vouchers airlines push.)

I raised the compensation issue in 2006 in a column, and the Department of Transportation opened an investigation, saying that *The Wall Street Journal* story was one reason it decided to examine the issue. The DOT solicited comment from travelers, travel companies, airlines, and anyone else who wanted to weigh in and decided that the maximum penalty should be doubled. Over time, a higher penalty will mean that airlines should be more generous in their offerings to volunteers, and may limit overbooking. Under current rules, airlines now have to compensate involuntarily bumped passengers with a payment, in cash or voucher, up to $800, depending on how quickly the airline can get you where you want to go.

WHICH AIRLINE BUMPS THE MOST

Here's a ranking of airlines, from the lowest rate of involuntarily bumped passengers to the highest, for 2007.

DENIED BOARDINGS (DB'S)

	Voluntary	Involuntary	Enplaned Passengers	Involuntary DB's per 10,000 passengers
jetBlue	13	43	21,386,573	0.02
AirTran	28,949	348	23,780,058	0.15
Hawaiian	1,061	119	7,098,609	0.17
United	90,639	4,448	62,732,171	0.71
Alaska	16,106	1,164	15,985,172	0.73
American	75,852	6,764	87,781,244	0.77
Northwest	72,115	3,969	47,779,125	0.83
Frontier	4,631	969	10,436,638	0.93
Southwest	88,248	11,288	101,910,758	1.11
US Airways	77,001	6,544	54,991,550	1.19
American Eagle	1,269	336	2,485,956	1.35
Continental	36,049	6,100	42,576,293	1.43
Mesa	15,590	1,120	7,262,198	1.54
SkyWest	19,507	1,339	7,937,530	1.69
Delta	78,837	16,691	67,455,072	2.47
Comair	5,455	556	1,763,507	3.15
Atlantic Southeast	9,913	1,968	4,377,102	4.50

POWER PROTECTIONS

So how do you protect yourself against this mess?

- Always reserve a seat in advance. If you have a seat reservation, it is much harder for an airline to bump you. Check the seat map before you buy to see if there are any empty seats. If not, consider switching to another flight. And if you can't reserve a seat online, call the airline and plead for a seat assignment.
- Print your boarding pass in advance. Once the boarding pass is issued, it's a lot harder for the airline to keep that seat from you.
- Get to the airport on time. Many airlines wipe out seat assignments if you aren't on the plane twenty minutes or more before departure for domestic flights. If you come running up at the last minute, your seat may be gone. And in those cases, you may have to fight for compensation, since you "violated" the ticket rules. Yikes!

If you do get bumped, here are a few absolutes to consider.

- Get a confirmed seat on the next available flight. Don't settle for standby.
- If you have to stay overnight in a city that's not your home, you are entitled to a hotel room and meals from the airline.
- Always demand cash; the airline can write you a check on the spot. The airline may try to give you a voucher, but why lock yourself in? You may want to use a different airline. You may want to travel on a busy holiday date blocked out on vouchers. Cash is good anytime,

anywhere. (If you voluntarily give up your seat, however, you can't demand cash.)

- If you are about to get bumped and you absolutely have to be on that flight, sweeten the pot for passengers with confirmed seats. Alexander Anolik, a San Francisco travel lawyer, suggests offering additional compensation on your own to people who do have seats to entice them to volunteer to give up their seat. I've heard people offering an extra $50 if someone would volunteer to give up a seat. Mr. Anolik gave a traveler $200 once, saving himself four hours of delay. Since he bills $395 an hour, he figured it was a bargain.

One last consideration: You are entitled to sue the airline in small claims court if you don't believe the compensation fits the crime. In some cases, for example, travelers have nonrefundable hotel reservations or cabins on cruise ships, and getting bumped from a flight means losing out. Whatever you get from the airline may not be enough to cover your losses. But to maintain your right to sue, you most likely have to refuse the airline's compensation. (The airline usually asks you to sign something saying the compensation represents a final settlement of all claims.) It's a big risk and major hassle—one I don't recommend for most people.

Thatcher Stone and his teenage daughter got bumped by Continental Airlines in Newark, New Jersey, as they were trying to get to a Christmas skiing vacation in Colorado. The airline couldn't get him to Colorado for six days, rendering his vacation useless. Worse, his baggage went on to Colorado, preventing the Stones from finding someplace else to ski. Mr. Stone, a New York lawyer who lectures on aviation law at the University of Virginia, refused the airline's $400-per-person offer, since he was out $1,800 in nonrefundable payments to his Telluride resort. Instead, he sued Continental in small claims court for breach of contract. He was awarded $3,110.

"The only reason I sued is because they weren't acting like mensches," Mr. Stone says.

Continental says when someone is bumped, the carrier tries to offer alternative flights, refund the ticket, help make other arrangements, or offer some form of denied boarding compensation. "But that is not always acceptable to the customer," a spokesman says. "We are always sorry when a customer is denied boarding involuntarily."

For people who don't happen to be aviation attorneys, the best course of action if your losses exceed the standard compensation is to document that to the airline and file a complaint seeking additional reimbursement. At least you should get vouchers from the airline for the additional amount of loss.

BUMPING RULES

Overbooking is one of the few areas where airline passengers do have some meaningful, enforceable rights. Here are the rules set out by the U.S. Department of Transportation.

✔ If a flight is overbooked, airlines must ask for volunteers to give up their seats.

✔ Airlines must establish boarding priority rules that dictate who gets bumped if a flight is overbooked. The DOT says the rules may include : "(1) a passenger's time of check-in; (2) whether a passenger has a seat assignment before reaching the departure gate for carriers that assign seats;

(3) the fare paid by a passenger; (4) a passenger's frequent-flyer status; and (5) a passenger's disability or status as an unaccompanied minor."

✔ Airlines have to give involuntarily bumped passengers written copies of all the rules that apply.

✔ If involuntarily bumped, airlines must pay passengers 200 percent of the fare, including taxes and fees, for that particular flight (not the whole trip), up to a maximum of $800. The compensation is only half as much if the airline can get you to your destination within two hours of your original schedule for domestic trips, or four hours for international trips. (If the airline can get you on another flight arriving within one hour, there's no compensation.)

✔ Airlines may offer transportation vouchers for the amount of compensation in lieu of cash, but passengers may decline the offer and demand the cash payment.

✔ Passengers lose out on compensation if they don't comply with ticketing provisions, such as check-in time requirements. You also don't get compensation if you were bumped because the airline had to substitute a smaller aircraft "when required for operational or safety reasons." On airplanes with thirty to sixty seats, you aren't compensated if the airline couldn't accommodate you because of weight and balance restrictions for safety reasons. Aircraft with thirty or fewer seats are exempt from the overbooking compensation rules.

POWER UPGRADES

You have a boarding pass for your coach seat and you'd like to be in first class. Once, you might have tried sweet-talking the gate agent or complimenting him on his tie, then casually asking if there were any upgrades.

Now though, the upgrade game has been almost completely automated. What matters is your frequent-flier elite level and the fare you paid for that trip—the higher the better for both. Some airlines now even give airport agents the ability to see how much your total spending has been on the airline in the past year or so. "I fly this airline every week!" you stammer. Umm, not so. Your total spending in the past twelve months has been $234. Busted.

The biggest differentiator of comfort in air travel is whether you can buy or wrangle your way into the first-class cabin. A first-class seat gives you room to work or sleep on an airplane. You get priority boarding and don't have to worry about room for your carry-ons or a closet for your coat. You get a bathroom with fewer people lining up for it. You get something to eat, and maybe even a smile from a flight attendant. In addition, first-class passengers get priority when airlines have to rebook passengers, and at most carriers, they get priority on standby lists if you want to change flights. Perhaps even more significantly, a first-class ticket lets you bypass security lines at many airports and get straight to the screening lanes. If you know you can go straight to the front of the line, you can plan your run through the airport more efficiently.

"For business travelers, getting into first class makes all the difference," says Travis Christ, a former vice president of marketing at US Airways Group Inc. And that's getting truer for leisure travelers as well. Who doesn't like to sleep, eat, and relax on vacation? There are ways to beat the system. Most of them require cash, however, but not the thousands of dollars that it typically takes to buy a first-class ticket straight up.

Top-level frequent fliers—people who fly 100,000 miles or more a year—generally get first crack at upgrades to first class. Some airlines give their best customers upgrades three days before a flight departs; lower-level frequent fliers—people who fly around 25,000 miles a year—get upgrades closer to departure if they are available. At most carriers, the lowest elite level gets a crack at available seats twenty-four hours before takeoff. Airlines vary on how they allot upgrades: Some give them to elite-level customers for free, while others use a credit system where you earn or buy upgrade points and then redeem them for first-class seats. Carriers also vary how their computers do the actual allocation. For some, it's first-come, first-served within your frequent-flier strata while others factor who paid the most for their tickets. They also have different strategies on how many seats to hold back, hoping to make a last-minute first-class sale. Airlines don't make the entire first-class cabin open to free upgrades. The walk-up customer who can't get a coach seat but is willing to pay thousands of dollars for a first-class seat is a gold mine for airlines, and they'll wait until the last minute, hoping someone with a fat expense account shows up. (The other last-minute hog of first-class seats: air marshals, those federal officers who travel incognito to thwart hijackings. They typically don't give airlines much notice when they will ride on a certain flight, and they usually require first-class seats so they are near the cockpit. If you think you have a first-class seat and you get bumped back to coach, it's often because of air marshals. Even worse for airlines, agents aren't allowed to tell customers they got bumped because air marshals are on the flight.)

If you want to buy your way to the front of the airplane, the first opportunity comes when you buy a ticket. Don't forget "Y-Up" fares and other ticket-buying tricks covered in Chapter 5. But that's not your only chance. Once you get to the airport, many airlines will sell upgrades, either from their kiosks or gate agents. US Airways and United have been the pioneers of selling upgrades, walking a fine line between angering road warriors who expect free upgrades in exchange for their loyalty and delighting customers who can fly like kings for as little as $50. Selling upgrades, both through the Y-Up kind of deals and the last-minute airport upgrades, has made it harder for premium customers to get upgrades, a result of the financial difficulties airlines have been under and the relentless push to find new ways to generate dollars. Airlines offer elite fliers seats in between—after the Y-Up sales and before the airport scramble. If you are willing to pay, you can probably play.

US Airways sells domestic upgrades for $50 to $150, depending on the length of a flight, and international upgrades at varying prices up to $500 or so. American sells domestic upgrades when empty first-class seats haven't been claimed in advance by top-level frequent fliers. The upgrades can cost $100 to $250 or so, but remember one benefit: First-class tickets exempt you from baggage fees on your first two suitcases. So the upgrade saves you $40 on American, making it more palatable.

United sells upgrades to its "Economy Plus" coach section but also has lots of opportunities for business-class and first-class upgrades, particularly on long flights, domestic and international. A colleague of mine was delighted when United offered for $700 an upgrade to business class on a fourteen-hour flight to China to cover the Summer Olympics—which was far less than the additional cost of a business-class ticket.

This is a case where it does pay to ask the gate agent if any upgrades are available—for purchase, rather than for pandering. Seat assignments in premium cabins can change quite a bit right up until the door to the airplane closes. Some high-fare customers may not show up, since their tickets usually give them flexibility. Some customers who had won upgrades may have taken an earlier flight or canceled at the last minute. Sometimes seats are reserved for airline crew members or airline executives who end up making other plans. It's worthwhile to check at various points in your wait at the airport if you are hungry for an upgrade—when you get to the airport, when you get to the gate, and just before you board.

POWER BOARDING

When boarding the airplane, a strategy can make your travels a bit less stressful. The biggest issue in boarding is the battle for overhead bin space—a battle made all the more intense by the fees airlines charge for checked luggage. To avoid fees, more people pack more stuff into their allotted carry-on bags (one bag and one personal item, like a purse or briefcase or backpack). Airlines have gotten more aggressive about policing carry-on baggage limits. Some carriers post baggage cops in airport lobbies and in front of TSA security checkpoints to intercept offenders, at least in the airline's eyes, and force people to check oversize carry-on bags. Most carriers have instructed flight attendants and gate agents to be more vigilant in checking the size and number of carry-ons, and forcing customers to check bags at the gate if they can. Be alert—they're watching you!

Of course, one of the frustrations for customers is that the silly sizing boxes that airlines try to use to enforce carry-on dimensions don't have much connection to reality. In other words, the boxes are smaller than the overhead bins. Does that make sense? Airlines say some planes in their fleets have smaller overhead bins than others, and so they set the sizers to the lowest possible size. I was traveling with Gordon Bethune, then the chief executive of Continental, and happily pointed out to him that his carry-on bag exceeded the size limits of his airline's sizing box. Like any other frequent traveler, he laughed and marched on board the plane.

Even the size limits vary among airlines. At American, United, and Delta, the maximum size of carry-on baggage is forty-five linear inches—the length, width, and height dimensions added together. At US Airways and Continental, the maximum is fifty-one inches—13 percent more. I have a Travelpro roll-aboard bag that I've taken all over the world, and every time I've raised it to slide it into an overhead bin, it has fit (sometimes snugly in older bins). The bag is twenty-three inches tall, fifteen inches wide, and twelve inches deep, when I don't unzip the expanders. At its standard size, its measurements total fifty inches—exceeding the rules at the three biggest airlines in the United States, while legal on Continental and US Airways. And airlines wonder why their rules confound travelers?

Your chances of finding space for your bag on board the plane are related to how early you board. Premium customers go first. Some carriers, though not many, will allow families traveling with small children to preboard. Ask to preboard if you have children with you or anyone who needs extra time, such as someone disabled or elderly. It's nice to avoid the pushy herd, and better still to get space for your carry-on baggage.

It's the later boarding groups that sweat. If it concerns you, you should think about boarding groups when you select your seats. At many airlines, the back of the plane boards first, so selecting seats in the rear will lessen the chance you'll have to check your carry-on bag should bins fill up. At other carriers, boarding is offered first to people with window seats, followed by middle seats, and then aisle seats. Game that system by making sure you have a window seat.

If you end up in a late boarding group, look at bins for bags that can be turned sideways to create more room. Many overhead bins are now deep enough that roll-aboard bags can go in wheels first. Look for coats that you can rest on top of your bag. Look for bins with pillows and blankets—take them out to make room for your bag, then make yourself popular by handing out blankets and pillows (if your airline still has such "comforts") to fellow passengers.

Because of the way overhead bin doors are shaped, propping up a longish item can allow a bin door to close and latch that might not close without the item being raised. Flight attendants know lots of tricks like that; don't be afraid to ask. They usually also have several compartments around airline cabins where they can stash a last bag or two—the bottom of a closet, the space behind the last row of seats in a cabin, or a bin in a galley once used for meals. And if all else fails and you have to check a bag during the boarding process, make sure you do several things before giving it up:

- Remove any valuables or breakables (jewelry, computers, cameras). Unless you are an elite-level frequent flier, odds are you may someday find yourself in the baggage-bin bind. It pays to pack carry-on bags for the possibility of getting checked by having your name inside and out and putting valuables in secure bags that you can remove without spilling earrings on the floor of a plane.

- Zip up all pockets.
- Retrieve your boarding pass and travel documents, especially passports.

Make sure you give the flight attendant your final destination, or see if the bag can be "gate checked" so that you can retrieve it on the jetway along with strollers. And when you get a claim check back from the flight attendant, make sure it shows that the bag is checked to a place you want it to go. Cursed would be the bag checked to San Diego (SAN) when you are headed to San Antonio (SAT) because someone handwrote the destination code incorrectly.

Finally, sit back, relax, and get ready to fly.

In the Middle Seat

The airline cabin is a hostile environment, where you can be made sick, disgusted, discombobulated, or just uncomfortable. Here's the inside skinny about everything aboard an airplane, from the risk of deep-vein thrombosis to the recycled air to the uncomfortable seats to ways to keep the inconsiderate in front of you from reclining into your lap.

Where to begin? Let's start with where to sit—front or back, aisle or window?

From a safety perspective, some researchers have made the case over the years that the back of the airplane may be safer than the front. Of course, it all depends on the type of crash, and crashes are so rare that the issue isn't too relevant.

I think the back-is-safer school of thought arose in the day when lots of planes had engines mounted in the rear of jets, such as the Boeing 727, McDonnell Douglas DC–10, and Lockheed L–1011, all of which had three engines in the tail, and the DC–9 and its follow-on, the MD–80, both of which have two engines in the rear. If you put all that engine weight in the back and subject the structure to the forces of being near powerful engines, you have to build a strong structure. From an engineering perspective, the rear structure of the airplane was a lot stronger than front sections. So when crashes occurred, the stronger tail sections often had a better chance of staying intact. And if the walls around you stayed together, your chances of surviving a crash were better.

This point was made obvious to me when I drove up on a major airline crash in 1985. I was flying from New York back home to Dallas, working for the Associated Press at the time. My flight passed through a turbulent cloud just before touching down, with swirling winds and striking colors—to this day I remember seeing odd purple and pink colors in the cloud. About fifteen minutes later, as I was exiting the terminal, the heavens opened, and an enormous thunderstorm pelted the airport. The rain was so intense that my wife, who had picked me up after she had a business meeting near the airport, pulled off the road at an underpass because we couldn't see.

Then we heard reports on the radio of an explosion at the north end of the airport, where we were heading. We drove on as the rain let up, still unable to see far ahead. In a short time we began seeing debris off in the grass, and then I saw the unmistakable: a large aircraft tire and sheared-off landing gear.

Delta Flight 191 crashed on August 2, 1985, roughly twenty minutes after I had landed on the same runway. As we drove on we saw the tail section of the L–1011 resting on the grass short of what was then Runway 17L at Dallas–Fort Worth International Airport. There was smoke all around—and nothing else of the plane to speak of but the tail section. The survivors of that crash were sitting in the rear of the airplane.

For some crashes, being up front has been perilous when the plane ran into something, like the 1999 crash of an American Airlines MD–80 in Little Rock, Arkansas, where the jet ran off the end of the runway and collided with metal and concrete posts for runway landing lights. The impact killed the captain and several passengers up front, including some in the first-class cabin. With other crashes where some people survived, tragedy befell people who went to emergency exits that were stuck or broken. Recently researchers have suggested there may be some advantage to sitting over the wings of a plane. Two people out of fifteen onboard an American Connection turboprop airplane survived a 2004 crash into trees as the plane was on final approach in Kirksville, Missouri. The two surviving passengers were seated over the wing spar, a beefy structure that supports much of the weight of the plane in-flight. The area where the wing attaches to the fuselage is structurally quite strong, and may remain in better shape than other areas of the plane. Those emergency exits may stand less chance of jamming, too, than front and rear doors. If survivability drives your seat selection, I'd suggest exit rows over the wing.

POWER IMPROVEMENTS

These days, airline crashes are rare. Technology has improved safety. Airliners and airports have better wind-shear detection systems, the development of which was largely driven by crashes like Delta 191, and pilots and air-traffic controllers are far more cautious about attempting to fly through potential wind-shear, a sudden shift in wind that can cause an airplane to lose altitude quickly. (Pilots are better trained, too.) Today's jets have better systems to warn pilots if they are flying toward dangerous terrain. They have better systems to warn of predicted midair collisions; their computers talk to other jets and coordinate instructions to both crews so they fly away from each other. Most crashes today result from some kind of human error—a mistake by pilots, mechanics, or controllers.

At the same time, airline cabins have become a lot more survivable in crashes. Seats are made of tougher materials that can stay bolted down and intact against much greater forces. If you survive impact, fire is the biggest threat, since jet fuel burns quickly and hotly. But materials used inside a cabin are designed to be slower to ignite and not give off noxious fumes, giving passengers time to escape. The time may only be ten minutes, but that's often enough to empty a jet. Perhaps the best example was the Air France A340 that ran off a runway in Toronto in 2005 and became engulfed in flames—after all 309 people aboard had gotten out of the aircraft carcass.

What does that mean for the average traveler worried about safety? Don't worry, and sit where you want. Today's jets, most of which are built with engines mounted under wings, don't offer the reinforced tails that older planes offered. Whether to sit in the front or the back boils down to some more pedestrian considerations:

- Sitting in the back lets you board early, giving you better overhead bin space availability.
- Sitting in the back can be unsettling to some people sensitive to motion. Some planes, particularly long jets such as the Boeing 757, have a tendency to sway just a tiny bit in the tail. Most people don't notice a difference. Some sensitive souls can end up feeling seasick.
- Sitting in the back puts you closer to bathrooms in most

coach cabins. Some people like that; others prefer not to be near long lines or any odors.

- Sitting in the front gets you out first, a real bonus if you have to run to a connecting flight or race to a taxi queue late at night.
- Sitting in the front can be quieter, especially on MD–80s, DC–9s, and regional jets with engines mounted at the rear.
- Sitting in the front typically means you'll get beverage service earlier. Airlines run out of specific drinks or snacks before serving everyone on some flights, and after waiting an hour for takeoff and flying through bumpy air while flight attendants stay seated, you may be parched before they wheel out a beverage cart.

Bottom line: It's a matter of personal preference. Most people prefer being up front—airlines often reserve seats in the front of the coach cabin for elite-level frequent fliers and even sell forward seats for an added fee. I wouldn't pay extra for a lower row number (unless it was first class or perhaps the extra legroom offered by United Airlines and jetBlue Airways at the front of their coach cabins), but I prefer to be closer to the front door. Getting off quickly can be a major benefit.

POWER SEATS

Aisle or window? To me, that's a bathroom question: How often do you have to leave your seat? I prefer aisles on long flights so I can get to the bathroom without making row mates stand, and so I can get up and stretch periodically. While aisle seats give you more space in which to work or slump, they have the downside of getting elbows and shoulders thumped when people and carts charge up or down the aisle. For shorter flights, I prefer windows. I'd much rather see the landscape.

Anywhere you sit, there's a good chance that the seat will be uncomfortable. Airline seats generally have flat seat-cushions and flat backs—nothing like the contours you find in automobile seats, for example, or in office chairs. They have no lumbar support in the lower back, and little upper-thigh support. If there are any headrests, they are usually ineffective. Aircraft coach seats are close to the same straight two-cushion design that came into vogue two decades ago.

Why? Cost, of course. Seat manufacturers can build a more comfortable coach aircraft seat—they already build cushy first-class and business-class seats. And some coach seats have improved, but it's still rare, and there's a long way to go. Manufacturers say they are handicapped by the peculiar restrictions and requirements of the airlines, each of which picks its own seat design. Aircraft engineers have to minimize weight while meeting rigorous safety and durability requirements. And aircraft seats, which are replaced by major airlines every five to eight years, have to fit all sizes and shapes of passengers. Thus, the simplest cushion is the most practical.

A contoured seat—as in a sports car—would not only provide more back support but would also make the plane feel roomier. If you contour around the shoulders, you don't feel as crowded to the person next to you. But airlines say that passengers like to raise armrests when seats are empty, and curling up in two or three seats would be more difficult if seats' backs and bottoms were contoured. Of course, finding an empty seat is rare these days.

The big drawback to contouring, however, is maintenance. Coach seats have to have removable covers for cleaning. Automobile seats now are made in one piece, with the fabric sewn to the foam so that wrinkles are eliminated in contours. Yet adding curves to aircraft seats would result in unattractive puckers in the covering. There is also the issue of how many seats airlines cram into coach cabins. Several years ago, new foams and seat-construction techniques allowed manufacturers to make seats with less bulk and more back support. The new seats freed up three inches of space between rows; but instead of giving passengers added legroom, airlines used the newfound inches to add seats. Seat manufacturers say that coach rows are so close together, there's not a lot they can do to improve comfort.

Aircraft manufacturers haven't helped either, as cabins have gotten skinnier for long-haul aircraft. A 1950s Harvard University study of New England passenger trains concluded that the minimum acceptable seat width was eighteen inches. Taking their cue from the study, Boeing and other aircraft makers designed many planes in the early jet era with eighteen-inch seats. And when they were built, passengers had smaller derrieres to plop into those seats. More space and less mass made for more comfort. Boeing, however, decided that planes designed for short trips, like the 1960s-designed Boeing 737, could have narrower cabins. That's more economical to fly, and designers figured that passengers could endure a seventeen-inch seat, such as what the 737 has, if they are in the seat for only an hour or two.

POWER SQUEEZE

The economical 737 grew into the most popular plane in the world among airlines, and airline executives pushed Boeing for new versions of the 737 with longer range, faster speed, and more seats. Airbus, Boeing's European competitor, upped the ante in the 1990s by launching a line of smaller jets—about the same size as the 737 but with much longer range (and wider seats). Soon, Boeing began losing orders to the Airbus A320. The crowning blow came in July 1992 when United Airlines, Boeing's biggest and most loyal customer, chose the A320 to replace its Boeing 727s. (The 727, like the A320, had eighteen-inch-wide coach seats.) Boeing launched a redesign of the 737, using more powerful engines and a new wing design to create a plane that could fly faster, longer, and higher than previous generations of 737s. Airlines could use the new 737 to fly over hubs in the Midwest like Chicago and Dallas and offer nonstop, transcontinental service to smaller cities on the East and West Coasts. You could fly nonstop from New York to Portland, Oregon, or from San Diego, California, or San Francisco to Hartford, Connecticut, for example. Travelers loved the convenience of avoiding connections when traveling across the country. Airlines loved the low operating costs, something Boeing had to maintain. After all, the biggest buyer of 737s now is penny-pinching Southwest Airlines, which at the time the new generation of 737s was designed was a short-hop airline not interested in long-haul comfort. To get the long range and better performance at low costs, Boeing gave up a bigger coach seat.

Realizing the 737 cabin might be considered small for long-haul flights, Boeing considered a two- or three-inch widening of the airframe, but the company said it found such a small change didn't make much difference inside. Customers—the airlines, in this case—told Boeing that a major widening, which would have made the plane heavier and more expensive to fly, wasn't worth it.

Boeing didn't widen the 737 cabin but instead simply

created a more open feel inside the plane, using ceiling panels that made the cabin look taller, and overhead bins with smooth curves. Seats designed for short trips became the seats for long trips. The larger Boeing 757 actually has seventeen-inch-wide seats as well—the cabin feels bigger because it's longer, but the squeeze at your hips is the same. In passenger surveys, wider planes like the two-aisle 767 or 777 outscore the 757, which has the same cabin width as the new 737.

Now as new planes come online, airlines are debating whether skinnier seats are just fine, even though passengers have grown, um, wider. Take the new Boeing 787 "Dreamliner." That's a 210-passenger jet designed to replace Boeing 767s and other long-haul wide-body planes with extreme comfort enhancements. The 787 will have big windows, far more comfortable cabin atmospheric pressure, and more humidity so people will arrive feeling less jet-lagged. Yet while the original design called for eight seats in each row of a 787 coach cabin, Boeing made the plane wide enough to fit nine seats. And guess what? About 75 percent of the airlines that have ordered the 787 are opting to install nine seats across a coach row, according to Boeing. That means travelers will plop into a seventeen-inch-wide seat, instead of the nineteen inches of room Boeing had hoped for in its patented 3–2–3 seating configuration.

Another example of the airline seat-squeeze: Emirates, a Dubai-based carrier that has grown with funding from petrodollars, has a reputation for high-quality service and richly appointed airplanes. But seating is cramped in coach class. Emirates installed ten seats across the coach rows of its Boeing 777s, offering seventeen inches of width to passengers. Most other airlines have nine seats across each row of their 777s in coach, with seats about eighteen inches wide. And on its superjumbo plane, the Airbus A380, Emirates opted for ten-across seating in coach as well, with only seventeen inches of width, despite the massive size of the double-deck flying giant.

In addition to width, legroom makes a huge difference in passenger comfort as well. As most travelers know, airlines have squished seats closer together, even when they had opportunities to provide more room without giving up seats when seat manufacturers came out with "slim line" seatbacks. The economics of having more seats to sell is just too compelling for airlines. American Airlines tried to give more legroom to every coach passenger, removing seats from planes and marketing "More Room Throughout Coach." Since there were fewer seats to sell, the company hoped it could get customers to pay more to fly American than a competing airline. But it didn't work. American's average ticket price didn't go up enough to cover the lost revenue of having fewer seats to sell, so it abandoned "More Room" and stuffed seats back into its airplanes. (Experiments like United's "Economy Plus" and jetBlue's extra-legroom rows, which are sold as add-ons, are different, since not everyone gets the benefit—you have to pay or qualify.)

POWER ROOM

Which airline gives you the most legroom? It's sometimes surprising. Discount airlines are sometimes the most generous—go figure. Southwest Airlines has thirty-two to thirty-three inches of space in each row of its Boeing 737s. (That's called "seat pitch" in airline parlance—the distance from one point on the seat to the same point on the next row.) Southwest's legroom is actual more ample than the 737s at Continental, which allots just thirty-one inches for rows on its 737s. Most of the industry has standardized in the thirty-one-to-thirty-two-inch range for seat pitch, although you can find seats with only thirty inches of space on some Northwest Airlines jets (DC–9s, Airbus A319s, and Boeing 757s), as well as some Boeing 767s at American and Delta and a few jets at Hawaiian, AirTran, and US Airways, according to SeatGuru.com, which tracks airline seats plane by plane.

In general, you can most often count on wider seats (eighteen inches) on these types of airplanes: Boeing 747, Boeing 777, Boeing 767, McDonnell-Douglas MD–80, and the three main models at Airbus, the A330, A340, and A320. A new generation of regional jets, typified by the Embraer 170 and 190s flown by regional airlines and jetBlue, also have eighteen-inch-wide seats. Planes that generally have seventeen-inch seats include the Boeing 757 and Boeing 737, and older regional jets such as the Embraer 145 and the Canadair CRJ–700. It looks like the Airbus A380 will be relegated to seventeen-inch seats in coach, at least with the airlines first to order the superjumbo jet.

In the early days of the Boeing 747 jumbo jet, airlines used all the newfound space they had to create cool customer amenities, like piano bars on the upper deck of the jet and plenty of room for passengers to mingle. When economic reality set in, airlines moved toward cramming seats into every available spot on planes, including the 747. The same pattern may well play out with the Airbus A380. The super-jumbo jet began flying in commercial service in 2008, and several carriers now fly the jet, including Emirates, Singapore Airlines, and Qantas Airways. Air France, Lufthansa, and Virgin Atlantic have ordered the plane. No U.S. airline has yet ordered the double-decked jet, and they may never. But it appears there will be dozens of A380s flying around the world, including into and out of the United States on international airlines.

Early owners of the A380 decked it out. Singapore added private cabins in first class with doors, and the ability to merge two suites together for couples who want to share a double bed in flight. Most other carriers opted for a bit less privacy for customers, perhaps not wanting to entice too many couples seeking to join the "Mile High" club. First-class suites have plenty of privacy at Qantas and others, but flight attendants can look over partitions and check on customers. The self-contained suites of modern first-class cabins have seats that fold into flat beds, often nearly seven feet long, plus a sitting area for colleagues, a large table for working or eating, and loads of in-flight entertainment on seventeen-inch LCD monitors or larger. (Expect a thousand channels or more.) Passengers get plush pillows, pajamas, and slippers. There's lots of storage. Emirates installed two elegant four-by-ten-foot bathrooms on its A380s, complete with hot showers. Passengers are limited to twenty-five minutes total time in the bathrooms, and five minutes total for the showers, due to water constraints.

Modern business-class cabins also have lie-flat beds, albeit a bit shorter at about six feet. (Many U.S. airlines are still playing catch-up and have business-class seats that lie flat, but at an angle instead of horizontal, meaning some travelers may slide as they sleep.) Business class on international airlines is generally a cut above what you get in business class on U.S. airlines. But with most any airline, you get key advantages with business class—airport lounges for meals or showers, or just relaxation before or after flights, plenty of room to sleep or work, good meal service, and entertainment options.

POWER RECLINE

Researchers have found that the biggest comfort differentiator for passengers is whether the middle seat next to you is occupied or not. Short of that, one of the biggest drivers of comfort and acceptable airline space in coach cabins is whether the person in front of you reclines. With seats pushed closer together, reclining a seat can prevent the person behind you from having room to use a notebook computer—and some laptop screens have been broken when seatbacks came hurtling back. To many people, declining to recline is a courtesy for your fellow sardines; for others, reclining is a God-given right. A Travelocity poll of 1,300 customers in 2004 found that almost one-third said they recline their seats "frequently" or "all the time."

Indeed, airlines say that when you buy a ticket, you buy the right to recline. You're entitled to use all the features of your seat, so airlines make it illegal to use products—wedges and such—that prevent a seat from reclining. Some seats, of course, don't recline, most often because the airline has to block customers from reclining into an exit row, restricting the space needed to evacuate a plane, but sometimes because the seat is broken. In that case, you can ask to be reseated, but you don't have any right to a refund.

Most U.S. airlines allow seats to tip as far back as four or five inches—a lot, considering the limited distance from your nose to the back of the headrest in front of you. The laptop issue, compounded by the bigger belly issue, prompted Southwest Airlines in 2006 to begin reducing the maximum recline in many of its seats. Bruised knees and spilled drinks also weighed on the decision, Southwest said. Southwest found that its seats had varying degrees of maximum recline, from 2 inches of movement at the top of the seat to 4.5 inches. The airline decided to standardize recline at 3 inches, adjusting seats as planes go in for major maintenance work. "It was impossible for a customer to use a laptop behind someone who had reclined fully in a seat that allowed 4 or 4.5 inches of recline," said a Southwest spokeswoman. The airline determined that a 3-inch recline provided maximum comfort and usability.

In a survey I conducted of seatback recline, Continental reported the steepest coach recline among major airlines at five to six inches of recline. That's tough on the knees when seats are set in thirty-one inches of space. United has a similar squeeze in its main coach cabin: five inches of recline with seats in thirty-one-inch rows. (United has the same recline in its "Economy Plus" seats as its regular coach seats, even though "Economy Plus" has four extra inches of legroom. Does that make sense?) American, Delta, and jetBlue say all their coach seats are set to recline four inches. Seat manufacturers say that seat recline should be tied to seat pitch—rows with small pitch should have limited recline; rows with more room can accommodate more recline. Either way, the current airline setup is a problem.

Weber Aircraft LP, a major seat manufacturer that is a subsidiary of France's Zodiac SA, has developed a seat that can pivot at its base to push the seat bottom forward as the chair's back reclines. That prevents the seat from moving back into the knees of the passenger behind. But the seat is more expensive than a regular airline seat, and while it has sold well at some foreign carriers like Emirates and Singapore Airlines, sales in the United States have been slow.

Battles over cabin space can get nasty, from annoying

kicking of the reclined seat to heated arguments. Many tall travelers admit to trying to send a message through a seatback by repeatedly bumping and kneeing the reclining passenger in front, or holding a newspaper up high so it brushes the head of the recliner. On some airlines you can wedge the top of your laptop into the lip on the seat where the tray table stores and prevent the person in front of you from reclining. The risk is that you will break your laptop screen. A longtime airline executive shared his favorite trick with me to reclaim the reclined space. If the person in front descends into his lap, he begins sneezing a bit. He'll ask a flight attendant for some water—no reason to be quiet about his possible "illness" after all. Once he gets the water, the fake sneezing increases. Then he works himself up to a big sneeze after dipping his fingers in the water. As the sneeze comes out, he flicks water onto the head of the reclined passenger in front of him. Presto— the passenger bolts upright and remains there for the rest of the flight. It's foolproof—and downright contemptible, I suppose.

Instead, here's a plea for civility. The proper way to handle the situation is to ask the person in front of you to refrain from reclining because you are trying to work. I find business travelers are sympathetic because they've been there. Infrequent travelers more often feel you are impinging on their freedom. If you feel uncomfortable making the request, you can also ask a flight attendant to speak to the person in front of you, or ask if you could be reseated. Better to be polite than to keep your knees locked into the back of the seat while the person in front of you fights to recline. Better yet, maybe airlines should segregate travelers into "recline" and "no recline" sections.

POWER PROTECTION

The airplane cabin is full of medical concerns. You can protect yourself by taking some commonsense precautions. Periodic concerns flare about "deep vein thrombosis"—blood clots that form often in legs and travel to vital parts of the body. Clots are believed to be more common when legs are immobile for long periods of time and the body is dehydrated—just the kind of conditions created by a long airplane flight. As a result, it is sometimes dubbed "coach class syndrome," though there certainly have been cases of business-class and first-class travelers who have had DVT problems.

Doctors have understood the problem of blood clots and immobility for many years, and connections to air travel began sprouting in medical literature in the 1950s. Long periods of immobility cause legs to swell because not all the blood gets pumped out. Clots—or clumps of cells—sometimes form in the deep veins of the calf and leg muscles. If clots move through the bloodstream to vital organs of the body, they can kill. In the lungs, for example, a clot can cause a pulmonary embolism, blocking airflow.

Anecdotally, DVT may be more widespread than many travelers realize. Ashford Hospital, less than a mile from London's Heathrow Airport, a hub on long-haul international flying, documented thirty cases over three years in which people collapsed and died of pulmonary embolism after long flights, according to a 2001 *Wall Street Journal* story. Ten of the thirty deaths came from the ultralong, twelve-hour Sydney-to-London route.

A hospital clinic at Narita Airport in Tokyo found twenty-five similar deaths over eight years, the *Journal* said. And many doctors believe the numbers are higher, since fatal blood clots can go undetected for days or weeks after a flight. Passengers who suffer symptoms such as pain in the chest, soreness in the leg, or shortness of breath are often unlikely to seek immediate help, especially as they scramble to head home or on to other destinations. A study published in the *Lancet*, a British medical journal, found that one long-haul traveler in every ten could be at risk for "symptomless" DVT—small clots, most of which dissolve harmlessly.

What should you do?

Drink something each hour on a flight.
Move about the cabin periodically. If you can't, exercise your legs while sitting. Most airlines now have exercise suggestions in seatback pockets.
Avoid caffeine and alcohol, which dehydrate.
Doctors advise older passengers to take aspirin to thin the blood.
Consider knee-high compression socks, which aid blood flow in the legs.

Many travelers also worry about the air inside an airplane cabin—is it polluted? Does it spread germs and disease? Most cabin air is recycled; aircraft today draw in only a limited amount of fresh air. Fresh air from outside jets is cold and must be passed through aircraft engines to be heated. (It passes through separate conduits, not through the core of the engine itself, so it is free of exhaust and noxious chemicals.) But that reduces the efficiency of the engine, so to save fuel, airlines limit the amount of fresh air cycled through engines. The recycled air does pass through some sophisticated filters—newer jets tend to have better filtration systems. The best of those filters can collect microscopic contaminants—even viruses. But like most things in the airline industry, reality sets in. Filters have to be cleaned and changed to be effective. Systems sometimes break down. You get the picture.

POWER FILTH

One of the public health realities of the airline business is that people are in close proximity for long periods, and they can spread things by breathing on one another, sharing dirty armrests, and a host of other germ-spreading activities. There's not much you can do about it. Wash hands often, try to avoid the sneezers, be careful what you touch in filthy airplane bathrooms—you know the drill. (One of the most unexplainable human behaviors I've ever witnessed: people prattling around barefoot in airline cabins, including trips to bathrooms, oblivious to the flotsam and jetsam on floors.) During a viral epidemic in Asia several years ago, airline passengers took to wearing hospital masks over noses and mouths. That seems extreme for everyday use. Then again, I think most of us realize we sometimes catch colds or other ailments on airline flights.

One of the most disgusting aspects of airplanes can be the seatback pocket, carrier of all kinds of filth, gobbledygook, and compost. Besides being a repository for magazines, newspapers, books, iPods, and air-sickness bags, seatback pockets get stuffed with all kinds of disgusting trash, from toenail clippings to mushy meals.

Travelers have told me tales of finding old french fries, a festering baby diaper, half a hamburger, cups of tobacco spit, used Kleenex, and wet napkins in seatback pockets. One man put a book in a seatback pocket and pulled it out to find the bottom covered in a melted candy bar. Dirty diapers are the most common problem, flight attendants say.

Some people try to hand them to flight attendants when they are trying to serve beverages and snacks. Watch out especially for middle-seat pockets—they tend to get the most trash because they are sometimes unoccupied.

The detritus problem is exacerbated by the fact that most airplanes are only lightly cleaned between each flight. Airlines say planes get a more thorough cleaning overnight and a "deep cleaning" about every thirty days. In many cases, seatback pockets aren't thoroughly checked until overnight cleaning crews work over a cabin. And blankets simply get folded for the next passenger, even if they have been used to wipe up bodily fluids.

The reality is that people do things on airplanes that they would never do in other public settings. They pluck eyebrows, polish nails, and pick noses. They stick chewed gum in places only other passengers will discover. They blow noses into blankets that get folded up for the next weary traveler. They prop bare feet up on bulkheads and seats. Sometimes they even engage in sex acts—and leave evidence for others to find. Though crammed together elbow to elbow in conditions more public than you'd find at a shopping mall, restaurant, church, or office, airline passengers sometimes behave as though the cabin were their own small nesting place—and one where they never have to worry about cleanliness, either.

Some psychologists believe that on airplanes, people feel anonymous, so they behave without their normal limits. When traveling, some people test boundaries or act out when away from spouses, friends, or any authority. For others, air travel leaves them psychologically off-kilter and more likely to do things they wouldn't normally do. Some lose control because the flying experience strips them of all control—you're told where to sit, when to sit, and when you will arrive. In addition, many people have difficulty being stuffed in close proximity with others and forced to share space, whether it's overhead bin space, armrests, or space taken away when the person in front reclines. As planes get more crowded, people get more cramped. Others experts say bad behavior has increased in relation to bad airline service—people retaliate against the airplane when an airline worker is rude to them or an airline makes them late, loses their bag, or denies an upgrade.

One other pollutant travelers may have to deal with in airline cabins: cellular phone conversations. Technology is making that possible, and while many travelers say they abhor the idea of having to listen to people negotiate deals or schedule dinners, some airlines around the world are already allowing in-flight chatter.

POWER CONNECTIONS

For years we've always been told that cell phones must be turned off in-flight. That's not so much out of concern for interference with the electronic navigation equipment on the airplane, though some scientists debate that point. The real concern is what airborne cell phones can do to cellular networks on the ground. A cell phone tries to stay in contact with the nearest tower. If you're five miles above the ground whizzing along at five hundred miles per hour, your cell phone can connect to lots and lots of towers and switch between towers at rapid speeds. That ties up a tremendous amount of tower capacity. Thus the problem. The ban on cell phones aboard airplanes originates at the Federal Communications Commission, not the Federal Aviation Administration. It's a phone company problem, not an airplane problem.

Now new technology is solving the phone company problem. Small antennas called "pico cells" have been developed to install on airplanes and corral all signals from nearby phones. Then the communications are packaged together and transmitted to phone company networks by antenna or satellite. This technology doesn't disrupt cell towers. The phones operate on much lower power because they just have to connect to the pico cell, not a tower miles away. Airlines in Europe have been experimenting with allowing cell phone calls—there may be less resistance there to in-flight chats than there seems to be in the United States. But don't be surprised if airlines relent because they can make some money off this service. If that happens, noise-canceling headphones, a popular accessory for many road warriors, may become more of a necessity for travelers.

POWER NAPPING

If that's not enough with which to cope, travelers have to battle the nagging problem of jet lag, that insidious ailment that can discombobulate you as you travel across multiple time zones. Jet lag can cause insomnia, irritability, indigestion, and disorientation in the days following air travel. Some help may be on the way.

Jet lag is typically exacerbated by dehydration—another reason why drinking lots of fluids is important in-flight. But it's a tough battle because the air you breath is dry inside an airplane—there's little moisture in the thin air of high-altitude travel. What's more, airlines pressurize cabins of jets to about eight thousand feet above sea level—about the altitude of Vail, Colorado, or Taos, New Mexico.

The Boeing 787, however, should be different, and may usher in an era where airplanes help curb jet lag. The 787 is made out of composite materials—superstrong plastics instead of aluminum. One reason today's airplanes need to be so dry is that moisture corrodes aluminum. But if the plane is plastic, like the 787, corrosion is less of an issue. With the increased strength of composite materials, the cabin can be pressurized to a more comfortable lower level, increasing the moisture. That, combined with some body-clock tricks Boeing has cooked up with a fancy cabin lighting system that can simulate nightfall during daylight or daybreak when it's dark outside, should make travelers arrive feeling more rested and less jet-lagged.

Until then, what to do? There are lots of home remedies for jet lag. In general, the best strategy I've seen, based partly on personal testing, is to try and move your body clock more toward your destination before departure, then reset as quickly as you can when you get there. Heading from the United States to Europe, for example, means going to sleep earlier before departure and sleeping as much as you can on the airplane. (I'm a big believer in sleep aids for travel, if that works for you.) When you arrive in the morning in Europe (though it's the middle of the night to your body), don't go to sleep—muddle through the first day as best you can, have an early dinner, and get as much sleep as possible. You should wake up the next day refreshed. For many people, going east always seems harder, losing hours instead of gaining them back. It's more disorienting, leaving you with days that are too short instead of too long. We all learn to cope with long days, but when half the night disappears, you're going to feel lousy.

Many people believe in diet to help—eating pasta and easily digestible foods before you travel, for example, or following a strict "no jet lag" diet promoted by Dr. Charles F. Ehret, a scientist at the Argonne National Laboratory

in Illinois (see www.antijetlagdiet.com), that alternates between feast and famine and sends you off on your trip with
high-protein meals in your stomach. (One caution: The
good doctor's Web site charges $10.95 to calculate your diet
for a one-way trip, and $16.95 for a round-trip meal plan.)
Others swear by herbal supplements and homeopathic remedies, such as tablets called No Jet Lag, available through
drugstores, health supplement stores, and some travel cata-
logs. (Cost: about $10 for thirty-two pills.)

Another popular jet lag strategy is melatonin to "reset"
your body clock when you arrive in a new time zone. Melatonin is a hormone secreted by the pineal gland in the brain
that helps control the body's internal clock. It's released by
our bodies based on sunlight—nighttime yields the release
of more melatonin. If you cheat yourself out of a night, you
lose melatonin and your circadian rhythm is disrupted.
Taking a small supplemental dose—doctors usually recommend 0.5 mg—about an hour before you go to sleep after
arrival, and perhaps a day or two into your trip, helps some
people recover quickly. Medical studies on melatonin supplements for jet lag have been inconclusive. It's worth a try,
but your mileage may vary, as they say.

CHAPTER 12

When Bad Things Happen
to Good Travelers

Your flight was terrible: You had lousy service, faced huge disruptions, and even suffered financial loss. The airline messed up. You can extract some revenge. Be warned: You may not get the satisfaction you want. You may just be flying off into more frustration, but you can get something out of it.

Mike Wallace of San Francisco was so mad about recent travel experiences and the airline's lack of response to his complaints that he searched the Internet for e-mail addresses at United Airlines and fired off an angry letter to more than sixty company officials. No response. A second e-mail to all the addresses he could find that used @united.com and @ual.com did get some attention. After corresponding with United a dozen different times about being stranded at airport hotels on two different trips because of United flight problems, Mr. Wallace and his wife got some measure of satisfaction: business-class upgrades for some future trips and a $400 voucher.

"It's a series of systems, policies, and nameless, faceless people in place to wear you out. Most people just give up, but I pursued and pursued and pursued before I finally got something," said Mr. Wallace, an environmental consultant and elite-level United customer. United says its goal is to "satisfy our customers the first time they call, write or e-mail us." That obviously doesn't happen all of the time.

POWER PROTESTING

Here are some tips to make your complaint to the airline more effective:

First, never tell an airline you'll never fly them again. If you do, the airline no longer has an incentive to try to win you back, some airline officials say. It's a common mistake that consumers make. Tell the airline why you'd like to keep doing business with them, but they should offer you something to buy back some loyalty and erase hard feelings about recent disasters.

Second, always tell the airline what you want in compensation and be realistic. A one-hour delay won't get you anything, but if the airline canceled your flight because of a mechanical problem, forced you to spend the night in a cheap motel and miss an important morning meeting, then lost your bag the next day, you can ask for something meaningful, like a free ticket. Remember, "sorry" doesn't cost the airline anything. It can automatically produce letters with nameless agents telling you how sorry they are you didn't like your last flight. Federal rules require airlines to reimburse customers for lost luggage and compensate them for bumping them from overbooked flights. After that, as with most any business, consumers are on their own seeking redress. If you want something, be specific.

There are differences in how airlines handle customer complaints. United and Continental, for example, still have phone lines to field complaints. More than two hundred Continental employees are trained to resolve problems and compensate passengers on the spot, a spokeswoman says. Most other carriers don't take complaints by telephone—mail, fax, or e-mail only. Once airlines respond to a written complaint, you typically can't talk to the customer service agent to appeal, either.

In general, most airlines pay more attention to complaints from top-tier frequent fliers, especially customers who spend lots of money each year with the airline. (They also pay attention to complaints from newspapers. I once went on a journalistic crusade to improve the coffee on Southwest Airlines. After several mentions of Southwest's lousy coffee in stories, and a published exposé on the source of the cheap grounds Southwest was buying, the airline relented, upgraded its coffee, and sent me a letter admitting it was giving in.) Airlines track customers not by miles flown but by dollars spent, and high-dollar customers get better compensation when they complain.

Airlines say all complaints do get heard, many get investigated, and all get a response of some sort, even if it's only a formulaic apology. Most carriers say they track complaints and compile monthly summary reports for executives, and many say they forward the complaint to the employee involved and supervisors. The most efficient way for them to field complaints is by e-mail. Because letters must be scanned electronically into computer systems, airlines tend to respond more quickly to e-mails than to mailed letters.

POWER PROCESSING

Automation is changing the airline complaint business. Many carriers now have systems that flag flights with lengthy airline-caused delays or nightmarish conditions, then generate letters of apology to passengers, some with offers of additional frequent-flier miles or vouchers offering discounts on future trips.

There's a lot more airlines could do in the future, too. New systems are under development that will track passenger experiences. If airlines spend the money to install the systems, reservation computers could flag previous bad experiences. When you check in, the agent could apologize for the six-hour delay on your last trip, or your lost baggage, and offer a free upgrade or coupon for a snack or drink.

Carriers say customers don't need to send complaints to the offices or e-mails of high-ranking executives because those complaints are routinely forwarded to the complaint department no matter how they come in. I have to question that claim. A slew of complaints to a CEO might catch the eye of an assistant doing the forwarding, and the trend might get mentioned. But there's little follow-up at airlines. Executives rarely follow complaints and inquire if they were ever resolved. Once in a blue moon, an elite-level frequent flier will get a call from a vice president or higher trying to resolve the complaint. Send it on to the executive suite, if you are so inclined, as well as to the generic customer service address.

If a second and third and fourth letter of complaint doesn't get you what you want, one recourse is to take the complaint to small-claims court. An airline ticket is a contract for service, and if the airline failed to live up to the terms spelled out in its "contract of carriage" (available on airline Web sites), you can pursue a claim in court. You have to be able to demonstrate real loss, not just be miffed about poor service or delays.

POWER POUTING

There is another way to pressure airlines into trying to resolve your complaint: Get the federal government involved. The U.S. Department of Transportation fields thousands of complaints about airlines each year, and government officials pass the complaints on to airlines. By law, each airline has to designate someone to respond to complaints sent by the DOT. (You can find the contacts listed on DOT's Web site, and use the names, addresses, and phone numbers yourself. Check http://airconsumer.ost.dot.gov/pubs.htm.)

Travelers get two benefits: a DOT-forwarded complaint may get more attention, and your complaint becomes part of the monthly report card that DOT issues on airline performance. Airlines and journalists pay close attention to those rankings, and carriers work hard to stay out of the cellar in the consumer complaint category.

Some airlines admit they do pay more attention to consumer complaints if travelers send them to the DOT. And the DOT says it sometimes uses complaint data in enforcement actions against airlines and in rule-making decisions—a history of lots of complaints can work against an airline. The agency also points out trends with airlines hoping to pressure change. "We're more than just a statistics-capturing office," said a senior Transportation official. "Airlines are sensitive to the complaints the department receives." Southwest, for one, says it does special reporting on complaints forwarded from the DOT, and a special report on DOT complaints goes out to company executives. "We pay huge attention to that," says Jim Ruppel, vice president of customer relations.

Government agencies generally don't post public scorecards on companies—the Federal Communications Commission doesn't list complaints against cellular-phone companies, for example, only the total number of complaints received. (They outnumber airline complaints two to one.) But the airline industry is unique—the DOT's reporting on airline performance is a holdover from the days before 1978 when carriers were regulated by the government.

The DOT has about twelve people in its Aviation Consumer Protection Division who handle airline complaints. The largest volume comes by e-mail (airconsumer@dot.gov), but DOT also accepts letters to its Washington headquarters (mail to: Aviation Consumer Protection Division C–75, U.S. Department of Transportation, 1200 New Jersey Ave. S.E., Washington, D.C. 20590) and calls to a voice mail (202–366–2220) where complaints can be recorded.

The DOT sends copies of every complaint to the airline involved, so involving DOT may be helpful to consumers frustrated by unresponsive airlines, particularly hard-to-reach foreign carriers. DOT officials decide if the complaint falls into a category requiring government investigation: lost baggage liability, late refunds, denied boarding on oversold flights, and civil rights, which include disability and discrimination issues. Airlines found to have violated federal rules can be fined by the DOT.

Most complaints deal with flight issues—cancellations, delays, and missed connections. Baggage issues are a close second, followed by customer-service and reservation-ticketing issues. Only a small percentage of travelers complain to DOT. Last year, the DOT recorded fewer than one complaint for every 100,000 passengers. Airlines say that's a sign that the vast majority of customers are satisfied, though several also acknowledged that they get four or five times as many complaints directly that the DOT never sees.

The monthly DOT tallies, available at http://airconsumer .ost.dot.gov/reports/index.htm, give consumers a valuable scorecard on which airlines are doing well in customer service and which are suffering problems. Complaints about United nearly doubled in 2000 over 1999 when the airline ran into labor problems that disrupted schedules. Huge travel problems in Philadelphia during the Christmas 2004 travel season pushed the rate of complaints about US Airways up to five times its December 2003 level.

The reality of the airline industry is that airlines frequently have to deal with bad weather and congestion both on the ground and in the sky. The worse the weather or congestion gets, the more complaints DOT gets. Under pressure, airlines disappoint passengers more frequently with lost luggage, long lines, interminable time spent on telephone hold, surly employees, and nights spent stranded at airports. Customer service in the airline business is often measured by how well companies perform under pressure.

Indeed, complaints to the DOT peaked in 1999 and 2000, when the airline industry suffered service breakdowns and congestion woes not all that dissimilar to the travel problems of the 2008 winter. Complaints hit their high-water mark in 2000 at 23,381, then fell to a low of 5,983 in 2003, when travel had declined considerably, leaving fewer planes and fewer passengers. By 2007, the number of complaints tallied by DOT was up to 9,444, and climbing. As travel rebounded, complaints increased. Wichita State University professor Dean Headley, who compiles an annual airline quality ranking, thinks the numbers are still depressed from where they might be because people have grown accustomed to service problems. "Airlines promise less and deliver less," he said. "Not much is left to complain about unless it's an extreme case." The DOT thinks the decline is more a reflection of congestion easing for several years. When airports and skies get more crowded, complaints rise, officials said.

POWER POLICING?

When airlines do break federal rules, the DOT itself hasn't always been a stern punishing parent. On Christmas Eve 2004, Comair's overtaxed crew-scheduling computer system collapsed, forcing more than a thousand flight cancellations and leaving thousands of passengers stranded. The airline, a regional affiliate of Delta, refused to pay some customers for hotel rooms, blaming the cancellations on a severe storm. The DOT ruled that Comair had acted illegally. Its punishment: a $75,000 fine that likely will never have to be paid.

The DOT's enforcement office aggressively prosecutes airlines for violations of wheelchair- and disability-access requirements, and keeps a sharp eye on airline advertisements to make sure fuel surcharges and taxes are flagged. But there's actually little enforcement of existing customer-service regulations in aviation. "When it comes to other areas of customer service, DOT enforcement is milquetoast," says Ken Mead, a former DOT inspector general who is a Washington attorney. "There's got to be a cop on the beat, and I don't see it."

The Comair case was one of the rare times the government documented a deception that many travelers believe happens frequently: airline employees lying to customers about the real reasons for cancellations, blaming bad weather so they wouldn't be financially responsible for hotels, meals, and any other possible compensation. It also shows how insignificant DOT fines are when airlines do violate contract terms in tickets or federal regulations. The

DOT forgives at least half of the fines levied under the consent orders it reaches with airlines if they promise not to repeat the practice for at least a year. The DOT also reduces fines if airlines spend money on improvements, such as retraining for telephone or gate agents who aren't up to speed on issues like accommodating disabled travelers.

United got out of most of a $75,000 fine for not having proper in-cabin storage for folding wheelchairs on some of its Boeing 737s by agreeing to put up eight new flight-information monitors at Chicago's O'Hare International Airport. That's something the airline likely would have done anyway—the airport is its biggest hub—but the DOT reduced the fine by $67,500 on the theory that the new screens would improve service for the hearing-impaired.

The DOT claims it has been more active in recent years, opening "several dozen consumer-protection investigations" as a direct result of concerns raised about enforcement. A spokesman says forgiving fines "provides an incentive for future compliance." Repeat offenders are given full penalties, he notes.

In one year's worth of DOT enforcement actions against airlines on customer-service issues, fifteen consent orders were signed with scheduled-service carriers large and small, domestic and international. Seven involved fare advertisements or displays on booking Web sites; three involved disabled-access issues. Four others involved infractions at small airlines, ranging from misreporting the cause of flight delays to failing to make prompt credit-card refunds to operating charter flights without DOT approval.

In the Comair case, DOT said in its final decision, "We view seriously any carrier's failure to honor commitments made to consumers." But officials agreed to forgive $50,000 of the $75,000 fine if Comair didn't get caught again blaming weather for its own service problems over the next year. The other $25,000 didn't have to be paid either, if Comair spent that much on extra accommodations for stranded customers over the next year. Just another example of how travelers are often on their own.

WHINE, WHINE

Which airline draws the most customer complaints? In 2007, it was US Airways.

	Complaints	Enplanements	Complaints Per 100,000 Enplanements
Southwest	266	101,991,150	0.26
Expressjet	78	17,426,271	0.45
Frontier	71	10,763,273	0.66
SkyWest	156	22,095,712	0.71
Hawaiian	51	7,102,463	0.72
Alaska	133	17,559,090	0.76
jetBue	165	21,045,088	0.78
Mesa	108	13,043,323	0.83
AirTran	197	23,773,103	0.83
Pinnacle	96	9,965,455	0.96
Continental	534	49,005,712	1.09
American Eagle	216	18,518,861	1.17
Atlantic Southeast	149	12,324,439	1.21
Northwest	768	53,736,983	1.43
Comair	138	9,571,231	1.44
American	1,617	98,165,082	1.65
Delta	1,325	73,051,467	1.81
United	1,540	68,386,110	2.25
US Airways	1,828	57,870,936	3.16

Source: U.S. Department of Transportation

CHAPTER 13

Airline/Air-Traffic-Control Operations

In a cavernous room longer than a football field near the Dallas–Fort Worth International Airport, scores of people run the largest airline in the world. They map out routes for jets, calculate how much fuel each flight needs, dictate where to load luggage—how many bags in the front, how many in the rear. Dispatchers talk to pilots routinely, both on the ground and in the air, and have joint legal

A radar image of 5,664 flights over the United States from FlightAware.com.

responsibility with the captain for their assigned flights. Other workers schedule pilots and flight attendants and scramble to find replacements when someone calls in sick or gets stranded in Seattle. Some airline workers inside the command center beg and barter with air-traffic controllers to prioritize certain flights, or get a long-delayed trip off the ground. The managers there answer the phone when there's a bomb threat. They pull out the crisis book when there's a crash. They retreat to a secure room with a hotline to Washington when there is a national emergency. They guess at the afternoon weather and study storm forecasts, deciding whether to cancel flights or not. They, and their counterparts at every other airline in the world, decide whether you'll get to your destination or not.

Each airline has its own operations center, as does the Federal Aviation Administration, which has a command bunker outside Washington, D.C., similar to NASA's "Mission Control," with giant video screens at the front of the room showing the status of air travel in the nation, and sometimes CNN news as well, then rows of experts sitting at computer consoles. It's a standard government-issue command center, with different desks for different functions, all pointed at the commander in the middle.

Scattered around the country, air-traffic controllers manage the flow of airplanes and instruct pilots. Across the globe, similar setups at airlines and air-traffic-control agencies move millions of people and millions of tons of cargo with extraordinary safety and, most of the time, remarkable speed. Our world depends on them to do their jobs efficiently. Most often, they do.

Air-traffic control is a huge four-dimensional puzzle, with each piece moving at five hundred miles per hour and carrying hundreds of people. The technology is rudimentary—a major handicap for travelers. You may be able to e-mail with a friend on the other side of the world, and airlines have sent text messages back and forth between cockpits and control centers for years, but an air-traffic controller can't e-mail a pilot. All communications in the mainland United States are verbal and over the radio, which limits capacity, slows down travel, and has the potential for error. Data-link technology is way behind schedule. You may be able to use satellite technology to zoom in and see your neighbor's backyard, or use the GPS device in your car to find the fastest route to a restaurant, but commercial airliners in the United States are tracked by radar and fly from one radio beacon to another. They don't even use much GPS—private airplanes all the way down to single-engine Cessnas use GPS to find their way through the sky, able to pinpoint the shortest, fastest route to a destination thousands of miles away. Airlines and the FAA are way behind.

POWER CANCELING

Travelers never see any of these professionals manage air travel across the country and around the world. For the most part, that's a good thing. You wouldn't want to watch when the "Manager on Duty" at an airline invokes a software tool called a "Cancellator" that searches out lightly booked flights to cancel when storms disrupt the flow of traffic and force airlines to reduce the number of flights in a day. You'd probably fume when a supervisor at the FAA's command center in Washington gets a call asking for priority routing for a plane carrying the Rolling Stones, and orders landing priority for that jet at Boston, or be miffed when jetBlue Airways asks for more direct routing for some cross-country flights so they don't have to make fuel stops in Denver and Salt Lake City because of circuitous routings. And you'd probably scream when a call comes in that a maintenance worker in New York cut a cable, and all traffic bound for La Guardia Airport must remain grounded until repairs to a landing guidance system can be made.

Despite all the command bunkers, computers, and air-traffic experts, managing the nation's air travel is a delicate proposition, more prone to clogs than a sink in a teenager's bathroom. A storm here can create lots of problems there because the system isn't flexible. Suppose a thunderstorm pops up over Rochester, New York, 260 miles northwest of Kennedy International Airport in New York. (I profiled this real-world example in a front-page *Wall Street Journal* story in 2007.) The storm shuts off one of the main routes into the New York area from the west, and all those planes coming from Chicago, San Francisco, and scores of other cities may be looking for a new highway. Air-traffic controllers reroute them to the south so that they can approach New York from another direction and avoid the storm. Some planes were directed as far south as Atlanta. Presto, there's a massive traffic jam over Washington, D.C., which is already a choke point for travel in and out of the Northeast. (The airspace over Washington is constrained by lots of military training areas just off the coast.) So Washington-area air-traffic controllers refuse to take any more planes— into New York or out of New York. A Delta flight in Fort Lauderdale, Florida, scheduled to fly to New York, Flight 88 in this case, sits on the ground waiting—for nearly four hours. And passengers are told the delay has been caused by bad weather. Bad weather? New York is cloudless. Fort Lauderdale is even sunnier and clearer. Those lying airlines!

One storm results in massive delays for travelers nowhere near the bad weather and who have no plans to fly anywhere near it. The problem is simple—a lack of capacity in the seemingly boundless sky. Because we restrict jets to specified routes in the sky, and have a limited number of sky highways drawn on maps, planes don't have a lot of room to maneuver. They can't take the back roads. If Interstate 95 is blocked, they have to move over to Interstate 85, and the traffic on Interstate 85 may have to move someplace else, too. The system, largely unchanged since the 1950s, is inflexible and overcrowded. Airlines have grown, the number of air travelers has skyrocketed, and the number of planes in the sky has increased dramatically in the past twenty years. And yet the air-traffic-control system is basically the same as it was two or three decades ago. Just as we need more runways on the ground to accommodate airplanes, we need more highways in the sky.

In 2007, 24 percent of all airline flights were delayed at least fifteen minutes, and the average delay was fifty-five minutes, according to the FAA. Passengers lost 112 million hours, up from a mere 100 million hours in 2006, according to estimates compiled by GRA Inc., a consulting firm, based on Department of Transportation data. That's 12,785 years' worth of waiting time. Delays cost airlines $8.1 billion in direct operating costs in 2007—mostly burning extra fuel and paying crews for the extra time during delays.

Many delays have been baked into the system—airlines padding schedules so that routinely delayed flights can get to their destination gates and open the door for passengers "on time." On average, U.S. airline flights were scheduled fifteen minutes longer in 2006 than in 1997, based on the same distances, according to a 2008 study by researchers Steven Morrison and Clifford Winston. I compared some current airline schedules to old timetables and found that it apparently takes twenty-five minutes longer to fly from

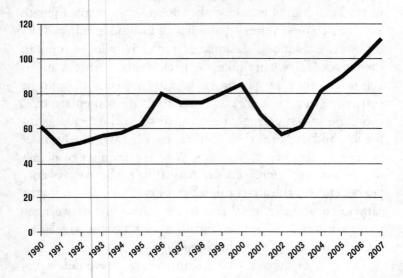

WASTED MINUTES, LONG TRIPS

Here is the total number of minutes, in millions, that passengers were delayed on airlines from 1990 to 2007.

Source: GRA Inc., based on ASQP and T100 Domestic Segment Data.

New York to Los Angeles than it did ten years ago. Flights from New York to Washington, D.C., a trip that normally takes only about thirty-five minutes in the air, are now routinely scheduled for well over an hour. It's not that planes are flying slower or airlines are somehow cheating just to boost their on-time arrival scorecards. It's the reality of the air-traffic system. Airlines don't like adding minutes to their schedules—that's expensive. They may need more airplanes to fly the same number of trips if minutes are added. Their labor costs will go up, since most pilots and flight attendants are paid the longer of either actual trip time or scheduled trip time. But the sad reality is that if you have to wait forty-five minutes every day to take off in the afternoon from New York, you better work that into your schedule.

POWER CONTROL

Understanding how the airlines and the FAA work—and how the system breaks down—will make you a savvier traveler, and help you make better choices. There may be instances when you can avoid trouble because you can anticipate problems. More likely, your travels may just be a bit calmer if you understand who controls what and why your flight is number forty-two for takeoff.

Let's start with airlines. Creating an airline schedule is a tricky thing. While travelers think of the schedule in terms of their particular flight, an airline thinks about the entire day's activity of that airplane. The key to good scheduling is finding the maximum use and maximum revenue potential for each plane each day. Timing is everything. An early morning flight to or from a major business center may generate strong revenue with lots of business travelers. Schedule that flight at 10 A.M. instead of 8 A.M. and those business travelers may buy tickets on another airline. Leisure travelers are less sensitive to time, but it's not always possible to have all your midmorning and midafternoon departures from vacation spots.

Most airlines in the United States—Southwest being the notable exception—schedule most of their flights into and out of hub airports. Funneling passengers through hubs helps fill up airplanes and allows airlines to provide jet service to cities that otherwise couldn't support it. A plane from Albuquerque, New Mexico, to Dallas may have passengers headed to thirty different destinations where the airline couldn't provide nonstop flights. With hubs, it can vacuum up those passengers and sort them across the country.

Planes rarely fly back and forth between the same cities, unless they are customized for certain markets like the Northeast shuttles between New York and Boston or the transcontinental flights between New York and Los Angeles. For the most part, that plane that flew from Dallas to Albuquerque will turn around and go back to Dallas, and then on to someplace else. From there, it might go back to Dallas, or it might head to another hub. If it began the day in Dallas it most likely will end up parked overnight elsewhere. During the twenty-eight days of a typical airline schedule, the plane may overnight in a different city every night. The schedule has to be created not only to cover every flight the airline has sold to customers but also to make sure each plane ends up getting all the necessary maintenance along the way. Periodically planes get simple checks like oil changes, then every few years they get a more extensive maintenance regime, then every seven years or so they have to go in for a major overhaul—a month-long process of taking the plane apart and putting it back together again after all kinds of inspections, repairs, refurbishments, and replacements.

Planes make money in the air, not on the ground, and thus airlines want to maximize their use each day. If you can squeeze a bit more flying out of each plane and thereby expand your schedule without buying more $50 million jets, you've improved the airline's finances. Schedules are precise. Adding a few minutes here and there can cost an airline millions of dollars annually, as pilots get paid by the minute at most airlines, and lots of maintenance items, such as engine overhauls, are dictated by total time in use. Those economics flies in the face of how imprecise airline operations are in reality, but explain why airlines schedule flights to leave at 7:27 and arrive at 9:18.

Southwest doesn't run flights back and forth into and out of big hubs, but it does work off the same type of month-long giant master schedule where each plane is assigned a line, and each day the line may be different. One day a particular Southwest 737 may start in Houston and fly to New Orleans, Nashville, Baltimore, Providence, Chicago, Phoenix, San Diego, and Oakland, then the next day fly a different hopscotch across the country. The schedule has to make sure the plane gets to an overnight maintenance base when necessary.

POWER EXCUSES

Once you understand the complexity of airline schedules, you get a better idea of the many issues that go into canceling a flight. Travelers often believe airlines cancel flights that are light on passengers. Often they are right, but it's not as underhanded as they might think. First, airlines would almost always rather fly the airplane than cancel. American Airlines drew fire from environmentalists for flying a wide-body Boeing 777 to Europe with only fourteen passengers on board—the trip had been delayed considerably, and most passengers found other options. Why didn't American just cancel instead of burning thousands of gallons of fuel for fourteen passengers? Because American had a full planeload of customers waiting in Europe to ride that plane back to the United States. And that's the same problem with canceling any flight—you may look around the gate area and see only a handful of people, but that plane may be needed the following morning for a full load of people somewhere. If it gets off schedule, it may not be in the right place at the right time.

Is it just coincidence that the flights that do get canceled seem to have light loads? No, not if the airline is working to inconvenience the fewest passengers possible. At hubs, when something goes wrong like a mechanical breakdown, planners in the airline operations center have various options. They can simply cancel the flight with the mechanical problem and try to accommodate those passengers on other flights. Or they can look for another airplane—perhaps a spare that could substitute and fly the rest of the broken-down plane's schedule for that day, or even longer. And if a spare isn't an option, airline operations planners often look for lightly booked trips where the flight could be canceled and the aircraft could be used for the more heavily booked trip—the one with the mechanical problem. So there you are, your plane pulls up to the gate and unloads and you're set to go, figuring it will be an enjoyable flight because there aren't many people waiting to board. And out of the blue the airline announces that because of a mechanical problem, your flight has been canceled. (If you followed that aircraft, you'd likely see it moved to another gate, or see passengers from another flight descend on your gate to board after you've been herded off to a rebooking desk.)

Is that fair? Some travelers find it devious—the people who actually had the mechanical problem get to fly, and people with a perfectly "healthy" aircraft get canceled. From the airline's perspective, the goal is to disrupt the fewest number of customers, so canceling a lightly booked trip is better.

Another common cancellation technique is to look for trips that are "out-and-back" round-trips for the aircraft and crews. That plane that went from Dallas out to Albuquerque and then back to Dallas might be a good candidate for canceling if storms force the airline to thin out its schedule in Dallas. Canceling the out-and-back trip means the plane will still be in place for its next trip later in the day, and will still end up at its scheduled overnight destination. Same for the crew. The disruption to the airline's schedule is minimal—though it's maximum for the Dallas and Albuquerque passengers, especially all those people making connections. The alternative is far worse for the airline. If you cancel a trip that doesn't come back to the same hub, you will end up canceling many more flights down the line because the airplane isn't there, or you may have to juggle the schedule to move a different airplane and different crews to cover the trips. That can be done, but it's often not as simple and it may be far more expensive.

There are times when you can tell where your aircraft is coming from and times you can't. If possible I like to track the inbound aircraft because I sometimes get earlier notification of delays. If you're in Jackson, Mississippi, and flying to Atlanta, you can look at the schedule and see that there's an inbound flight from Atlanta to Jackson that's flown with the same type of aircraft you're scheduled to fly. Odds are good that's your plane, and if it's late coming in, it will likely be late going out. Worse, if it's canceled you may end up canceled, too. A flight-tracking alert for the inbound plane can give you a heads-up. On the other hand, if you're in Atlanta going to Jackson, there's no way to tell what aircraft the airline will use for that trip, due to the amount of traffic and number of planes in and out of Atlanta each day. And even when you think you do know—you notice that a flight from Cleveland to Atlanta has the same flight number as the Atlanta–Jackson flight and appears to be the first leg of a two-leg trip—don't be surprised if the airline switches aircraft. It happens all the time. The airline can substitute airplanes, so don't assume your flight will be canceled just because the Cleveland leg was canceled. And with international trips, don't assume flights continue on with the same aircraft. In 2008, United scheduled a Boeing 777 as Flight 991 from San Francisco to Washington, D.C., and then on to Paris, a Boeing 777 as Flight 991. The same Boeing 777? Easy to assume —same flight number, same type of aircraft, same ticket. But no, Flight 991 is actually a connection to Flight 991. The flight was listed on United's Web site as a one-stop, but there was also a note that the itinerary required a change of aircraft.

POWER PREPARATIONS

As complex as scheduling is, that's the easy part. The hard part is actually flying the schedule. Preparations for a flight begin hours ahead of time. Catering gets adjusted, depending on how many passengers are expected, though when most flights are running full, there's not much need to tinker with how many Diet Cokes and snacks-for-sale to load. Dispatchers, who have to be licensed by the FAA, check any security concerns for each flight, and look at whether any VIPs are on board or other passengers with special needs. They estimate how many bags will be checked for each flight and how they should be loaded. Weight and balance are crucial to an airplane— the center of gravity needs to be pinpointed, based on what's loaded, including passengers—to make sure that the plane won't be tail-heavy or nose-heavy and have trouble flying. The center of gravity can also affect how much fuel the plane burns, so it must be optimized. In general, you want to make sure you have enough weight in the rear to help keep the nose pointed slightly up as the plane cruises. Dispatchers calculate how much fuel the flight will need, which can be a controversial issue these days.

By law, all airline flights have to take off with enough fuel to fly to their destination and make an approach, then fly to an alternate airport selected by the dispatcher based on good weather conditions, make an approach there, and still land with forty-five minutes of fuel remaining. (Long international flights also have to carry 5 percent more fuel than is calculated to be burned during the cruising portion of the flight to cushion for wind shifts, weather changes, and navigational errors. The FAA dropped the percentage from 10 percent in 2004 to account for more accuracy in airline predictions and navigation.) It's a solid cushion that has stood the industry well—planes rarely have to make unplanned stops for fuel. Many airlines even operate with slightly bigger cushions: US Airways, for example, plans for its flights to have sixty minutes of fuel remaining instead of the forty-five minutes the FAA insists on.

Pilots always want as much fuel as possible. You never want to be up in the air wishing for more. There are lots of instances when the fuel burn doesn't go as the dispatcher calculated before takeoff. Headwinds may be stronger than forecasted, for example, or air-traffic controllers may give the plane a longer routing because of traffic congestion. If the skies over Chicago are clogged, it's nice to have the ability to fly up over Canada for a while. But before doing that, pilots have to make sure they have enough fuel to meet all the regulations, including getting to the alternate airport and landing with forty-five minutes of fuel still in the tanks.

Carrying fuel is expensive—a gallon of jet fuel weighs about six pounds, so an extra hour of fuel can result in thousands of additional pounds, and it takes more fuel to fly that extra weight. Airline managers have pressured pilots and dispatchers to minimize extra fuel, sometimes to the detriment of passengers. Flights that end up diverted to other airports because they didn't have enough fuel to circle and wait out a brief storm, for example, end up many hours late, or even canceled, simply to save money.

In June 2004 American's Flight 70 took off from Frankfurt for a ten-hour flight to Dallas, where thunderstorms were forecasted for the flight's expected landing. The captain, whose account of the trip's ordeal was posted on pilot Web sites, said he questioned whether minimum fuel was enough, given the forecast. The dispatcher insisted on the 5 percent fuel reserve and nothing more. "I'm tired of fighting with these *?!! Penny-pinchers, so I figured if we end up diverting, so be it," the captain wrote.

Sure enough, once over the Midwest, air-traffic control gave the American flight a new roundabout route to avoid thunderstorms. When the pilot punched the circuitous path into the Boeing 777's flight computer, the flight crew realized it didn't have enough fuel to accept the new route. Instead, the flight diverted to Chicago, where it had to wait after landing nearly three hours for a gate, according to the captain's account. The crew reached time limits on its work day and couldn't fly. American didn't have another crew to fly the plane to Dallas. The flight was canceled, and passengers scrambled for other ways to get home.

The cost to American of hotel rooms for the crew of Flight 70 (the unfortunate passengers were probably on their own for hotel rooms, since American claimed weather caused the problem), extra flying time to get the plane to Dallas, and passenger rebookings, among other issues, surely, the captain argued, far outweighed the cost of flying extra fuel across the Atlantic Ocean. All that could have been avoided with an estimated $400 in extra fuel burned for carrying the seven thousand pounds needed to meet the 10 percent reserve for the flight.

American officials argued the plane wouldn't have reached Dallas regardless of fuel reserves because of the weather, and Chicago was a good place for the wide-body jet, where passengers could clear customs and immigration. American and other airlines say tighter fuel loading hasn't added to the number of diversions experienced by travelers. In general, flight statistics back them up. But there surely have been flights that could have gotten to their destinations had they carried more fuel.

Dispatchers file a flight plan electronically with the FAA for each flight and hope it gets approved. On some routes, the FAA has designated preferred flight paths—it wants all jets flying between New York and Atlanta on the same path, for example. Airplanes don't fly the shortest route between two cities—that's one of the major inefficiencies in the system, and why it takes longer and longer to get from one city to another.

POWER HOPSCOTCH

Jets still fly along designated highways in the sky—a grid laid out, named, and numbered. The nation's airways evolved from air-traffic routes established in the 1920s when the government was developing airmail service. Pilots followed established ground routes, generally flying low enough to trace actual roads and spot one geographic landmark, then another. In 1926, the Air Commerce Act authorized the government to build a network of other navigational aids, beginning with bonfires later replaced by illuminated towers and, eventually, radio beacons and radar.

The radio beacons broadcast on a set frequency, and planes tune into that frequency just as you or I would call up a radio station on a digital radio. Navigation equipment on an airplane can tell pilots where they are in relation to the beacon, and what direction to fly to reach it. Draw a line between two beacons and you have a stretch of airborne road. Connect the path to more beacons and you have a highway in the sky. The highways are eight miles wide because of the inaccuracies of both radar and the radio beacons. Satellite-based technology would be far more accurate for both, which would enable the FAA to create more highways in the congested Northeast, where there's not much room to maneuver before you hit another highway's boundaries. Satellite technology would also allow planes to fly closer together, getting more throughput out of the airspace, and it would allow much more direct courses than the zigs and zags of passing from one beacon to the next. Planes today have the capability to do that, and sometimes you'll hear your captain say they asked for a "short cut" or if you listen in on radio broadcasts such as United's popular "Channel 9" air-traffic communications feed you'll hear pilots ask air-traffic controllers for permission to go "direct" to a fix. In each case, they are trying to cut a corner off a jagged flight path to save time and fuel. A plane in Seattle could fly the shortest path to Miami—that's what the GPS does in the single-engine Cessna. But air-traffic controllers don't have the technology to keep up with that—a spaghetti mix of jets flying where they want. Someday, FAA computers will have the predictive power to clear a flight directly to its destination, checking for any conflicts along the path. Today's air-traffic control technology—much the same as what was in use forty years ago—needs planes to stick to those highways so it can keep them safely separated.

Each major airport is laid out with similar specificity. Think of the airspace around your home airport as a giant square—a cube, really—as that's how the FAA maps it out. Each corner of the square has a navigation beacon, and most of the time all jets entering the area have to fly over one of those corner posts. Planes come in over the corners, but jets that have just taken off fly out of the area through the sides of the box. That's a quick way of keeping the departures out of the way of the arrivals, and vice versa.

POWER FIXES

All of these serious navigation routes and points often get silly names. Nations label their navigation fixes with names so pilots and controllers can easily communicate about them over the radio. Names of fixes—a particular point in the sky placed on maps—are drawn up with five-letter identifiers, and the FAA has had lots of fun naming points in the sky. Making them more memorable enhances safety, the FAA figures, and lessens the chance for confusion.

To arrive in Nashville, for example, planes pass over PICKN and GRNIN and then HEHAW. Airplanes approaching Newark International Airport in New Jersey toward the northeast will cross either HOWYA or DOOIN. Louisiana has RYTHM, Kentucky has BRBON, and Massachusetts has BOSOX. Kansas City has SPICY, BARBQ, and RIBBS. To pilots, Montpelier, Vermont, is known for its HAMMM, BURGR, and FRYYS. Andrews Air Force Base near Washington has a Republican bent these days, with an approach from the south that goes from FORRD to RREGN and one from the north that moves from DUBYA to BUUSH. And if you fly the approach to Runway 16 in Portsmouth, New Hampshire, you might think you're in a Sylvester and Tweety Bird cartoon. The route takes you from ITAWT to ITAWA to PUDYE to TTATT. If a pilot can't land, he is told to hold by way of IDEED. ("I thought I saw a pussycat. . . . I did!")

Some are of questionable taste. On one of the arrival routings to Cincinnati, pilots are likely to be instructed to "cross DRESR at eighteen thousand feet." The FAA also allowed BUXOM, which is in Oregon, and JUGGS, which is in Idaho. Sports themes are popular. In Phoenix, one arrival route to the airport moves from SLAMN to DUNKK to BBALL to SUNSS to HOOPS. Football-crazed Houston has an arrival with the following fixes: GOALL, PPUNT, DRPPD, FTBAL, COACH, QTRBK, TAKKL, RECVR, FMBLE, and, seven miles west of Hobby Airport, TCHDN. So are celebrities. When actor and pilot Kurt Russell approaches Brackett Field near La Verne, California, he passes GOLDI and HAWNN, which honor his longtime partner.

Once a flight plan is filed, the FAA's "Traffic Management Unit" tries to figure out if that will work. Computers predict how many planes will be in a specific area at a specific time—will one controller in Cleveland or New York or Atlanta be particularly overloaded at a certain hour if too many flight plans are approved for the same paths? Expected arrival times are also calculated—what time will the plane pass over the corner post, and is that the same time as another jet whose flight plan has already been approved? If there is a conflict, a plane might be given a later takeoff time than it wants. "Wheels up" at fifteen past the hour— so planes sit at the end of a runway waiting for clearance.

Of course, if the traffic managers aren't managing well, then the system can bog down. One summer, airlines complained that the FAA's Cleveland air-traffic center, which manages a vital chunk of airspace that's a gateway into and out of the Northeast, wasn't handling its volume. Controllers insisted that planes be spread out sixty miles one behind the other on some days (five miles is the required minimum). Sometimes routes were shut down based on just the *forecast* of bad weather, resulting in massive delays. After I wrote about the issue, an air-traffic controller in Cleveland called me up irate that I had identified Cleveland Center as the problem. "The problem isn't Cleveland Center. The problem is the Traffic Management Unit. They won't let anybody through—they are being way too conservative," he said.

"And where is the Traffic Management Unit?" I asked.

"UPSTAIRS!"

When problems develop, or traffic just gets heavy, the FAA's command center tries to coordinate action across the country. It issues "Ground Delay" programs to slow down takeoffs for clogged airports. High winds or low visibility that force controllers to spread out landings and takeoffs often trigger ground-delay programs—all takeoffs for La Guardia may be delayed an hour, for example, and if the airport doesn't catch up, the delays compound and get longer and longer as the day goes on. A more severe hammer in the FAA toolbox is a "Ground Stop" program: Nobody takes off for a certain airport (unless you somehow are considered a VIP). You can check for ground-delay and ground-stop programs on the FAA's Web site for travelers, www.fly.faa.gov. It has lots of useful information, including a map on the opening screen that shows any trouble spots impacting travel.

After several years of poorly coordinated operations, which resulted in more delays for travelers, the FAA has made a major effort to communicate with its "customers"— airlines—a lot better. The FAA command center hosts a conference call with any airline that wants to dial in every two hours. Airlines and the FAA discuss weather forecasts— one airline says its meteorology service says the storms near O'Hare won't materialize while others think they will fire at 5 P.M., and the FAA is planning for the storms to arrive at 2 P.M. The difference: If the FAA goes with the 2 P.M. forecast, it may start delaying flights across the country far earlier than if it plans on 5 P.M. storms. And if the storms never materialize, people get delayed when there is no bad weather. The alternative may be worse—launch all flights and then have storms arrive. Scores of planes will be circling for long periods if they have enough fuel, or scattered at airports across the Midwest and unable to get to Chicago. Taking all the different forecasts into account, the FAA tries to come up with a "collaborative" decision-making plan—a game plan everyone agrees to play by for that day.

On the conference calls, airlines get to air grievances against the FAA or one another. The FAA now makes tools available to all airlines, for example, that show the expected arrivals over time at busy airports. If it asked for all airlines to thin out their New York arrivals, for example, but one airline doesn't do it, the others will squawk. The conference calls also provide the opportunity to work out alternative plans when certain routes get blocked, such as a storm in Rochester that ended up moving air traffic as far south as Atlanta. The FAA's different regional centers are on the call and can agree or refuse to take additional planes. "We need to move the flow from Florida to the Northeast over Memphis," the FAA command center says, because of storms over the Carolinas. Memphis says it can't do that unless flights from the Los Angeles basin going east are bumped to the north over Chicago and then Cleveland. To make that happen, Chicago and Cleveland ask for changes. You get the picture—after all, it may be your flight from San Francisco to Boston that ended up over Canada because of storms in the Carolinas.

While command center communications between the FAA and the airlines has improved, there are still major problems with communications on the ground that can impact your flight, and problems with some of the rules governing pilots in long delays. In June 2008 Peter Arakelian flew on a US Airways regional carrier from New York back home to Raleigh, North Carolina. The plane left on time then sat in a long line of jets waiting more than two hours to take off from La Guardia. High winds slowed everything down at the airport. Then an afternoon thunderstorm in the New York area messed travel up further. After nearly three hours of sitting, the plane had to get out of line to go get more fuel, a result either of poor planning by the airline or the limited fuel capacity of a fully loaded regional jet, or both. Getting out of line means losing that place in line—a major problem for airlines with the FAA's crude conga line system. After gassing up, Mr. Arakelian's flight again had more than twenty planes ahead of it.

After five hours on the plane, Mr. Arakelian and some others decided they wanted to get off and try again in the morning. The captain refused, saying the flight would again lose its place in line if it returned to a gate. But soon after that, the captain relented and canceled the flight. "Keeping folks on a plane for five and a half hours is just inhumane. It's horrible," said Mr. Arakelian.

POWER NIGHTMARES

This issue arose, of course, after the horrific accounts of both an American Airlines flight stranded in Austin, Texas, for nine hours and a jetBlue Airways flight stuck in New York during an ice storm for ten hours with little services and grotesque conditions on board the plane. Why can't long-delayed flights make a pit stop at a gate, get some food and bathroom service, and resume the long wait if they are trying to take off? The FAA's answer to that question is that airlines have a representative inside the FAA's command center and that person can ask for help on particular flights. That's not a workable solution.

Another problem with long delays: duty-time limits for flight crews. Federal rules give pilots a total work day of sixteen hours, with only eight hours at the controls of an airplane. A pilot can't start a new flight with a scheduled time that would push over eight hours in the cockpit, but the pilot can continue any delayed flight up to the sixteen-hour limit.

The rules discourage pilots from taking planes back to gates. Suppose the pilots have been on duty in the cockpit for a total of six hours so far that day, and they have a two-hour flight ahead of them. They have plenty of time available to finish that flight—up to the sixteen hours limit for their day, but if the flight goes back to the gate, the day technically ends. Pushing back from the gate means a new flight begins. If the pilots already had six hours in the cockpit, they can't end the flight without busting the eight-hour limit. Those pilots can't start a "new" flight—the airline would have to find another crew.

Does that make any sense? Wouldn't the pilots be better rested if they could hang out in the terminal like passengers, maybe get some food and relax? Instead, the FAA is, in a sense, forcing them to stay in the cockpit. The FAA claims the way to avoid that problem is for a stranded flight to return to a gate early and preserve enough of the pilot's eight hours of available flying time to complete the trip once the weather clears. That means losing a flight's place in line and angering passengers who want to get out of town. Frequent travelers are willing to sit for a few hours, but often not six, eight, or ten hours—and who can blame them?

That's how clunky the system is today. As a result, one important tip: When you board a flight that may sit for a long time because of traffic congestion or bad weather, ask the captain as you say hello how much duty time he or she has left that day. That way you'll know if the pilots will "time out" and have to cancel the flight after a few hours, or whether they have plenty of available time and you have a good chance of getting where you want to go. I wouldn't run off a plane if the pilot said something like, "We have to go within the next two hours or we have to cancel," but I might get on my cell phone and try to make a hotel reservation for the night in that city that can be canceled without payment, knowing there is a high probability I may be stuck. Better to get a hotel room before dozens of other passengers are scrambling. You can also warn spouses, clients, or whomever else that you may have trouble getting out of town.

One burning question confronting airlines is whether more weather detection technology has increased delays. Did planes used to fly through more bad weather in the past than pilots are willing to do today? On older radar screens, air-traffic controllers never saw storms—many had local TV weather on in radar rooms to see if bad weather was developing. Today, controllers can paint storms on their screens. That's a tremendous advantage for controllers and pilots. It also means that air routes may shut down more often. The same can be said for better on-board weather radar. Are pilots more cautious about flying through bad weather? Or is the system today so inflexible that pilots can't get the freedom to pick their way through a cluster of storm clouds as they might have in the past?

Pilots along with airline and FAA executives are divided on the issue, and there's been no serious study about it. Some technology improvements have improved safety, and added to delays. Airport ramp areas, the tarmac area around gates, must be shut down when lightning is in the area. That's for the safety of workers. But better lightning detection gear means ramp areas get shut down more often, leading to more travel delays. The technology has improved safety, but there is a consequence.

POWER DELAY PROGRAMS

More aggressive management of the nation's air traffic system has undoubtedly improved safety as well, but there can be a consequence in more delays. Ground-delay and ground-stop programs are examples—the tight management of traffic flow lessons dangerous situations like lots of planes circling over the same spot on the ground, but it also can increase delays. On those conference calls, the FAA sets arrival limits at airports and expects airlines to cut their schedules accordingly. If Chicago's O'Hare can normally take eighty arrivals an hour during afternoon hours, but needs to reduce that to fifty an hour, airlines adjust. They may cancel some flights, delay some others, and if there are high-priority flights that *need* to get to O'Hare, they can make trades in position in the landing queue. Arriving international flights often get priority from controllers—they've been in the air a long time and don't want to get into fuel-shortage issues or other problems. It's not always first come, first serve in the airplane business.

Some trades are made for reasons that have little to do with aviation. If American has one flight scheduled to land at 2 P.M., and another scheduled to land at 3 P.M., the FAA does allow the airline to trade landing times for its jets, as long as they can get to where they need to be at the right time. Airlines do that kind of swapping for flights carrying VIPs. Many track U.S. senators on board, for example, or corporate bigwigs, and tag those flights as high priority. You don't want the senator to be delayed and angry about your service, especially if it's someone who gets a vote on airline funding issues.

Among the VIPs that Continental Airlines used to track were GB1, GB2, GB3, and GB4. I was in the Continental operations center one day when all four GBs were flying. GB1 was the operations center code for Gordon Bethune, the chairman and chief executive of the airline at the time. GB2 was Greg Brenneman, the number two executive at Continental at the time. GB3 was George H. W. Bush, the former president, who lived in Houston and flew the home-town airline, since he didn't have the services of Air Force One after leaving office. And GB4 was George W. Bush, his son who was governor of Texas at the time.

Flight swapping isn't only for VIPs. Airlines often make some flights a priority if they have loads of connecting passengers—a flight feeding a departure bank of international flights that the airline doesn't want to delay for the connecting customers and their luggage, for example. Or if a plane happens to be transporting a pilot needed for a departing high-dollar flight, the plane may get priority. Consider the cost of delaying a jumbo jet, and it is easy to see why an airline would be willing to delay other customers to get that pilot in ASAP. If an airline can't trade flights around, it can always beg for help from the FAA. The industry even staffs a desk inside the FAA command center where airlines can call and ask their representative to go around the room and plead their case. I've seen jetBlue call begging for help with a flight from the West Coast circling near Boston and about to run short on fuel, forcing it to divert to its alternate destination. Couldn't they get a break and get clearance for Boston? Yes, indeed. Corporate jets have their own staffer inside the command center, too, through the National Business Aviation Association. That's how the Rolling Stones and many others get priority for their flights.

Next time you find yourself on a flight with a VIP (it happens all the time, especially if you fly in to or out of New York or Los Angeles), see if you get clearance to take off without ever tapping the brakes and land in what seems like record timing.

POWER MODERNIZATION?

What's remarkable is that at any given moment, more than five thousand jets are airborne over the United States, and many others crossing oceans, and it's all done with extreme safety. Yet everyone involved in air-traffic management admits that it could be a lot better—faster, more efficient, and even safer still. Modernizing the air-traffic control system is a national necessity, vital to the economy, crucial if airlines are going to have any chance for long-term financial success. Upgrading the FAA should be a huge national priority—it saves fuel and money, helps the environment, makes Americans more productive, and promotes travel and tourism.

Yet the effort to modernize has been a disaster over the years. In 1981 the agency launched what was to have been a ten-year, $12 billion program aimed at improving its domestic air traffic management. The program tripled in cost, and some of its biggest projects were plagued by technical setbacks. As a result, the FAA had to postpone, at least until 2002, the deployment of a key satellite-based navigation system that was supposed to be in place by 1998. It's still postponed. Now the FAA talks about a "Next Generation" system by 2025. Projects have run far over budget and way behind schedule. Some have ended up complete failures. Other nations have been able to produce excellent systems far faster than the United States, even though the need and the finances are greater here.

In 1995, the FAA awarded a $140 million contract to Hughes Aircraft Co., since acquired by Raytheon Co., to develop a satellite-based system for tracking flights across oceans. There's no radar coverage out over oceans, so airliners fly a designated track and radio in their position every ten minutes or so. Controllers space planes out by a hundred miles because they can't see them. And in the United States, flights across the Pacific were tracked in Oakland, California, for many, many years by controllers with little plastic toys they called "shrimp boats." Each little toy represented a plane and controllers pushed them along a Plexiglas table map of the Pacific as they radioed in their position.

The contract was for a satellite-based system that could track flights even more accurately than radar. Airlines would install equipment on board jets to broadcast their position to controllers over satellite links. Computers would take that data and present it on a controller's screen—presto, you have radar, even when you don't have radar coverage. Instead of scratching high-frequency radio channels, pilots and controllers could communicate by text message. And because the system would be so accurate, separation standards between planes could be reduced, creating more capacity in the skies. Airlines could tailor routes to each day's wind conditions and shave thirty minutes on average off a fourteen-hour trans-Pacific flight, a huge fuel savings.

The Hughes contract flopped—the FAA pulled the plug in the late 1990s after three years of cost overruns and repeated technical failures. Raytheon, which has developed successful systems for Canada, said the FAA kept altering its goals and specifications. For example, the agency decided a year into the program that predicting conflicts between flights should be the top priority, even though conflict-prediction technology wasn't included in the original contract. The program's failure infuriated the airlines, which had spent more than $1 million per plane to upgrade their cockpits to handle the new satellite-based technology.

The FAA concedes it has mismanaged many of its past modernization efforts (but says it is on track now). So far, the United States has spent more than $50 billion trying to modernize its air-traffic control system and has only modest, mostly routine upgrades to show for it. In the meantime, Australia has developed its own oceanic system, as has New Zealand. Australia, with a privatized air-traffic services provider, had great need, since much of the nation was without any sort of radar coverage, and it vitally depends on trans-oceanic flights. The same could be said for New Zealand, which gave the project to a group of about twelve engineers and computer scientists at the University of Christchurch. Australia and New Zealand both reduced their separation standards over oceans to sixty horizontal miles, while the United States insists on keeping them a hundred miles apart. Canada, too, had come up with its own and was controlling transatlantic flights with an advanced system. They all produced remarkable systems—so good that when the United States had to rebid for an oceanic system, the winning contractor, Lockheed Martin Corp., had partnered up with New Zealand to employ its technology. Only now is an advanced oceanic system coming online in the United States—the shrimp boats lived long lives in Oakland. And any hope for such an advanced system for the continental United States remains years, if not decades, away.

Every day, travelers pay the price.

CHAPTER 14

The Best Perks

Travel is best when you have the personal space you need and comfort you desire; when you don't have to stand in long lines or fight through colossal crowds; when you get attentive service, along with correct answers, accurate information, and helpful suggestions, and when you travel on your own schedule rather than someone else's.

You can get all of that, but more times than not, it will cost you. You can get outstanding service and comfort riding first-class on international airlines. You can skip past lines and have your own valet and find yourself whisked away once you reach your destination. This chapter will show you the best of the best.

The place to start is with private jet service. There's a reason why people pay hundreds of thousands of dollars for a piece of a private jet—because there's no other travel experience like it. You arrange the departure time when it is convenient for you. You drive, or you are driven, to the airport—often an uncrowded airport that caters to private planes or an area of a large commercial airport far from the masses—and you spin through a gate out onto the airport ramp area and pull up right next to your plane. You may have a walk of ten feet, perhaps fourteen feet, to reach your airplane. An attendant, or maybe one of the pilots themselves, fetches your bags and stows them for you. You might have parked for free in front of a private terminal where attendants smile and greet you by name. The terminal will likely have clean bathrooms with amenities like mouthwash and cologne on the counter. (Always remember to use the bathroom at those terminals—restrooms are one of the few primitive areas and major drawbacks of private planes.) You might grab a freshly baked chocolate chip cookie before you walk out to the plane. You might notice what is missing: There's no security screening to contend with, in fact no TSA at all. There's no concourse to trudge down, no road warriors to bump into your shoulder, no loudspeakers blaring unintelligible pages and gate changes, no CNN repeating in ten-minute intervals. And if you're thirty minutes early, no matter, you can depart early. If you're forty-five minutes late, that doesn't matter much, either.

On board, you'll find comfy leather seats and couches and well-appointed fixtures. There may be tabletops for working or eating, or seats that fold down into beds. The flight might be catered with fresh seafood and champagne. You can face colleagues and brainstorm, or use your on board Internet connection to stay in touch. Stretch your legs and look around—where's the middle seat? There's no such thing! And then marvel as you take off within minutes of firing up the engine and set a course for your destination, avoiding much of the congestion that befalls airliners on the ground and in the air. You may also be able to land at a small airport closer to your destination—fly right into the town where the plant or factory is, or the golf resort or family cabin.

As expensive as it is, private jet travel is a monumental leap in comfort over commercial airline travel and a time-saver as well. That's why wealthy people and deep-pocketed companies pay the steep price. A study by the Stanford Transportation Group LLC, a consulting firm, found that for every hundred first-class-type passengers carried by airlines there were forty-one passengers flying in private jets. Premium passengers at airlines—those that pay for the privilege, at least—have stalled and even declined, while private jet travel has surged. Economic woes may temporarily slow that down, but unless airline service improves tremendously, there remains a huge diversion of the best customers out there away from the airlines.

POWER JETTING

There are ways for you to take advantage of private jets from time to time without buying into a major financial commitment. You can make private jets work for you for a trip or two, and it might even be more economical than buying a bunch of expensive tickets for your family or colleagues.

In years past, chartering an airplane and crew was a complicated, potentially risky affair—you had to find a local operator, negotiate a price, and hope that the plane was in good shape and the pilots, too. It was daunting, and many people didn't take the plunge. Then fractional ownership, in which companies sell a share of an airplane, came along and made it much easier to charter a jet. Companies like NetJets and FlexJet opened up the private jet world by making planes easier to buy and schedule—you got one-stop shopping at a reputable, national firm that took care of hiring and training crews, maintaining airplanes, and making sure everything was on time and safe. But when fractional programs proved too expensive for many—hundreds of thousands of dollars per year—and fractional companies realized they had lots of expensive planes that could fly more often, jet-card programs came along. Jet cards let you buy as few as ten hours of flying for about $44,000 at 2008 prices, plus fuel adjustment charges. A larger pool of travelers could afford that, and snapped up cards.

Now charter brokers are bringing the cost down even more by making it simpler to hire planes for single trips, called "on-demand" charters, on a pay-as-you-go basis—no buying into an airplane or prebuying hours of flying time. Several firms have simplified the process by collecting bids from charter companies for interested fliers and making arrangements, from car service to on board catering.

A one-time charter is still more expensive than first-class airline tickets. But it can be affordable to many people without CEO salaries or trust funds who might want to splurge once or twice a year on a special trip. A typical New York-to-Florida one-way flight costs $8,000 to $20,000 for a six-passenger jet, depending on whether the plane goes home empty or not. If the charter company doesn't find another customer for the flight home, you pay for that trip, too.

XOJet offers one-trip on-demand charters as well as programs for people who fly more than a hundred hours a year in private jets. Virgin Charter has brought the backing of British entrepreneur Richard Branson into the private jet world. Virgin Charter selects operators from around the country to be part of its network. When you call up looking for a plane from New York to West Palm Beach, the company does the searching, pricing, and negotiating for you. You get some comfort from having a known brand name vetting the airplanes and even the pilots. OneSky

Jets, based in Manchester, New Hampshire, is a similar company setting up on-demand charters. OneSky has its own command center to track flights and make customer arrangements. You can pay about $12,000 to $13,000 for a three- to four-hour flight. Take some friends along and the cost per passenger gets a bit more reasonable.

Air Partner PLC, a U.K.-based company that flies the White House press corps and is the largest air charter broker in the world, says it is seeing more clients come from ownership programs into one-time charters. "The savings can be huge," says David McCown, Air Partner's vice president of business development.

Chad Monroe, a Tampa, Florida, shopping center developer, took seven friends to New York in 2007 for a surprise weekend getaway, chartering an eight-passenger plane through Air Partner for $20,000 round-trip. He brought a boom box and Cristal champagne on board for the flight, and the group had so much fun he surprised them with a trip to the Bahamas in June on another private plane. "It's a lot of money for what you're getting, but it's great fun for special trips here and there," says Mr. Monroe.

With many brokers and more than a thousand jet operators in the fragmented field, a company called JetDirect Aviation Holdings LLC has been trying to form a national charter company by buying up local jet operators. It also merged in 2007 with Sentient Jet Inc., a membership program that offers fixed rates on charters but requires a $100,000 initial deposit. Delta Air Elite, a unit of Delta Air Lines Inc., also offers both a card option and one-time charter.

One way to lower the cost of private jets is to try to snag "empty leg" trips—repositioning flights that take passengers at discounted rates. Brokers post them on their Web sites. OneSky Jets has an e-mail alert service that can zap messages to you when empty leg flights become available. Lots of other Web sites offer empty leg postings, such as Jets.com. In general, most operators with empty legs post them in several places and the Web sites search aggressively, so using one should find all potential prospects. Shaircraft Solutions LLC, a firm that advises clients on the best way to charter for a particular trip, also offers its members, who pay $495 a year, a ride-share board so they can take advantage of empty seats on one another's flights.

Empty legs are a crapshoot, and I haven't seen too much success chasing that golden seat. In theory, they'd be most readily available on busy jet routes—to Aspen or the Bahamas, for example. And yet most operators can pick up a return charter from busy destinations like that. For out-of-the-way destinations, you have to be lucky to find a plane flying empty from Fargo to Hartford. Rarely do the planets line up, and to make it work you have to give up a lot of the flexibility that is the attraction of private jet travel in the first place. If you may have to wait two days for the empty-leg trip, you should just ride the airlines.

POWER SAFETY

With all these companies making it easier and perhaps even cheaper to take a private jet instead of an airline, there is a smart way to protect your own safety. This is important, because there are lots of unsavory operators in the charter airplane business, people who might operate a plane that isn't in proper mechanical order or fly with pilots who aren't currently certified to fly that particular plane. Many crashes result from pilot error. Shortcuts, like failing to have the plane properly de-iced when taking off in a Colorado snowstorm, calculating the weight-and-balance of the plane improperly, or setting the navigation radios wrong and flying the plane into the ground in fog can lead to injuries and fatalities.

The private jet world's two main safety rating agencies are making it possible for consumers to check charter companies and individual pilots to make sure their flight has aviation's equivalent of a Good Housekeeping seal of approval. Whenever you arrange a charter, ask for an ARG/US TripCHEQ or a Wyvern rating. Aviation Research Group/US Inc., or ARG/US, and Wyvern Consulting Ltd., a unit of CharterX Corp., are the two biggest private jet safety firms. They audit charter companies and check out pilots, from conducting criminal background checks to figuring out how many hours of experience each pilot has in the cockpit of a particular type of airplane. Corporations have used ARG/US and Wyvern for many years to make sure that jets chartered for executives were as safe as possible.

Now both companies are making it easier for consumers to get the same safety checks. ARG/US offers a simple "TripCHEQ" that rates a particular flight with a green, yellow, or red light, based on the record of the operator and the experience of the pilots (www.aviationresearch.com). "We see more and more consumers using the system," said Kathy Tyler, director of sales at ARG/US. "They want to make sure the good, the bad, and the ugly are known."

You can buy a TripCHEQ for $250, or ask the broker you use or charter operator you hire to provide it. Of 42,000 charter trips ARG/US checked one recent year, 12 percent failed to meet its standards. In most cases, the pilots failed to meet the firm's strict experience requirements. In order to get a green-light rating, the two pilots must have combined time in that type of airplane of 250 hours, among other criteria.

Wyvern offers a Pilot & Aircraft Safety Survey, or PASS, report (www.wyvernltd.com). A basic membership gets you five PASS reports a month and costs $299. You can specify the safety criteria you want or use Wyvern's recommended standards. Virgin Charter offers PASS to all its customers.

Wyvern audits charter operators and labels them either "Wyvern Recommended" or not. At any given time, only about 10 percent of the 1,200 or 1,300 jet charter operators in the United States are recommended. Separately, each trip can be evaluated as to whether it is "Wyvern Compliant"— that is, it meets Wyvern's standards, regardless of whether the operator is recommended or not. There has never been a fatality on a "Wyvern Compliant" flight, Wyvern says.

POWER TERMINALS

If you have to fly commercial, first-class is by far the best perk going. We've already explored ways to buy your way up to the front of the plane at affordable prices. On board airplanes, airlines don't have a lot of opportunity to differentiate from other competitors, and new ideas are copied easily. The same manufacturers sell seats or in-flight entertainment systems to all airlines; the same kitchens cater different airlines, too. But on the ground, carriers are getting more creative because they can offer something that competing airlines may have a hard time replicating. And as a result many airlines—mostly outside the United States— are taking the ground warfare to new heights, far beyond offering fancy clubs with showers and meeting rooms.

There's a first-class frenzy going on among international airlines, from Middle Eastern carriers installing lavish closed-door suites in the front of planes to Virgin Atlantic's "Clubhouse" at London's Heathrow Airport, with a beauty salon, cinema, and Jacuzzi. British Airways built six lounges for first-class and business-class customers in its giant new Terminal Five at London's Heathrow Airport. One elegant meeting room has leather seats from the last Concorde supersonic jet made into boardroom chairs. The competition is particularly intense in Asia, where carriers have been longtime leaders in first-class luxury. Qantas Airways opened new first-class lounges in Sydney and Melbourne, Australia, with spas, libraries, and chair-side waiter service. Cathay Pacific's Hong Kong first-class lounge, called The Wing, has been voted the best first-class lounge in the world by companies that survey travelers. The lounge includes a noodle bar, library, and a bath facility dubbed "the Cabanas."

Typically these separate ground facilities are offered only to international first-class passengers and the top elite-levels of an airline's frequent-flier program—the big spenders, in other words. What do you get? Elegance, comfort, status, and convenience, complete with your own security screening queue and a car that will drive you across the tarmac out to the door of your airplane.

In Frankfurt, Lufthansa's first-class terminal is a separate facility that doesn't look at all like an airport terminal—think hip boutique hotel instead. With leather seats in the lobby, halogen lighting, cocktail glasses filled with nuts, and jazz playing in the background, there's nary a "Lufthansa" sign visible. On arrival, a valet takes your luggage and parks your car. An attendant greets you, walks you through a private security and immigration check and tells you when it's time to leave. You can enjoy a bubble bath with a rubber ducky or have a smoke in a cigar room. There's a gourmet restaurant with white tablecloths and waiters. And a few minutes before departure, you are driven to your airplane in your choice of a Mercedes or Porsche for boarding up the staircase used by baggage handlers and pilots, bypassing the herds and hordes completely. Lufthansa says about three hundred passengers per day use the terminal, which employs two hundred people. The facility opened in 2005 and Lufthansa says that in its first two years, sales of first-class tickets increased more than 40 percent.

Lufthansa found that the lounge has prompted passengers to arrive twice as early for flights than the airline planned—ninety minutes instead of an anticipated forty-five minutes. Some come hours ahead to enjoy the restaurant and bar with eighty kinds of whiskey. (On New Year's Eve, a couple with first-class tickets came to dine, then canceled their tickets for a full refund and left the airport.) It was so successful that Lufthansa opened a similar first-class terminal in Munich.

Lufthansa's terminal success prompted Air France to come up with its own special facility for first-class customers, which opened in 2007. Air France doesn't have a separate terminal for its "L'Espace Première" service, but it did create a first-class-only door at Charles de Gaulle International Airport (CDG) with a brass hotel cart for baggage and personalized greeting by airline attendants who study passenger lists in advance. One attendant escorts a Première customer through a special first-class security line and takes the passenger to a Première lounge, where a French immigration officer in plainclothes does a passport check. Air France also provides a special telephone number for Première passengers to call if they'll be late to possibly delay the plane's departure.

With flights spread over five different buildings and construction seemingly a constant hassle at CDG, creating a single entrance and lounge for first-class passengers and driving customers to airplanes proved to be a significant time-saving benefit. First-class passengers can arrive only thirty minutes before international flights and still make a flight. The swank service is offered only to first-class passengers. Air France won't upgrade business-class customers into empty first-class seats, either. The airline says if it gives the product away to some customers, why would others buy it?

Virgin Atlantic Airways, known for its posh service, offers its "Upper Class" premium service at business-class prices—about $10,000 round-trip across the Atlantic. With that you get a car service, a seat that folds down into a flat bed, and, until high oil prices forced cost cutting, an in-flight masseuse. In London, Virgin opened a special entrance to its "Clubhouse" in 2007 for its best customers. The airline takes your car information, and your driver can pull right into a secure area at Heathrow, dropping you in a circular drive where attendants greet you. The Clubhouse has a restaurant; TV viewing areas; and bath, shower, and hot tub facilities. There's a giant old wood table covered with newspapers and magazines that once was in Sir Richard Branson's dining room—over that table, legends of rock 'n' roll wrote songs and carried on with the music promoter, who used earnings from his record label to build his Virgin Group Ltd. and launch a host of companies, including his airline. The Clubhouse has gotten a lot of acclaim for its free beauty salon, offering facials, haircuts, massages, and other pampering by appointment. Virgin Atlantic CEO Steve Ridgway likes to tell a story of a London business executive who thanked him for the free haircut he got while waiting for a flight. "The ticket cost $10,000, so the haircut wasn't exactly free," Mr. Ridgway said, chuckling.

POWER SPLURGES

For the rest of us, who don't want to pay $10,000 for a haircut or a flight, there are lots of perks you can nab on the ground. Some of these can have far greater impact on the stress and strain of your trip than the particular seat you get on the airplane.

The first thing worth splurging on is airport valet parking. Not having to make a long walk from the car to the terminal or having to hoist your luggage into a bus and then out again before you even set foot in the terminal can prevent both back pain and perspiration. It can also save you some time and some hassle when you return to the airport dead tired from your trip.

Airports are increasingly offering affordable valet parking options. At Los Angeles International Airport, for example, you can use valet parking for thirty-eight dollars. only eight dollars more than the airport's regular daily parking rate. And you might just feel like a Hollywood star pulling up to the curb and dropping your keys with a valet. (Watch out for paparazzi—they stake out LAX looking for celebrities.) At Dallas–Fort Worth International Airport, valet parking at the terminal is twenty-two dollars a day; regular parking at the terminal is seventeen dollars a day (of course, remote parking is cheaper). Your car is parked in a covered secure lot, and it will be driven up to the curb and waiting for you upon your return. You can arrange for a car wash, oil change, dent repair, or other services while you're away. In Pittsburgh, a car wash is fifteen dollars, and new wiper blades can be installed for thirty dollars.

An even better perk is to hire a car service, either to get you from home to the airport or to pick you up at your destination. A black car service is certainly pricier than a taxi in almost any city—having a sedan waiting for you probably costs at least double or triple the local cab fare. But it can be more convenient, certainly more comfortable, and maybe even more secure. There's nothing worse than standing in a long cab line at an airport late on a bitterly cold night, or wondering if you are going to survive the wild ride with a lead-footed cabbie and a car that hasn't had shock absorbers replaced in years.

Most car services are locally based, so you can find offerings by doing a quick search on the Internet. A few sites, including bookalimoUSA.com, limos.com, limolinkexchange .com, and USLimoDirectory.com, offer listings for various cities. Book A Limo offers rates on its site—a sedan from New York's La Guardia Airport runs about $82, including tolls and tips, and Kennedy Airport runs about $111, also with tips and tolls included. That's about double what cabs cost. On USLimoDirectory.com you can request quotes— you have to give them your contact information, however, to get quotes. A few companies offer multicity coverage, such as Carey International Inc., which has a worldwide network of cars available and claims to be the first limousine company in the world, and the first with a global franchise network. EmpireCLS is another major black car and limo provider, formed by the merger of a New York-area company (Empire) with a Los Angeles-based car service (CLS). The merged company has offices in five U.S. cities and relationships with car services that cover 650 cities.

POWER TRICKS

For celebrities and VIPs, airlines have special staffs of experienced handlers who can pulls strings and tricks and whisk the rich and famous through airports in a jiffy, or sneak them out through a terminal back door to avoid photographers. Even though many have their own jets these days, many celebrities still rely on airlines for international travel. And some still want to be the focus of the photographers' lenses—a glamorous march through the airport can get them on magazine covers worldwide. Airport and airline officials say gate agents or skycaps who check in celebrities often tip off photographers—and earn a percentage of the revenue a photo generates.

To shield celebrities, airlines have special rooms, some hidden behind unmarked doors adjacent to gates and some private lounges inside airport clubs, reserved for politicians, movie stars, sports heroes, and other dignitaries. At some key airports, American Airlines has motorized privacy carts to ferry VIPs to gates with fringe hanging down from the roof that obscures the faces of the VIPs. Airlines allow celebrities to order special meals—and some travel internationally with their own chef, who is allowed to cook in airplane galleys. Stars get private phone numbers to airline officials for help with bookings. Carriers sometimes even send employees to stand in long lines at immigration and border security checkpoints if agencies won't grant special status for traveling stars.

In general, if you have to ask for it, you probably don't qualify for special treatment. But even if you haven't won an Oscar, you can purchase a bit of special coddling for yourself for as little as $100.

American has special concierge handling called "Five Star" service available at LAX and New York's Kennedy International Airport where an airline representative meets you, shuttles you through check-in and security screening, and on to a gate or into an airport club. The airline sets up the service for movie studio VIPs, and American doesn't advertise the service. You won't find mention of it on the airline's Web site, but it is available to anyone in the know. (Psst. The phone number is 877–578–2702.)

Private firms offer similar services to the public as well as the rich and famous. Airport Assistance Worldwide (888–444–4919 or www.airportassistance.com) is based in Los Angeles but lists the more than 140 airports where it has agents available worldwide. Basic service can be arranged for as little as ninety-five dollars, plus tips. The agents will meet clients at the curb and help them get to a lounge or gate, carry bags, watch children while you make a pit stop or whatever else you need them to do. Often they have greased the wheels a bit with airlines—good concierges know airline agents and will be ready with boarding passes, baggage tags, and anything else needed for the trip. Using the service allows you to bypass any check-in lines, and perhaps even bypass security lines. The concierge may just look official or be pushy, moving clients to the front of lines without any conscience just by appearing authorized to do it. Private services said they can't guarantee clients will be able to bypass lines—that's up to TSA officials and airline workers. "Our reps are pretty aggressive when they need to be," said Michelle Kohler of Airport Assistance.

One offbeat suggestion: Try giving those kinds of services as an unusual, memorable gift to someone in need. A group of Los Angeles mothers started giving one another certificates for airport service for fun—the escort can be a huge help when traveling with infants, if only because you get an extra set of hands at the airport.

POWER CLUBS

Once you're inside the airport, you can buy yourself a day pass to the luxury and convenience of an airline club. Carriers have clubs at their major airports and hubs. You can find a quiet cubicle for work or phone calls, relax and watch television in a nice leather chair, saddle up to a bar, or even make use of meeting rooms and shower facilities at most airports. Annual memberships cost anywhere from $300 to $500 a year or so (elite-level frequent fliers sometimes get discounts). That may make sense for road warriors who spend lots of time at airports, or frequent overnight fliers who need a club for a shower and shave after landing. "It's worth every penny to me," Bill Salvin of Phoenix said of his Admirals Club membership at American Airlines. "The peace and quiet is a huge benefit, especially if you're stranded."

Continental Airlines says selling memberships to its Presidents Clubs is the most valuable perk it offers frequent fliers. Membership is $400 a year (cheaper if you have elite-level frequent-flier status with Continental). Credit cards can get you memberships as well. The American Express Co. Platinum card comes with airport club access at participating clubs run by American, Delta, Continental, and Northwest airlines. Continental's Presidential Plus Card from MasterCard gives you club membership for a $375 annual fee, plus elite-level frequent-flier status on Continental, double frequent-flier miles on travel spending, and elite status at both Hyatt and Avis.

Most airlines will also sell day passes to their clubs for twenty-five to fifty dollars a day (international arrival clubs may be more). Those clubs can be quite handy for rebooking or getting upgrades—the front desks at clubs are staffed by the most experienced, highest rated customer service agents, so they are whizzes at finding you seats or flight options. Day passes can even be a clever way to avoid a long line at an airport lobby—buy a day pass at a kiosk, go through security, and walk right up to an agent inside the club for much faster service. It can be a small price to pay if it means the difference between getting home that night or scrounging for a hotel room on your own.

POWER DRIVES

One splurge favored by many travelers is the rental-car upgrade. Live a little! If you're in California, get the convertible, or the Prius. Why not cruise around Boston in a well-appointed Volvo, or race around Phoenix in that Infiniti G35? Hertz, for one, sometimes puts its "Prestige Collection" on sale. But even without sales, you can often score a substantial upgrade for about $50 more per day on your rental. Here's one choice offered for a summer weekend rental in Miami: a Ford Focus for $57.49 per day or a Ford Mustang convertible for $82.49 per day (and the Mustang includes Sirius satellite radio). Wouldn't the twists and turns and breathtaking beauty of the road to Hana be a lot more fun if you rented an open-air Jeep Wrangler at the Maui airport for $95.49 a day instead of a Toyota Camry for $64.49 a day? Hertz rents an Infiniti G35 in San Francisco for $107.99 a day, compared to $57.50 for a Chevrolet Impala. In Los Angeles, would you rather be driving around in a $73.99 per day Hyundai Accent, or a $119.99 per day Ford Shelby GTH Mustang convertible?

As with airlines and hotels, elite status at a car-rental company can get you free upgrades. At many car rental companies, gold cards are free to frequent renters or employees of companies with corporate contracts. Renting cars equipped with GPS may be the most useful upgrade of all. GPS systems can keep you from getting lost, save time racing between appointments without fumbling around with maps, or find the nearest In-N-Out Burger. Priceless.

And if you want a fine meal in your coach seat, check your hotel before you leave and see if they pack box lunches or meals to go for travelers. High-end hotels often send you on your way with fancy meals, and that poached-salmon dinner for sixteen or twenty dollars may be far more appetizing when you're up in the air than whatever you could forage at the airport, or the beef jerky snacks that airlines sell.

We often get wrapped up in the expense of travel, in opening the wallet at every turn and spending far more than we are accustomed to paying for food and services at home. But travel is an adventure, and I often think people could enjoy it a lot more if they didn't worry about being frugal *all* the time. Sure, you have to watch money when you travel, but you can make the trip far more enjoyable if you spend a bit more in wise ways. Treat yourself—there are ways to get the star treatment without paying outrageous prices.

Hotel Secrets and Strategies

With hotels, forget everything you just learned about airlines. Hotels are the exact opposite in every aspect, from buying to upgrading to enjoying. The hotel world is what airlines would like to be, an industry where consumers don't view every competitor's product as the same, where people will pay for something nicer, and where profits can be earned on a consistent basis. Paying more gets you a nicer room, unlike radically different airfares, which buy the same service regardless.

Different hotel brands can still command different room rates. You're not likely to find a Ritz-Carlton selling rooms at Motel 6 prices because hotels work harder at maintaining an image and sticking to their prices, even if it means vacant rooms. Unlike airlines, hotels have been able to segment customers by having different brands under the same umbrella. Starwood Hotels & Resorts Worldwide Inc. has upscale brands like Westin and W, midrange brands like Sheraton, and more budget-oriented brands like Four Points. Marriott Hotels and Resorts has everything from Ritz-Carlton to Springhill Suites and Fairfield Inn. Airlines couldn't sustain separate brands—United tried with "Ted," Delta with "Song," and US Airways with "Metrojet"—because in the end, the service was the same and customers were only confused, not segmented. Hotels have even been able to brand things as basic as beds: Westin's "Heavenly Bed" campaign has proven to be a major marketing success.

Hotels also do a better job than airlines in keeping track of customer information. (Airlines hope to get to the point where check-in clerks and kiosks know a good bit about you and respond personally. If you take a ski trip every Christmas, Continental Airlines says it can figure that out and send you an e-mail next year in the fall with ideas and fares for winter skiing destinations. But generally, they aren't skilled at using it to market to us yet.) When you check into a hotel, however, the desk clerk may well have all kinds of information about you. At Millennium Hotels and Resorts, for example, members of the company's frequent-stay program are tracked on all kinds of preferences, Chief Executive John Arnett says. If you ask for a feather pillow at one Millennium Hotel, the request goes in your file and other hotels on future visits will provide feather pillows for you. If you request delivery of *The Wall Street Journal* in the morning, you should get it in the future as well. If you mention to a hotel employee that you and your spouse are celebrating your wedding anniversary, you may end up with an e-mail in about eleven months offering some ideas for special anniversary trips. Most major hotels are marketing to customers this way.

Everyone should sign up for frequent-stay programs, even if you are hell-bent on collecting airline miles and can't be bothered with hotel programs. It's through those programs that hotels offer special deals they wouldn't dare advertise or offer in travel booking systems where competitors could see them. "It's a war. Everyone is trying to hang on to customers, and so we need to understand our customers and take care of them," says Mr. Arnett.

More important, the hotel tracks how often you stay and what you spend. When you check in, a desk clerk can see how good a customer you are. Trying to get upgraded to a suite by boasting about how many times you've stayed at the hotel may only get you a dry smile if you haven't been at the hotel as often as you claim.

POWER GODS

How do you land that suite upgrade? Hotel insiders say you just have to ask—nicely. Airlines have automated the upgrade world to specific algorithms based on how much you spend with the airline, how much you fly, and when you requested the upgrade. At most hotels, desk clerks are still gods, and they have the power to allocate the inventory as they want.

The sophisticated tracking systems alert desk clerks to customers they might want to upgrade. Elite-level members of hotel loyalty programs may be eligible for automatic upgrades. And you can earn elite status without spending a hundred nights a year on the road. Starwood's American Express card, for example, grants Gold Preferred status at Starwood hotels, with free available room upgrades, when you use your card for $30,000 in purchases within a calendar year.

It doesn't end there—hotel upgrades are available to those who ask. Hotel industry experts say that rather than trying to be aggressive about upgrades, hotel employees respond better to indirect, low-key requests. "Gee, I'm so tired. . . . Last time I was here I got to stay in one of your suites and it made my day. . . . Not any chance you might have a suite available is there?" You get the idea.

"Desk clerks like to surprise customers," said Thom Nulty, a longtime travel expert who has worked for airlines and travel agencies and now is senior vice president at the Preferred Hotel Group. A couple of rules do apply. If you are checking in for a long stay, don't expect an upgrade. Hotels don't want to give away suites they might have a chance of selling, and if they give it to you for five nights, they may be throwing away money. The best chances for an upgrade often come when you check in late for short stays—there's little chance the hotel is going to sell the empty suite at that point.

Some travelers believe they can score suites by being finicky, complaining about every little thing in their assigned rooms and hoping an apologetic hotel manager will upgrade them to satisfy them. I've known people who insist that a particular room is too noisy or too cold or too dark; they may even "discover" water spots or sudden malfunctions in order to leverage their way to something nicer. I can't condone or recommend such skullduggery, and remember, hotels track your profile. Too much complaining and you'll find the hotel far less sympathetic in the future—they know all the tricks.

That said, there's no reason to tolerate real problems, especially at pricey hotels. If your room is too close to a noisy elevator or equipped with a weak showerhead, call to get the situation resolved. If there's a problem with the air-conditioning, let them know before you end up sleepless. If you've endured some legitimate problem, the hotel should compensate accordingly. Don't be afraid to ask for more towels or glasses or even lamps. If the hotel is well run, it should respond. If it doesn't, post a review online noting the problem and let the management know you'll take your business elsewhere in the future.

U.S. hotels sell about one billion room nights a year. New construction for hotels has been slow—the supply has increased only about one percent a year for several years. Hotels have gotten a bit fuller each night, and room rates have gone up. On average, hotel room rates increased steadily from 2003 to 2007, climbing from $82.52 a night, on average, to $103.64 per night in 2007. Even as new hotels are built, others are converted to condominiums or offices, keeping down the supply of new rooms. For developers, there was more money to be made constructing new housing or office buildings. That may change as the housing and office markets face economic difficulties—hotels could catch up. Hotel room rates did soften in 2008 with the weak U.S. economy, and many areas that rely on airplanes to fill rooms, such as Hawaii, Las Vegas, and Orlando, resorted to special deals to attract vacationers after airlines cut capacity in response to high fuel prices. Yet even as hotels in many less traveled cities have had to discount prices, others remain high. In Manhattan, $500 rooms became commonplace at Sheratons and Marriotts. Even the two-star budget Comfort Inn in Manhattan is often priced at over $300 a night.

POWER LOCATIONS

In many ways, choosing hotels is a far more important factor in the success and cost of a trip than picking airline flights, and yet we spend far more time fretting about airlines. We fret over $50 in airfare for a week-long trip, spending perhaps $400 with the airline, then book a hotel room that may end up costing three times as much as the airfare. Saving

$10 a night on a hotel room might have bigger impact on the total trip cost than our airline shopping, but we rarely pay such close attention to hotel rates. That's a result of long-standing habits and frustrations—it's a lot easier to buy hotel rooms than airline tickets. And the likelihood of problems is greater with airlines.

That's probably a mistake. A hotel's location and amenities can alter the success of your trip, for business or leisure or both. When was the last time you checked to see if a hotel you booked was near a subway station, or had a good health club, or had good restaurants within walking distance? If you are scheduled to arrive late at night, does the hotel you booked have twenty-four-hour room service, just in case you can't stomach airport food or end up spending eight hours sitting in a plane waiting for takeoff? Did it make sense to book a hotel $20 cheaper if you spend $30 more in cab fare during your trip? The lack of smart shopping can leave you overpaying for a subpar property.

Another major consideration: What kind of hotel do you want? Be honest, because there are all kinds of hotel personalities. Some may look cool but may not really be for you. The latest trend is hip boutique hotels—even the chains are opening boutique hotels. Many offer elegantly appointed rooms, handsome lobbies, bars, and nightclubs, fancy restaurants, and an A-list clientele. That all comes at a high price, of course, and it often comes with a certain attitude. Workers at boutique hotels often prance around in all-black attire with an air that suggests they are just too pretty to be troubled with your stopped-up sink or request for museum directions. Rooms at boutique hotels can be small, and for some people, the whole scene can be hard to navigate. Try the experience and see if you like it, but don't be afraid to stick to bread-and-butter Hiltons if that's where you feel most comfortable.

POWER DEALS

Hotel shopping is actually more complicated than you might think on price, too. Unlike airlines, which generally post the same prices to different ticket-selling outlets, many hotels sell their rooms wholesale to travel suppliers for resale at whatever price they can get. Expedia and other online travel vendors negotiate deals directly with chains and with hotels themselves. For that reason, you're likely to see different prices on the same hotels for the same dates. To take advantage of the deals, you have to shop multiple sites.

I looked for a five-day October stay in Seattle and found fairly consistent pricing on chain hotels. Expedia, Travelocity, and Priceline all offered the Westin Seattle at $250 a night. Expedia and Travelocity also had the same price on the Seattle Marriott Waterfront at $297, and Marriott's Web site had the same price without the service fee that Expedia and Travelocity charge.

On independent hotels, prices varied considerably. Expedia offered the Hotel Monaco at $277 per night, cheaper than Travelocity's price of $326. The Alexis Hotel was $271 at Expedia and $331 per night at Travelocity. And the Hotel Vintage Park was $221 per night at Expedia and 21 percent more at $267 on Travelocity. All three of those are well-rated boutique hotels that are part of the Kimpton Hotel Group—it appears Expedia cut a deal with Kimpton. Travelocity, on the other hand, had cheaper prices than Expedia on several high-quality hotels. The Red Lion on Fifth Avenue was $249 on Travelocity but $289 a night on

Expedia. The Sorrento Hotel was $40 a night cheaper on Travelocity than Expedia's price of $269 per night. A room with two queen beds and free Internet service was $305 on Travelocity but $325 on Expedia. Other services weigh in with their own deals as well. For the Hotel Monaco, for example, Orbitz had a price similar to Expedia's low price; Priceline.com was higher than Travelocity's prices. Ebookers .com was in the middle at $312 per night.

There's no consistency in which site has the best deals. As the online booking industry has consolidated, you will find that more sites have the same prices. Expedia owns Hotels .com, for example, so they share the same inventory. Orbitz owns Cheaptickets.com. You can search multiple sites from one site. A service called IgoUgo.com will send your search criteria to multiple booking sites, triggering as many as a dozen searches. You put in your dates and select which sites you want to search, and IgoUgo saves the time of setting up searches independently at each site. Alternatively, a site like Mobissimo.com will search multiple hotel bookings sites at once and display different prices on the same properties available at different booking sites.

Another alternative: Hotwire.com offers unnamed hotels you can pick by star rating and neighborhood. Prices tend to be cheaper—hotels can dump unsold inventory on places like Hotwire and Priceline, and as they are anonymous, they don't wreck their basic rate structures. The risk, however, is that you buy something when you don't really know what you are getting. Plenty of travelers are pleasantly surprised when they get an outstanding deal at an excellent hotel, yet others find disappointment when a hotel doesn't seem up to the star rating it was pitched at, or the definition of a neighborhood seems liberal. In other words, your definition of a "four-star" hotel may not match the booking service's definition, and the hotel may be a lot farther from downtown than you think, or worse, on a shady side of downtown. Like airline consolidators, the hotel consolidators offer savings at a steep price, making them more attractive to "adventurous" travelers.

Another caution: Many hotel bookings now require deposits or even full payment in advance when chasing discounted rates online. Most of the rooms are still refundable if you cancel, but check the cancellation rules. You may have to pay the entire amount in advance by credit card or check to guarantee the booking. One way to avoid that, in many cases, is to see if the hotel's own Web site offers the same price. Hotels rarely require that kind of prepayment directly from customers.

In general, it pays to always check the hotel's Web site anyway. The Web site is the cheapest way for a hotel to process a booking—book directly online and the hotel company doesn't have to pay fees to a booking service or have more reservationists on staff. Hotels offer incentives to drive bookings that way, and almost always the hotel's Web site has whatever the cheapest available rates might be. You'll also find lower rates online than by calling the hotel directly, in most cases. Years back people could call a hotel and sometimes negotiate a good deal over the phone: "I stayed there for $250 last time—can't you give me that rate again?" But these days, the rates available over the phone are typically higher than online, since booking with a real person costs the hotel more.

Some hotels offer special deals on their Web sites that aren't available elsewhere, like rates with free parking, packages that include goodies like champagne and strawberries or couple's massages, free Internet service, free breakfast, or maybe a pass for a day spa. It's also smart to sign up for e-mail alerts from your favorite hotels and chains. Like airlines, hotels zap out offers of special rates or attractive add-ons to regular customers. Most of the offers you'll delete from your in-box, but occasionally a deal will coincide with a time you want to visit.

POWER REVIEWS

Most hotel booking sites offer customer reviews on particular properties. Sometimes you may find hundreds of reviews posted on major properties, and a rating number or ranking becomes more trustworthy. Sometimes you may find only one or two reviews on a hotel, and it's hard to know if the two people who posted something were just malcontents or guests who had the misfortune of staying during a bad week, or perhaps the glowing reviews were posted by the hotel manager or relatives of the night clerk. Fodors.com offer its hotel tips online for free—click on a city and you can see "Fodor's Choice" hotel recommendations. As mentioned in Chapter 4, TripAdvisor.com has an extensive database of reviews—it claims fifteen million reviews and opinions—and the site ranks hotels in a particular city based on those reviews. (A good test: Search hotels or restaurants in your hometown, and see if you agree with the rankings.)

Once you've made a booking, record the cancellation date on your itinerary or calendar—some hotels and booking services have forty-eight-hour policies, or longer, to cancel without penalty instead of the good ol' standard twenty-four hours. And when you get to travel, have the hotel's phone number handy. I think it's a good practice to call the hotel if you are running late and tell the front desk clerks of your expected late arrival. Tell them you're still coming and ask them to make sure not to give away your room if the hotel happens to be overbooked for the night. There are few worse moments in travel than arriving at a hotel in the middle of the night after a torturous airline trip only to be told that the hotel is going to put you in a taxi and send you to another property with a room for you. It's called being "walked," and it stinks. You can minimize your odds by calling to confirm that you'll be there, only late. In addition, when you do call, you might ask if the hotel has a shuttle service that could meet your flight, or even arrange for a car service for you if you are landing in an unfamiliar city in the wee hours of the morning. Instead of dealing with rickety cabs and questionable drivers at 2 A.M., you might appreciate having a black car service meet you with a driver holding a sign with your name on it. A good hotel can arrange that for you at the last minute.

POWER STRANDINGS

If you end up getting stranded at an airport unexpectedly and can't make it to your destination hotel, make sure you call so that your entire reservation isn't canceled. Hotels will have sympathy for those kinds of disruptions from weather or airline problems, and maybe even waive no-show penalties if you miss the first night. The bigger concern for you, however, may be the immediate scramble to find a hotel room while hundreds of other stranded passengers are doing everything they can to avoid sleeping on the floor of an airport terminal. You should have the phone list mentioned in Chapter 7's preparations so you can call while standing in line. It may pay to wait in line for help from the airline. Airlines contract with hotel booking companies for hotel services for their crews and stranded passengers, and they may have better access to rooms. Airlines pay for hotel rooms only if it's their fault that you got stranded. For issues "outside the airline's control," such as weather problems, airlines won't pay to put you up. (Chapter 7 also discussed some insurance options for that situation.) But they can sometimes offer discounts and help you find rooms.

Regardless of who is paying, the companies that book hotels rooms for airlines vacuum up available rooms in hub-airport cities whenever there is a whiff of bad weather or airline operational problems. They call airport hotels and beg and barter for inventory—May I have a hundred rooms? Will you split your last ten rooms with us? Hotels sell them the rooms at discounted bulk rates, but may hold back inventory that they can sell themselves to customers who walk in or call at the last minute with a credit card willing to pay full price. It's on-the-fly yield management, hundreds of rooms being booked and sold within a few minutes, with hotels trying to decide whether to gamble on full-fare customers or take the sure thing of selling rooms to the bookers. And the bookers have to guess accurately how many rooms they will need.

The end result is that you can call a hotel and be told it is sold out, then ten minutes later an airline can hand you information on its hotel booking service, which may offer you a room at that same "sold out" hotel. The booking service controlled the inventory. You may be furious at the airline and frustrated at having to stand in a long line, but that voucher from the airline may be your best bet for a bed and shower.

The important thing to remember with hotels is that most of the industry does care about customer service, and your best bet—always—is to ask. If a room isn't to your liking, you can often be moved, repaired, or even upgraded.

It pays to be a regular customer with a particular hotel, or at least with a particular hotel chain, but there are plenty of times when you'll want to book a hotel with the best location, or the perfect amenities for your trip. If you're on a business trip, don't forget to consider gym facilities or even proximity to golf, swimming, sailing, or any other activity you may enjoy. (Why don't more hotels have bowling alleys or movie theaters for guests, huh?) If you're on vacation, you might want to check for computer access so you can check e-mail without lugging a laptop. There are lots of choices and far better options with hotels than with airlines. If you choose carefully, you can improve your trip.

CHAPTER 16

Cruise Strategies

O ne of the great trends in travel over the past twenty years or so has been the rise in popularity of cruise ships. If you haven't cruised, you should try it. There are cruises for most every type of traveler, from adventurous types to lay-out sun worshippers. A cruise can take you to exotic islands or European capitals, providing a floating hotel at each stop. It can move you through Caribbean hot spots or even complement your stay at Disney World. Some cruises are built around hobbies or sports affiliations, a chance to spend a week with knitters or get up close and personal with football legends. And believe it or not, some ships have gourmet food, excellent live entertainment, and attentive service.

Since 1990, the cruise industry has averaged annual growth of 7.4 percent per year, growing from about 3.8 million passengers worldwide in 1990 to 12.6 million by the end of 2007, according to Cruise Lines International Association, the industry's trade group. About half of all cruises are six to eight days in duration; 30 percent are shorter, at two to five days, and shorter cruises have been growing in popularity.

There are about two dozen different cruise lines, with some offering just a couple of small ships for specialized sailings to giants with megaships. Royal Caribbean and Carnival are the two biggest cruise lines, each with more than twenty ships. The trend has been to add bigger and bigger ships. Royal Caribbean has a ship under construction called "Project Genesis" scheduled to begin sailing in late 2009 with the capacity to carry 6,400 passengers—a whopping 50 percent more than its current largest ship. Genesis will be 1,180 feet long—nearly four football fields, or roughly one quarter mile long (and eighty-eight feet longer than the USS *Ronald Reagan* aircraft carrier). The Genesis ship, as yet unnamed, will be 154 feet wide at water level and 240 feet high—as tall as a twenty-story building. More room gives the cruise line more real estate to play with to offer more games, restaurants, and ways to spend money and have fun.

Enticed? The first thing to do when considering a cruise is to decide which is most important to you: the boat or the ports? For some people, the ship is the focal point of the vacation. Some cruisers may desire a small vessel offering luxurious sailing without thousands of people in backpacks and flip-flops, perhaps exploring Galápagos or Antarctica or the West Indies. Most prefer the eye-popping variety of big boats. For some, a ship with gourmet food options or an elaborate spa and heath club may make an enjoyable vacation. Others want an active boat with cruise directors, entertainers, multiple restaurants, and activities like rock climbing. Some ships have ice-skating rinks, golf driving ranges, water park attractions like surfing wave generators, and lazy rivers for tube floating. The casino may be your thing, or bingo, or musical acts, or just drinking and dining and enjoying the nightlife of a cruise catering to young singles. There are cruises marketed specifically for families with children, young singles, or gay and lesbian travelers. Those people don't particularly care where the boat goes—the fun of the trip will be on the boat. And so selecting the right boat is top priority.

For others, the ship is simply a vehicle. Those people want a cruise through the Mediterranean or Alaska or an itinerary of the best beaches in the Caribbean. They'll still need to select a cruise line and a vessel carefully, but their first consideration will be the ports of call. It's a great way to tour through Europe or other areas—no packing up, fighting crowds at train stations or airports, checking in and out of hotels. You get on the boat, unpack, and let the cruise line move you around. Once those people decide where they want to go, then it's time to pick a ship that gets them there.

POWER BOATING

Here's a rough guide. For families with kids, the Carnival Cruise Line works well and, of course, Disney Cruises. Condé Nast Traveler's annual cruise section also suggests Royal Caribbean's *Freedom of the Seas*, a 3,600-passenger giant that has teen facilities from which parents are banned that have video games, musical instruments, all kinds of activities, and snowball fights.

For foodies, Condé Nast recommends several boats from different lines: Crystal Cruises' *Crystal Symphony*, a medium-size 940-passenger ship with signature chef restaurants; Regent Seven Seas Cruises' *Seven Seas Voyager*, which carries 700 passengers fed by chefs trained at the French culinary institute Le Cordon Bleu; along with two large ships: Holland America's *Eurodam* (which has a culinary arts theater for cooking demonstrations) and Norwegian Cruise Lines' *Norwegian Jade* (twelve restaurants with everything from French to Tex-Mex).

For luxury lovers, consider small ships such as *Seabourn Legend* from Yachts of Seabourn (uniformed stewards wade into the water with trays of caviar and champagne at a beach barbecue). Condé Nast also recommends *SeaDream I* from SeaDream Yacht Club (a staff of ninety-five to care for only fifty-five couples) and *Silver Whisper* from Silversea, which offers professional butlers in its finest suites.

Spa-goers will enjoy Celebrity's *Solstice*, which has a class of cabins built for people who like to check into spas and never leave, with an adults-only lap pool in the solarium, a "Persian Garden" steam bath, and a café with spa cuisine. Costa Cruises' *Costa Serena*, with a 23,000-square-foot spa, Norwegian's *Norwegian Gem*, and Cunard's *Queen Victoria* are other enticing candidates for spa lovers.

Party people should consider *Carnival Freedom*, with nightly parties and karaoke, twenty-two bars, adult comedy shows, and a risqué version of *The Newlywed Game*; *Crystal Serenity*, which is anything but serene at night with top-flight entertainers and a lively casino; or easyCruise's *Easy-Cruise Life*, which pulls into Riviera ports around noon and sets sail early the next morning, allowing all-night onshore club hopping. (easyCruise is no-frills, low-priced cruising from the same Greek entrepreneur who launched easyJet, one of Europe's major discount airlines.)

POWER HEALTH

You can find all kinds of rankings and reviews of ships on the Internet. One of the least obvious but most helpful is the Centers for Disease Control, which posts results of cruise ship inspections on its Web site, www.cdc.gov. You can search for ships you are considering, or even get a list of ships that had "unsatisfactory" scores. The CDC also offers tips for staying healthy on cruises, which basically amount to washing hands frequently because of the danger of viruses spreading quickly, and being careful about what you eat. Commercial sites offer more partisan opinion on different cruises. CruiseCritic.com has extensive ratings of ships, for example, but the ratings are based on reader reviews, and the number of readers who actually review a ship can be small—fewer than thirty on some ships, while others have closer to a hundred reviews. The CruiseCritic site does have lots of tools to help you select a cruise that will likely be well suited to your interests. CruiseMates .com has a forum where you can see what others have said about particular cruises or post questions. If you don't want to trust the advice of anonymous people posting opinions, the services of a good travel agent who specializes in selling cruises can be invaluable, not just in terms of getting a good price or picking the right cruise, but also in securing a desirable cabin, booking good shore excursions, and finding the best airfare to get you to the sailing.

Cruises are one area of travel in particular where it does pay to do as much research as you can, because there are lots of choices to be made, even after you select a ship and itinerary.

POWER CABINS

The most basic choice you face is picking a cabin—whether you want a room opening to the outside of the ship, often with a balcony, or whether you are fine with a cheaper interior room, with no windows or outside views.

To many people, the interior room is just fine because you can save lots of money and you won't spend much time in the room. There's ample opportunity to find a chaise somewhere and lay out if you want to gaze at the ocean or watch land rise up from the horizon as the ship nears port. Interior rooms can be dark at night—no moonlight trickling in through the draperies. Some people find that helpful for sleeping; others find the total darkness unsettling.

A balcony can be a blessing—a private sanctuary where you can sit, read, snooze, or just hold hands with someone and the rest of the world won't go running by. Having a window lets you better control light and even noise, if you like the soft sound of a ship punching through waves on the open sea. Outside rooms tend to be larger on many ships, and they definitely are more expensive. (Personally, I'm a balcony guy. I love having my own spot to read a book on a cruise, or just sit and watch the sunrise. A good solution for families is to get one of each—an inside room for the kids and an outside room across the hallway for the parents.)

Once that decision is made, you need to think about what part of the ship you want to live in—a decision largely dependent on whether you think seasickness may be an issue or not. If motion bothers you, consider a cabin in the middle of the ship, which doesn't have as much up and down as the bow or stern. Many people sensitive to the motion of the ship prefer lower-level midship cabins. (And some people love the motion of a ship—it rocks you to sleep!)

Upper decks generally are considered more desirable by passengers because they are closer to the action—often a walk to restaurants and other attractions instead of riding elevators up and down. Whether you prefer being forward in the ship or toward the stern seems to be a matter of personal taste. Some people like the front of the ship because those cabins are often closer to restaurants and nightclubs; others prefer being aft to be away from loud music at night. It's important to check the layout of the ship when considering cabins, and check what is above and below your cabin, plus the location of elevators, which can be noisy. Having a nightclub on the other side of your cabin ceiling may not be conducive to sleep, for example. (If you seek quiet, get a cabin near the ship's health club, which will likely be empty at night.) Then again, being close to a source of coffee in the morning may be nice.

You can get a discount on your cabin if you buy a "guaranteed rate" at a certain level, but allow the cruise line to assign your specific cabin when you check in. Most people reserve an exact cabin number when they book. But some can gamble—the cruise line guarantees you'll have an outside double above a specified level, for example, but has some leeway in what cabin to assign. When you check in, you may well end up with the least desirable cabin on that deck—probably the one next door to the smoke-filled casino. On the other hand, you may luck out and find yourself upgraded to a suite, or sent to a much nicer stateroom on a higher level than you bought. Your cabin is not something you want to gamble on, but if the room is not that important to you, it may well be worth it to save some money and at the same time have the opportunity to get an upgrade.

In general, cruise pricing is not as frustrating as airline pricing, but it does share some similarities. You can buy from online travel agencies or "brick and mortar" travel agents, or you can buy from the cruise line itself. It depends on whether you want the assistance of someone else—that will likely cost more, though sometimes travel agencies swing discounts from cruise lines that more than compensate. Buying early gives you the best selection and cheapest prices—prices go up as ships fill up. And like airlines, you might be able to swing an upgrade in your cabin—many cruise lines base upgrades on what you paid compared with other passengers. These days, with ships so full, chances of an upgrade to a suite are slim, but it can happen, especially in off-peak seasons or on less traveled routes. It never hurts to ask.

After you've settled on a cruise, a cabin, and a price, check to see what the cruise line can offer in terms of airfare to and from the departure port, and compare that to what you can get on your own. Sometimes cruise lines have group discounts with airlines or even their own chartered flights to get passengers to ships, and buying air service as a package can be cheaper. You should also check what the cruise line charges to bus people from the airport to the dock—sometimes a good deal and sometimes excessive.

One final transportation check: times. Check to see what time you have to arrive for the bus to the dock, for example—it may be quite early. And whatever you book for a flight, assume the flight will be delayed. Since air travel has gotten so unreliable, it makes sense to arrive a day early for a cruise sailing so you don't literally miss the boat and find yourself scrambling for a one-way flight to Cancun or Juneau.

And when all the travel arrangements are in place, consider whether you want to insure this major purchase. As always, check the terms of travel insurance before you buy it. Can you cancel for any reason? What medical issues allow you to cancel? What kind of hurricane protection do you have? What if the boat sails even though a hurricane is brewing, and you just don't want to go? Are you covered? And would you be covered anyway by the cruise line and the airline, which often let customers rebook in the face of serious storms?

POWER EXCURSIONS

Wait, you're not done spending money, even though you're still months away from sailing. If you think airlines lure you on board with below cost fares and then soak customers with fees that raise the true cost of flying, wait until you walk the gangway into a cruise ship. The selling begins before you board, and it doesn't end until you drive away from the dock.

The major expense you'll face will be "shore excursions." Those are fun trips and activities you can prereserve from the cruise line, or venture out and buy on your own. At any given port, you'll be offered beach packages, horseback riding, bicycling, and Jeep adventures, sailing, snorkeling, swimming with dolphins, helicopter rides, cooking and dining tours—you name it. The cruise line arranges a catalog of offerings that, in general, are more expensive than what you can book on your own without paying a commission to the cruise line. Then again, the cruise line offers some quality control.

Prices can be steep. An afternoon snorkel and scuba dive costs $249 per person in Cozumel on Royal Caribbean; a horseback ride through a jungle in Cozumel costs $89 per person. Even one hour of parasailing is $79 per adult. And prices zoom for more exotic adventures, like a helicopter ride and three hours of trekking on an Alaskan glacier, which Celebrity offers for $514 per person.

There are some ways to save money and end up with a better adventure as well. There are lots of independent operators at ports around the world who have a loyal following among cruise mavens who offer excellent value in shore excursions, and it's worthwhile to do a little Internet hunting to seek them out. (You might also find recommendations in cruise guidebooks and magazines.) In Cozumel, an independent company, Island Marketing Ltd., offers a two-hour horseback ride through a jungle area for $52 per person, $37 less than Royal Caribbean.

Which way should you go? The first rule is to plan something ahead—don't rely on the street vendors who will greet the boat and bombard you with offers as you disembark. You have no way of knowing if they have any sort of license, insurance, knowledge, or code of ethics. But after that, opt for either the cruise line's offerings or your own bookings—whichever makes you feel more comfortable.

For many, there is safety in sticking with the cruise line. The biggest benefit may be that if your tour happens to run late, the ship will wait for one of its own groups before setting sail. If you're off on your own and don't return by the specified sailing time, you might be left behind and have to find a way to fly yourself on to the next port to rejoin the ship. That's generally a small risk—reputable tour companies know what time the ship will sail and they can be counted on to get you back, and cruise lines do record who boards so they know if they are missing someone. But for some, it can be a worry.

Another advantage is that possible complications have generally been removed by the cruise line, so the shore excursion should be hassle free. I've heard from passengers on a Carnival cruise in Russia who discovered that people who didn't book through the cruise line couldn't get through customs; those with tickets to the cruise line's shore excursion went on their way without delay.

The other advantage of the cruise-sponsored shore excursions is that some vetting has gone into the contracting, though you'll find that in some cases, that often doesn't really mean much. Excursions contracted through the boat may end up being shorter and more pedestrian than independent contractors. Like many others, I found myself feeling cheated when the cruise-line-backed sea kayaking tour amounted to paddling some boats about two hundred yards to a Mexican beach area where street vendors hawked jewelry and trinkets. We sat there until seemingly all cash had been spent by the group, then paddled back single-file, and scolded by a guide on a Jet Ski if we didn't move fast enough or directly enough (he tried to tow one kayak in because the paddlers weren't proficient enough for his schedule). The van ride to the area was longer than the kayaking—not exactly the fun day on the water I thought I had purchased for several hundred dollars.

Other cruise veterans talk of such shore excursions as one in Istanbul that was light on history and sites, but included two hours in a rug store where a merchant gave lengthy sales pitches (perhaps the leader's cousin). Indeed, a common complaint with cruise-line shore excursions is that they often include too much captive-audience selling by locals. You see great pictures of horseback riding in the surf or climbing the steps to an ancient monument, but that ends up being a sidelight to high-pressure sales games.

Some passengers say they have gotten partial refunds and other accommodations from cruise lines after complaining about the quality of a shore excursion, while others say the cruise line turns a deaf ear and claims no relationship with the shore excursion provider.

Venturing out on your own does introduce more risk, but you can save money and you can end up with a better, less crowded experience. Independent shore excursion companies that rely on Internet-posted reviews, repeat customers, and word-of-mouth recommendations often try harder to please and may give you a much better kayaking experience. Careful researching can pay off—search for offerings at your port of call and look for reviews and recommendations. Does the vendor have a good Web site? Is there a telephone number you can call and discuss arrangements? Is it licensed by the country's tourism board? Is it a member of a trade group like the American Society of Travel Agents? Those are ways to get a better sense of how legitimate the business is.

Another thing to look for: Does the vendor provide transportation from the ship to its site, or are you expected to get yourself there by local taxi? Local taxis can be fun and interesting because you can learn a lot about the local scene from taxi drivers, and sometimes in the Caribbean it's great to hire a car for the day and visit different beaches, shopping, or whatever you want to do. But don't let yourself be surprised—find out in advance if transportation from the pier is provided in your tour, and then decide if you're up for dealing with local drivers. (One tip on drivers—always agree on a set price before you get in the car.) If you don't want to do a little bartering, or feel queasy about riding in a car that may be older than you are, you may want to stick with the ship's offerings, since transportation is included right from the dock.

In general, look for tours either from the cruise line or from independent vendors that stop at points of interest rather than driving by them. You also want to make sure the vendors promise specific times spent on different activities—four hours of actually deep-sea fishing, for example, rather than just an afternoon adventure that may include two hours docked at a peddlers village.

You can hunt for independent excursions simply by Googling your port and "shore excursions," or by checking cruise advice books and sites like ShoreTrips.com, which has offerings from around the world and reviews for customers, and CruiseCritic.com and CruiseMates.com, both of which have articles on things to do in various ports of call. Many popular ports have their own shore excursion sites, like CozumelCruiseExcursions.com or JamaicaCruiseExcursions .com, CancunVista.com, and Caribbeanshoretours.com. Scout around—offerings change all the time, and you really can find fun things to do.

POWER MATES

If you're concerned about trying something new on your own, you may be able to find partners before you ever set sail. CruiseMates.com has a "Meet on Board" section where you can look for others who have booked the same cruise, then compare notes with them. You may find suggestions from previous cruising passengers about great shore excursions, and you may be able to rustle up company for an adventure. In fact, many tour companies offer discounts to groups of three or more, so you may save some money and make some new friends at the same time. It's a neat twist on "do it yourself"—like college roommates freshman year e-mailing back and forth so they get to know each other before they move into the dormitory together.

The bottom line to shore excursions is that it pays to plan ahead, whether you opt for the cruise line offerings or independent companies. With cruise lines, popular tours can sell out, and the last thing you want to do is spend a lot of time on the boat waiting in line at the shore excursion booking desk. (You may end up there anyway. Sometimes if too few passengers sign up for tours, they are canceled and you'll simply get a note slipped under your cabin door telling you to rebook.) The cost of all this can be a significant add-on to the price of what you thought was an "all-inclusive" cruise, so budget accordingly. But no matter how you do it, getting off the boat and exploring ancient ruins, local cultures, beaches, or shopping can make your cruise so much more interesting, or partaking in glacier hikes, coral reef snorkeling, horseback riding, parasailing, deep-sea fishing, sailing, or whatever fun you want can yield lasting memories.

Once you've planned out your excursions, you probably need to think about how you're going to pack. Packing for a cruise can be a challenge because multiple outfits may be required for each day. You may want beach or pool attire, workout clothes, long sleeves and long pants for shore excursions, and formal wear for dinner—all in the same day.

Veterans say don't be fooled—pack light, as you would for any trip. No sense ending up paying an airline hundreds of dollars in baggage fees to tote many trunks on board your ship. You really can get by with simple, casual wear, color coordinated so you get many outfits out of a few basics, and perhaps a nicer outfit for special occasions during your week. If you want to partake in formal shipboard dinners (many "freestyle" cruises leave their formal nights optional), you can either pack one suit or formal dress, or arrange to rent a tuxedo or formal attire from the cruise line—they are usually pretty reliable about such rentals. One tip: Don't take lots of jewelry. Most vessels have in-room safes, but there will be times when your luggage is out of your control.

As you board the boat, the cruise line will issue you a pass card that will likely be both identification for disembarking and reboarding and your personal charge card for extras on the boat. There are plenty of opportunities to spend lots of money of course, and not just on T-shirts and souvenir plastic drinking mugs. Ships may have art auctions. Massages and facials and a host of other services may cost you money. Alcohol, naturally, will be charged to your card. You may be asked if you want to prepurchase a "plan," such as a "soft drink plan" that provides unlimited sodas for a set fee. Before you buy, decide if you can drink twenty dollars a day's worth of diet soda, or whatever the offer is. Be careful—the card can make it far too easy to spend money. You may never even see prices or be given receipts and you won't realize how much you swiped that card until checkout time. One other credit card issue: If you're hopping from port to port in different places, make sure your credit card company knows you'll be traveling and where. Some companies, Citibank in particular, have aggressive "fraud detection" units that will suspend your card if charges start appearing from places like Mexico or Honduras or Turkey—places the credit card company thinks could spell fraud. The credit card company may start rejecting charges, and your cruise line pings the company twice a day to make sure your credit is still good while you're running around the ship swiping that pass. Surprise! The pass will be rejected and you'll be sent to the purser. You may have a hard time contacting your credit card company from sea. A better plan is to alert the company before you sail and hope it figures out that your spending is really your spending.

POWER CALLS

Communications on board can be expensive, too. Many ships now offer wireless Internet connections, but Internet service at sea is expensive. Your BlackBerry or smartphone can find service on the ship, too, but at rates that may not be part of your monthly service plan and may surprise you with an extra hundred dollars or more on your bill when you get home. If you're concerned about the cost, you may find it more economical to buy some minutes on one of the ship's computers—they'll have plenty available for checking e-mail or surfing the Internet. Leave your laptop computer at home, anyway—you're on vacation! And if you must check in with the office, wait until you reach a port and use the local phone service, which will probably be cheaper than the ship's.

Before you pay off your account, pack up, and dock for the final time, you'll most likely be hit up for tips for workers on the ship. On many cruise lines this is a formal process with suggested rates for everyone from your chamber attendant to your dining table waiter and the dining room captain. Tipping ends up being a major portion of income for workers on the boat. Whether you think it's right or not, the cruise line is counting on you to pay for its labor, and the workers you get to know are there for the tips. It takes some planning—tipping may amount to several hundred dollars for a family, spread among several workers.

Like many vacations, a cruise can end up costing more than you planned. But cruising can be also be an outstanding value—just be careful and plan ahead. Whether you want an active vacation, a relaxing, lay-out kind of getaway, a giant drunken party, a chance to explore nature, or a sightseer's delight through fascinating cities, great museums, and historical treasures, a cruise ship can be an ideal vacation.

Conclusion
Will Travel Ever Get Better?

I often joke that if airlines ever figured out a way to run their business well—delighting customers with good value, an easy-to-use product, dependable service, friendly employees, clean and comfortable equipment—then I'd be out of a job as a writer and "traveler's advocate." But as one of my colleagues likes to say, this industry, from a reporter's perspective, just keeps giving and giving.

Air travel seemingly gets worse and worse. We endure busts and booms with airlines, neither particularly enjoyable for passengers. In the late 1990s, when the economy was booming, airlines jacked up prices, angering customers. Service deteriorated, thanks to air-traffic congestion and delays and labor feuds between pilots and management that left customers sitting on canceled or delayed flights. Then the economy softened and the terrorist attacks of 2001 sent the airline industry into a tailspin. Airplanes were grounded, employees laid off, and service cut back so much that air travel became more and more unpleasant. Food was taken off flights and penalties were increased and imposed on passengers. At one point, half the entire U.S.

industry was operating under protection of federal bankruptcy courts. What an industry!

Then, just as airlines emerged from bankruptcy reorganization and started making money again, oil prices shot up. Airlines slashed costs, changed how they operate to get more efficient, and thought they had figured out a way to be profitable even when oil cost $70 a barrel in 2007. (Some Wall Street analysts had predicted as oil climbed from the $30s and $40s that the industry would be dead if oil prices ever reached $60 a barrel.) Then oil prices doubled again and the airline industry was left reeling. Then oil prices come crashing down, but so does the global economy. Airlines bounce from one crisis to the next. Is there any other business so sensitive to economic changes and global politics? Possibly not.

Will the industry ever find the stability, profitability, and ability to provide good service? That's unlikely, given the basic structure of the business. First, no other industry is so competitive on price. Consumers can comparison shop with a couple of clicks, seeing all the prices for the industry at any given moment. Imagine if your computer could compare prices of groceries or automobiles or televisions for you, showing the cheapest price at every auto dealer in town, for example. Pricing displays, whether they are in front of travel agents or in front of average travelers, are set up to list the cheapest prices first. Woe be the airline that doesn't match the cheapest price—or so airlines say. If you try to hold out for a higher price, you often end up with nothing—no sale and an empty seat.

On top of that pricing pressure, airlines are expensive to run, with high capital costs for airplanes, airport terminals, computing heft, and the labor costs of skilled mechanics and pilots. It's a business that still operates with lots of workers, many of them highly trained and highly paid. It's a cyclical business, tightly tied to the ups and downs of the broad economy, and is highly seasonal and even variable day by day. The result is that you have an industry with high costs and commodity pricing, yielding a low-margin business. And that's when things are good for airlines.

The domestic United States skies offer the largest air-travel market in the world, and it is also the most competitive in the world. Whenever one airline starts making money on a route, a competitor can easily move an airplane in to try and reap rewards as well. Airplanes are the factories and office buildings of the aviation industry, but unlike factories and office buildings they are mobile. That makes the business all the more competitive. On top of that, it's easy to start an airline, and start-ups have the advantage of low costs—employees with no seniority, no pension obligations, no aircraft debt, and, if you lease new planes, little maintenance obligations. History has shown that anytime an airline can find a stable, profitable market base, a new entrant is likely to appear on the scene and start chipping away. Airlines do well when they can keep the supply of seats in line with demand so that they can charge airfares high enough to cover their costs. But whenever that happens, new capacity comes in, prices get slashed, and profits become elusive again.

POWER BENEFITS

In the short run, the intense competition is good for consumers. We all enjoy a good fare war, and the price of an airline ticket has become an incredible bargain. Between 1978, the year the airline industry was deregulated, and 2007, the price of the cost to fly one mile domestically rose 53 percent, not adjusting for inflation. Over the same period, a gallon of milk increased in price by 154 percent, according to the U.S. Bureau of Labor Statistics; the average selling price of a new car ballooned 345 percent, according to the National Automobile Dealers Association, and the average cost of a year at a public university skyrocketed 799 percent, according to the College Board. If you adjust for inflation, the average airline ticket costs half what it did in 1978. Cheap and plentiful air service has changed the way we live, allowing frequent vacations or fun trips, allowing us to live far from parents or children and still get together and maintain family ties, allowing us to work or attend school farther from home than our parents or grandparents may have ventured. The airways are the interstate highways of our modern lives.

Despite recent years with hefty price increases, air travel is still a decent bargain. In the long run, consumers need airlines to be profitable. Consumers want to see airlines invest in new airplanes, better seats, and more service on the ground and in the air. Consumers deserve friendly and helpful airline employees, not surly traffic cops angry about the latest layoffs or management bonuses. Consumers need dependable service, whether that means delivering your luggage back to you without damage or delay, or just getting the flight to New York as promised. We don't get that from an industry always seeming to circle the drain.

The turbulence in the skies means we should demand better from both our government and our airlines. Consumers need important protections when traveling, and yet Congress and several presidential administrations have done little. We don't have any sort of "Passengers Bill of Rights." Canada, the European Union, and other governments have written some basic protections into law. Haven't U.S. travelers suffered enough to earn some relief? We don't have a modern air-traffic-control system and we, as travelers, should demand one.

Until we get reliable and efficient air travel, we're on our own and we must take more control. We've seen how we can take steps to improve our journeys and minimize our own hassles. Follow the Ten Commandments of Travel. Power Travel works, even when airlines don't work so well.

Appendix
Resources

Here's a list of useful Web sites to help navigate travel.

FOR PLANNING

How to find me and current travel news:
The Middle Seat Terminal: http://blogs.wsj.com/
middleseat/ WSJ.com

Government statistics and complaints:
http://airconsumer.ost.dot.gov/
http://ec.europa.eu/transport/air_portal/

Reviews and suggestions:
BestTripChoices.com
CruiseCritic.com
TripAdvisor.com
AirlineQuality.com

FOR SHOPPING

AirlineConsolidator.com
BookingBuddy.com
CheapoAir.com
Cheaptickets.com
Orbitz.com
Expedia.com
ExpertFlyer.com
Farecast.com
FareCompare.com
Hotels.com
Hotwire.com
ITAsoftware.com
InsureMyTrip.com
Kayak.com
Lessno.com
Mobissimo.com
SideStep.com
SquareMouth.com (Insurance)
STAtravel.com (Student discounts)
StudentUniverse.com
TotalTravelInsurance.com
Travelocity.com
USACA.com (Consolidators)
Yapta.com
And don't forget individual airline and hotel Web sites.

FOR FLIGHT INFORMATION & TRACKING

FlightArrivals.com
FlightExplorer.com
FlightStats.com (One of my favorites)

FlightView.com
Fly.FAA.Gov (Very useful FAA site)
FlyteComm.com
SeatGuru.com (Excellent information)

FOR FREQUENT-FLIER PROGRAM HELP

AwardGrabber.com
FlyerTalk.com
FrequentFlier.com
InsideFlyer.com
MilesMaven.com
Yapta.com

FOR DESTINATIONS

AirportAssistance.com (Concierge service)
bookalimoUSA.com
Fodors.com
IgoUgo.com
limolinkexchange.com
limos.com
LonelyPlanet.com
Mapquest.com
Google Maps
MobilTravelGuide.com
OpenTable.com (Restaurant reservations and reviews)
ShoreTrips.com
USLimoDirectory.com
VirtualTourist.com
Weather.com
Zagat.com

FOR SAFETY

Private jets:
AviationResearch.com
Wyvernltd.com

European "Blacklist" of airlines:
http://ec.europa.eu/transport/air-ban/list_en.htm

IATA safety audit:
http://www.iata.org/ps/certification/iosa/registry.htm